DYNAMICS
COUPLES ▮▮▮▮ Y

D0870458

Jürg Willi was born in Zurich, Switzerland, in 1934, the son of a professor of pediatrics. He studied medicine in Freiburg, Vienna, Paris, and Zurich, before specializing in psychiatry at the renowned Bürgholzli Clinic under Professor Manfred Bleuler, son of psychiatric pioneer Eugen Bleuler. From 1964 to 1967 Dr. Willi was Assistant Medical Director at Bürgholzli. He then transferred to the Psychiatric University Clinic of Zurich and in 1973 was appointed its Director.

Since 1970, Dr. Willi has worked extensively in the field of couple and family therapy. In collaboration with the Institute for Marriage and Family in Switzerland he has pioneered outpatient programs in couple and family therapy. He also teaches at the University Hospital in Zurich and in 1977 was appointed Professor Extraordinary specializing in Medical Psychology.

Dr. Willi's first publications included papers on the psychopathology of hysterical and neurotic marriages. He subsequently developed the Joint Rorschach Test, a diagnostic tool used in the study of couple and group relationships. This became the subject of his first book, published in 1973. Over the next five years, drawing on his own observations and stimulated by the work of Henry Dicks of the Tavistock Clinic in London, Dr. Willi elaborated his concept of the role of *collusion* in couple relationships.

DYNAMICS OF COUPLES THERAPY was published in Germany in 1978 as a companion volume to the highly successful COUPLES IN COLLUSION. Both works are published by Hunter House in the **Concepts in Psychology for Everyday Living** series.

Dr. Willi and his wife Margaretta Dubach, an artist and art teacher, are co-authors of a children's book, *Viktor, Noch, und Sadi-Madi*. They have two sons, Kristof and Dominic.

Series Title:
Concepts in Psychology for Everyday Living

Translated from the German
THERAPIE DER ZWEIERBEZIEHUNG
by
Jan van Heurck

Hunter House Inc., Publishers
Claremont, CA

Jürg Willi, M.D.

DYNAMICS OF COUPLES THERAPY

Understanding the Potential of the Couple/Therapist Triangle

Originally published in German under the title THERAPIE DER
ZWEIERBEZIEHUNG © Rowohlt Verlag GmbH, Reinbek bei Hamburg,
1978

Authorized English translation by Jan van Heurck © Hunter House Inc.,
Publishers 1984

This paperback edition published in 1986 by Hunter House Inc., Publishers

Library of Congress Cataloging-in-Publication Data:

Willi, Jurg.
    Dynamics of couples therapy.

    (Concepts in psychology for everyday living)
    Translation of: Therapie der Zweierbeziehung.
    Bibliography: p.
    Includes index.
    1. Marital psychotherapy.   2. Psychotherapist and patient.   I. Title.
II. Series.
RC488.5.W55513   1986   616.89'156   86-2980
ISBN 0-89793-018-5 (pbk.)

Cover design by Qalagraphia; painting by Luis R. Caughman
Set in 10 on 12 Times Roman
Manufactured in the United States of America

CONTENTS

PREFACE

This book does not provide an absolute answer to the perennial question of what is *the* correct or true therapeutic method or theory. Experience has given me a greater flexibility for entering with each couple into a process that is unique in its dynamics and changes. In doing so I have learned to make better use of the therapeutic readiness and possibilities inherent in such a process.

The systemic-structuralist method (Minuchin, Sluzki, et al.) proved most successful during the initial phases of therapy when the partners were often so bitterly entwined that no meaningful dialogue could be reached without the direct introduction of structures and rules. In these cases, the structures and rules served to calm the setting to the point where existing conflicts and overpowering feelings of fear, aggression and hate could be considerably reduced. The systemic-strategic method (Watzalawick, Haley, Selvini, et al.) was most helpful for me in those cases where I, as therapist, had the impression that the partners were basically unwilling to change their destructive game. From sexual therapy (Helene Singer-Kaplan) I learned how a graduated series of exercises, undertaken in small steps, can help to overcome not only the fears that block the partners but also the helplessness of the therapist.

Then there is the rather large group of couples searching for therapy who, according to my experience, profit more from a dynamic, growth-oriented method because for them the central issues are the meaningfulness of their partnership and the clarification of their feelings, ambivalences and constraints. This book is about the therapy of such couples.

I learned about the limitations of the directive therapeutic method at the same time as I discovered its advantages. Insofar as systemic therapeutic methods deliberately avoid paying attention to the feelings and insights of the patients, these methods also neglect the feelings and insights of the therapists who go through training. The originators of the directive methods for the most part still underwent psychoanalytic training but their pupils seldom do so. When therapists with only systemic or communications theory training neglect to take their own feelings and fantasies into account, their patients and they run the risk of getting trapped in blind alleys. The escape routes they try under these circumstances generally result in "more of the same." (Watzalawick, Weakland and Fisch). Because of personal insecurity there is a tendency for systemic-structuralistic therapists to attempt to achieve the hierarchically superior position at any price. They engage in a power struggle with their clients, which results in a loss of credibility for the therapist. Alternatively, systemic-strategic therapists may make use of paradoxical methods of intervention in order to justify their own communications fears and to find an elegant resolution for their own feelings of impotence.

If what the therapeutic sciences tell us is correct, namely that the therapeutic relationship is of greater importance that the method, then it follows that the clarification of the therapist's own reactions are of value in the formation of the therapeutic relationship. It is in this sense that I hope this book will be a contribution to couples therapy that goes beyond different schools and methods.

Jürg Willi
Zurich, 1983

DYNAMICS OF COUPLES THERAPY

1

THE THERAPEUTIC TRIANGLE

Critique of the Collusion Concept

The Ego-Stabilizing Effect of Marriage

The Ego-Limiting Effects of Marriage

Formation of the Therapeutic Triangle
as an Attempt to Compensate for
Defects in the Partnership

Critique of the Collusion Concept

The collusion concept, as I depicted it in 1975 in my book *Couples in Collusion,* involves the unconscious interaction of two partners in such a way that they play into each other's hands. I believe that this concept is significant in couples therapy but that it cannot cover all facets of the actual therapy situation. Thus I would like to cite certain criticisms of the collusion concept that help us to see it in its proper perspective relative to couples therapy.

In *Couples in Collusion* I described how the disposition to involve oneself in collusions is determined either by unmastered conflicts in one's relationship with one's parents, conflicts *whose roots reach back to early childhood,* or by fear of suffering the same kinds of problems one's parents had in their marriage. But in addition it should be noted, as *Richter* (1976)

1

rightly points out, that psychoanalysts should take care to avoid viewing their patients' present-day problems exclusively in terms of the repetition of early childhood experiences. For the adult is confronted by a host of social conditions that are quite new to him and that he can neither completely understand nor effectively deal with, practically speaking, purely by using the models provided by his childhood experience. Consequently he must discover brand new answers to questions involving his own sexual relationships. Psychoanalysis should make accessible not only the reexperience of buried memories but also the unconscious influences at work in the patient's actual present-day situation. These include the immediate pressures and anxieties about living up to sex-role demands, as well as the insecurities surrounding the contemporary ideal of marriage—questions about marriage as an institution, the division of labor between husband and wife, having a family, extramarital relationships, and so on. All these insecurities intensify the conflict between the conservative, traditional aspects of a couple's relationship and their moves towards emancipation. This conflict promotes the growth of collusions.

There is also the danger of defining the couple relationship as a self-enclosed dynamic system within the framework of the collusion concept. It is wrong to accuse psychoanalysis of an excessive preoccupation with the intrapsychic structures of a hypostasized individual, only to turn around and lapse into exactly the same bias, this time not with regard to the individual but the couple. The couple relationship is a recent sociocultural development. In many cultures there is no such thing as the formation of exclusive pairs who have a life of their own, separate from the group. In such cultures marriage does not so much unite two partners as two families. A man views his wife less as a love-partner than as the mother of his children. Often the family group regards too much intimacy between two love-partners as a disruptive force and deliberately thwarts it. Here the central family conflict is not between man and wife but, for example, between mother-in-law and daughter-in-law; or there may be more complex fields of conflict from which the marital relationship cannot be isolated. But even in the modern Western world a love match is not an everyday occurrence. Men and women often marry out of practical necessity, for example if the woman becomes pregnant, or for social and economic reasons, or for security. A genuine love match, with all its attendant deep-seated expectations of happiness, fulfillment and self-validation, does not develop, and as a result the deep-lying, unconscious urges that lead to the formation of collusions are not actualized to the same extent. *In many marriages external contingencies do not permit the development of an intimate marital dynamic.* For example, this may be true of working-class couples whose confining housing situation and large numbers of children never allow them to be alone together. In addition the problems of earning a living, or conflicts deriving from social conditions, may play so primary a role that the notion of *therapeutic work on unconscious expectations and fantasies strikes people as an irrelevant luxury.* Phenomenologically the couple relationship is an abstraction whose reality varies greatly, depending on cultural and social conditions. Despite the contemporary critique of marriage, people in the Western industrialized societies now attach more importance than ever before to the enduring relationship between a couple as a source of personal happiness and fulfillment. This also means that the couple relationship is under more stress and fraught with more problems than ever before. The collusion concept refers to the problematic interplay between the partners in which they are captives of one another through mutually unresolved conflicts that are acted out in irrational behavior.

The Ego-Stabilizing Effect of Marriage

My main concern in *Couples in Collusion* was to show the unconscious and problematic interplay of two partners. Two people may *pair off because of certain basic shared attitudes, which are fantasies rooted in deep-lying fears and needs. But such shared fantasies do not lead them to adopt identical postures in their relationship. Instead they lead as a rule to polarization, the adoption of diametrically opposite positions:* a progressive, "adult," often overcompensatory position by the one partner, and a regressive, often decompensatory position by the other.

By its very nature marriage affords room for both progressive and regressive behavior. To a certain degree marriage should satisfy regressive needs, such as the need to be looked after, needs for protection and support, tenderness and sexual gratification, and projective identification with a partner one admires. But marriage should also demand progressive traits from the partner, such as the sense of responsibility for and an unselfish devotion to the partnership, the ability to tolerate stress and frustration, maturity and consideration for one's partner. These capabilities should be fostered while at the same time the marriage provides sexual and personal validation. In every marriage the partners effect a role and chore division and work as a team to increase the efficiency of the partnership and provide mutual gratification. A couple relationship can contribute greatly to *ego-stabilization by dividing up defensive functions.* The ego of one partner can be relieved of some of the burdens of self-defense by delegating them to the other partner, at the cost of increased dependency. Likewise the ego can be stabilized through *identification with a particular role in the service of the dual community or the formation of a kind of group ego,* which also reinforces the bond. The couple relationship can become a haven from emotional insecurity and from external threats, and can assume much of the burden of defensive and adaptive functions (cf. the discussion of adaptive mechanisms in *Parin,* 1977). Given the increasing alienation that people are experiencing in their work situations, as well as increasing social mobility and the fleeting nature of human relationships, the couple relationship is playing a more and more centralized role. *But the greater the demand placed on a marriage as a defensive and adaptive institution, the more subject the partners will be to the demands of their partnership.* Of the wealth of personal potential in both partners, the qualities manifested will be the ones required and permitted by the partnership. The partners tune in to each other and develop interrelated "interactional personalities" (*Willi,* 1973, 1975). In the process each individual assumes one of the characters accessible to him, but forfeits the ability to develop freely. *Often it is not easy to tell whether someone has been stabilized by a marriage, and found identity, structure, a guideline, or simply lost his flexibility and become rigid, stale and stodgy.* It is, to be sure, difficult to decide to what extent the formation of an "interactional personality" has contributed to maturation and personal growth, to what extent to stagnation. It would of course be wrong to regard the ego-stabilization achieved through marriage *exclusively* as a defensive or adaptive phenomenon. The response of a partner is an important element in the discovery of personal identity (*Erikson,* 1956/57). The possibility of finding satisfaction and meaningful activity in a lasting relationship and the necessity of standing up for oneself and living up to certain demands are part and parcel of becoming a mature adult. In this area no clear distinction can be made between healthy and neurotic traits, and there is often a blending of the two.

The Ego-Limiting Effects of Marriage

Vulnerable and disturbed partnerships are characterized by an overabundance of fears that are supposed to be warded off by the structural interplay of the partnership. Vulnerable partnerships are also characterized by the overabundance of needs that are satisfiable only in the partnership. But neurotic partnerships cannot be directly equated with partnerships made up of neurotic partners, for it is by no means true that all severely neurotic people expect a marriage to cure or alleviate their suffering, inhibitions and unmastered conflicts. A collusion—that is, an unconscious agreement by two partners to *interact in a way gratifying to both*—is neurotic to the *degree that it leads to a compulsive determination of each partner by the other and does not allow either one the possibility of breaking loose from this constraint.*

Just as a partnership can help, on the one hand, to stabilize the individual ego and fortify its defensive and adaptive functions relative to internal and external threats and stresses, it can, on the other hand, threaten the individual and place him under stress, inducing neurosis in a personality that is relatively healthy in other areas. A marriage is not a fixed state but a *process demanding continual adjustments to ever-shifting internal and external circumstances.* A marriage in which the partners, as interactional personalities, are too dependent on and influenced by each other does not allow them to participate in this process, for it leaves them little scope for development, for experimentation and new experiences; these arouse intolerable fears that the defensive structure the partners have built together may break down, or the relationship disintegrate.

When a couple have lived together for a long time their mutual interpenetration poses real problems, because all the ego, id and superego functions that a person turns over to his partner make him increasingly dependent on the partner's readiness to fulfill the delegated tasks reliably. Should one partner no longer be prepared to do what is expected of him, the other will feel more frustrated at having to solve problems on his own than if he had never allowed himself to expect the partnership to help him with his problems in the first place. In therapy, patients often maintain that before marriage they were independent and capable and had no unrealistic and unfulfillable expectations. Not until, with the greatest misgivings, they had entered into the partnership did they become so regressive, dependent and demanding. They also recognize that in delegating certain tasks to their partner they were doing what the partner really wanted, and that the latter is now dependent on the ego-stabilization derived from his or her need to perform these tasks. On the other hand, the assumption of delegated duties may be not only ego-stabilizing, but can also be ego-confining in that it fixes a person in a clearly defined role behavior. For example, in a case in which the fantasy of total fusion has helped bind two partners together, it is demanded of both that they avoid anything which might point up the fact that they are still separate. But in the long run, the progressive partner will feel trapped in the idealized image that the regressive partner has formed of him. He will feel manipulated and forced to assume a false identity, and may react in angry and hurtful ways in an attempt to get the other partner out of his system. Moreover, the regressive partner, who has sacrificed his identity for the progressive partner, cannot neglect his own self-development with impunity. In his fantasies, feelings and behavior he will persecute the progressive partner and will create guilt feelings in him in the attempt to keep him from becoming more independent and separate. The partners are trapped in a conflict in which they can neither get close to each other nor clearly tell which is which.

Troubled couples are caught in a tormenting ambivalence. One partner formulates efforts towards emancipation, the other supports the status quo, upholding their original contract. One moves forward, the other backward, while the relationship ceases to develop at all. During therapy many therapists challenge the partners to formulate clearly what they want so they can reach a compromise between their opposing needs. This technique does not take into account the fact that each partner wants to head in a certain direction only so long as the other wants to move in the opposite direction, because both are suffering from ambivalent feelings. Another characteristic of disturbed couples is their dread of any change in their relationship. Though each may clamor for a change in his partner, each will just as clamorously resist any actual change in the other because this change would necessitate his changing too, and this might endanger their original definition of their love. This makes the therapeutic treatment of marital conflicts immensely difficult. On the surface it seems simple to give a troubled couple good advice, expecting them to listen to reason, to be a bit more tolerant and considerate, and finally to resolve to do what they know to be positive and refrain from doing what they know to be negative, or arrive at a compromise. Often the marriage counsellor fails to acknowledge the underlying reality, the fact that the partners secretly resist the very thing that on a more superficial level they appear to want.

Formation of the Therapeutic Triangle as an Attempt to Compensate for Defects in the Partnership

Problems are particularly likely to arise in partnerships where the need to adapt to the constantly shifting internal and external circumstances produces in the couple a state of unbearable stress and consequently a resistance to change. Many factors determine whether the stress of marital tensions will lead to the actual breakdown of the marriage. Outside factors that support the partners and relieve their tension can have a particularly stabilizing effect. These include support from third parties—children, parents, relatives, friends—and support from religion or world views. People can find compensation in their work and other surrogate gratifications and contacts.

Bateson (1958), *M. Bowen* (1966), *Haley* (1977) and other American family investigators regard the marital twosome as an inherently unstable system that tends to turn into a triangle as soon as it comes under stress. As a rule this triangle is a system involving two against one. Two members of the triangle become polarized against a third party, and although the original partners are separated, at the same time the dynamics of the triangle continue to hold them together. The third party in a triangle can be children, parents or friends; or it can be a therapist.

It is important for the couples therapist to recognize that given this constellation, he cannot help being part of the triangle. The inner dynamics of the triangle are such that the couple's first concern is how the constellation of two-against-one composes itself. The therapist is placed under tremendous pressure to take up a position. Will he side with the wife against the husband; with the husband against the wife; or will the two partners form a united front against him? The therapist can try to avoid the dynamics of the triangle system by struggling to maintain the position of a neutral, objective observer or of an active animal trainer. But he can also try to accept its inevitable dynamics, enter into its swing and try to use its laws productively. *Haley* (1977) writes that whatever rules a couple follow, the therapist is a part of them. The leverage that the therapist has becomes therapeutic and effective as he changes these rules whenever they are applied to him.

This book depicts couples therapy in terms of the therapeutic triangle, that is, in terms of the psychological involvement of the therapist with the couple.

2

THE FIRST TALK
WITH THE COUPLE

Making the Appointment

The First Interview

Some General Points of View Regarding
the First Interview

Making the Appointment

Generally a couple's first contact with the therapist is made through a telephone call. Often the caller wants to go into detail about his reasons for deciding that he needs a therapist, and to describe the marital crisis with which he wants help. I try to define my therapeutic attitude from the outset by telling the caller that if possible I would prefer not to be given any information about the relationship unless the other partner is present. Given the dynamics of the therapeutic triangle, it is clear that the partner who did not telephone the therapist may feel at a disadvantage from the very beginning. Therefore I immediately ask the caller whether the other partner would be willing to come along to our first talk, which for the time being we may assume will be the only one. This makes it clear that I view the couple's conflict and their possible therapy as a matter concerning them both. Quite often the caller has not even informed the other partner of his intention to call me, and is obviously envisioning our sessions as tête-à-têtes in which we would confer about how best to get the troublesome partner under control, and what psychological techniques could most readily be used to train him to perform as he should. Often the reply to my query about the other partner's willingness to attend our session is that the partner would not be willing to accompany his spouse to any talk with me. I emphasize that for the time being we would only meet once to clarify matters, that it is of great concern to me to know what the other partner thinks about the marital crisis, and that each one of us will be equally free to decide whether, in the end, he feels it makes sense for us to work together in therapy. If the other partner refuses to meet with me even once, I tell the caller that I fear that any therapy would be more or less doomed from the start.

The other partner is almost always willing to talk with me just *once*. If he is not, the question arises as to how the caller presented my invitation to his spouse. Often the reason for the refusal lies in some resistance on the part of the caller, who sabotages plans for a three-way talk because initially he wants to have the therapist all to himself. *Greene* recommends that in this case the therapist himself should telephone the other partner and ask him to come to a session.

The First Interview

I view couples therapy as a therapeutic triangle devoted to work on the couple's relationship, and so from the very first meeting I hold sessions with both partners, and at least in the beginning hold no individual sessions whatever. Many experienced couples therapists, including *Greene*, begin the therapy by holding individual sessions with each partner, and even consider it extremely beneficial to give each one the opportunity to confide secrets to the therapist. I do not regard it as an incontrovertible law that there must be no individual talks at the beginning of a therapy. I simply find that this approach simplifies my relationship with the couple and gives me more freedom in the therapy. In particular, seeing both partners together makes it possible for me to interpret nonverbal communications between them and to discover inconsistencies between what they say and how they say it. On the other hand, combining joint sessions with individual sessions gives a therapist a clearer grasp of the interactional personality of each partner. At joint sessions one partner is often timid, mute and passive, but in a private session he may be quite capable of expressing himself freely and openly; or one partner may wear a defensive armor during a joint session but manage to show his vulnerable side in a private talk. Because as a rule I hold only joint sessions, I often fail to get information about the partners' past history. Therefore I give them questionnaires and ask them to write something about their background.

The first interview is an exciting and intensive encounter between the therapist and the couple. Each makes a strong impression on the other. The purpose of this initial talk is to clear up the question: Do the three of us want to enter into the therapy process in order to get a better understanding of what is making it hard for the couple to live together and to set the stage for them to learn from the present crisis?

Two things concern me as a therapist:

—What can I *learn* from the couple, during this first talk, about the nature of their problem and the appropriate therapeutic approach to it?

—What can I *communicate* to the couple about the nature of the therapy?

To some extent I structure the first interview so that our talk often follows the pattern described in Chapter 12. But some couples give the talk quite a different pattern. Generally, this initial talk, like the later sessions, lasts between 75 and 90 minutes.

After I greet the couple, explain the therapeutic setting and take some personal data (age, how long married, profession, etc.) and information about the outer situation and circumstances, the first interview passes through the following phases:

Phase 1: Both Partners Describe Their View of the Conflict
Addressing both partners, I begin our talk by asking, "So, what exactly is the problem?" Then one partner will begin to give an account of their troubles, at which point a certain dynamics may begin to develop, which at first I do not attempt to structure. During the first few minutes, the couple present themselves to the therapist. It is important to note which partner introduces them, how they divide the responsibility for describing their problems, and what they choose to tell the therapist first. Often it is already possible to begin diagnosis. For example, does each partner immediately try to get the therapist on his side and assign him the function of judging who is right? Does each one accuse the other and immediately try to justify himself? Does one partner look to me to act as a father to whom he can cry out his misery in the hope that I will set the other partner straight? Does one present the other as a sick person whom the two of us must get together to care for? Or does the couple's description

already reveal a certain insight into their problems and desire to use therapy as an aid to working on their problems together? Often the conflict is expressed less in what each partner says than in nonverbal forms of communication, and especially in the behavior of the partner who is not speaking at the moment. Is he taking an active interest in what the speaker is saying, or does he turn away with indifference? Does each partner seem to relate to the therapist as an individual only, or do the two of them try to describe their situation jointly? Does one claim the right to do all the talking, not giving the other a chance to tell his side? Does one partner maintain a regressive silence, as if he had not yet learned to talk, so that the other continually takes over and finishes his sentence for him or the therapist is forced to pay him special attention? Or does one partner give the impression that he cannot talk because he is afraid the emotions he has been damming up for years could suddenly pour out and place excessive demands on the therapist?

During the first few minutes I also try to notice what kind of mood the couple put me in, and how the couple view me: as a judge, a helper, an enemy, an ally, a lover, an authority, a rival, etc.

As a rule I let them speak for a few minutes without any intervention on my part. Then I begin to structure the conversation. I ask each partner what he has felt about the preceding comments of his mate. The purpose of this stereophonic form of communication is to enable the therapist to attune himself to the way the couple are relating and to use the differences in the ways they depict their problems to pick up on the essential elements of their conflicts. If, from the very beginning, I find one of the partners unlikable and feel an urge to identify with the other, I concentrate more attention on the unlikable one because I am certain that from his viewpoint, and in terms of his experience, he has good reasons for choosing to present himself in a way that makes an unpleasant impression on me. By having each partner describe everything from his/her own point of view, I try to communicate my attitude to the couple in the first few minutes: "Here you both have the right to say what you feel about what goes on between you. I'll do my best to understand you both; and whatever happens between you, I'm sure it concerns you both, not just one or the other. I expect both of you to get actively involved in therapy, and I won't let either of you be passive and uninvolved, or monopolize the conversation. I'll try to keep you from hurting each other or humiliating each other in front of me. I don't intend to take sides with either of you: I want to relate to you as a couple."

Phase 2: The Connection Between the Present Conflict and the Choice of Partner at an Earlier Time

Towards the middle of our session I try to place what I have learned about the couple's present-day problems within the larger context of their marital history and determine the connection between partner choice and marital conflict. I am particularly interested in how each of the couple came to choose his partner. "How did you meet? What was your first impression of your partner? What were your hopes and expectations regarding your relationship? What were your anxieties and fears? What were the basic principles which you felt would give your relationship a solid foundation? How did your partnership change your relationship with other people, especially with your parents? What things did you feel you were willing to give up to be together?"

Often these questions release a sort of shock wave, trigger feelings of bewilderment and difficulty in remembering exactly what had initially made one's partner seem so attractive. Frequently I phrase the question even more pointedly, "How did it happen that, out of all the partners you might have chosen, you chose this particular one?" I proceed on the assumption that virtually everyone has an intrinsically unlimited choice of potential partners, but that he has become acquainted with only a few and ultimately has married only one. Naturally external circumstances may have had a decisive influence on the couple's decision to marry—for example the woman's pregnancy; the desire to escape an intolerable home situation; a panicky feeling that time is running out; or the attempt to escape a disappointment in love by marrying on the rebound. But I rarely regard such factors as the crucial reason for the marriage. Very often the couple's description of the reasons for choosing their partners shows that the very qualities which years ago were attractive have now become the source of irritation and conflict. As a rule the partners are forced to admit that when they married they could see only positive qualities in each other, but after a number of years this is no longer the case. Often they feel so resentful towards each other that they cannot imagine having ever loved each other.

Frequently the discussion of the relationship between partner choice and partner conflict comes as a kind of revelation to the couple. Often they are not sufficiently aware of the extent to which their present conflict was already implicit in their partner choice, and often they know little about their partner's motives for falling in love. They jump to the conclusion that they did not see what their partner was really like, or married the wrong person. But in most cases they have much more in common than they realize. The first talk should make them sufficiently aware of this fact so that they feel they have a stake in examining their problems more closely.

By asking these questions I try to communicate to the couple the fact that the crisis in their marriage is not simply a momentary difficulty but a process whose roots reach way back to their choice of partners. I wish to show them that this crisis is not an irrational but a comprehensible event, the logical result of what has gone on before. The point is *to make productive use of the crisis, to grow by meeting its demands.* I try to motivate the couple to look at themselves and each other, and to grow through their insight into the positive and negative aspects of their life together. At the same time I am already making apparent to them my workstyle. My concern is to help them achieve mutual understanding, and only secondarily to change their behavior. Sometimes the situation is so chaotic and destructive that it is absolutely necessary to introduce a strict reorganization, with rules and firm structures, in order to develop a somewhat constructive atmosphere for discussing the couple's problems.

Phase 3: Tentative Interpretations and the Clarification of the Therapy Process

When the couple and I have been talking for fifty or sixty minutes I try to order and clarify in a somewhat more systematic way the impressions I have gathered so far. Generally, I formulate a few observations summarizing what has been said, and take particular care to point out the interdependence of the couple's behavior: "You say 'The only reason I am this way is because you are that way.' Don't you think you'd have to expand that to read, 'The only reason you are that way is that I am this way'?" Whenever possible I try to suggest the focus of the treatment by drawing up a collusion formula (v. Chapter 3). Trial interpretations of this kind enable me to sound out the couple's ability to make sense of the things I say. For example, it is important to me to know whether the partners will simply project the blame onto each other, or whether each shows at least some signs of willingness to look at his own problems. But during the first talk one cannot expect much cooperation. I have often found that one partner is so filled with bitterness and pain that he must continue to express this pain throughout several sessions before he feels capable of looking at himself and dealing with his own contribution to the crisis. Patients like this are particularly grateful to have someone just accept their bitterness and let them say everything they have to say without putting any pressure on them. But on occasion bitter behavior on the part of one partner is also meant to test whether the therapist is genuinely willing to become involved. This situation gets tricky if the therapist continues to give one partner special treatment.

The trial interpretations turn into a discussion of how all three of us would like to proceed from here. I ask each partner whether he would like therapy and what he would expect to gain from it. As a rule the two partners are not equally motivated to seek treatment. It is essential to talk about fears, doubts and reservations, as well as to reduce premature optimism and give each partner a more realistic sense of what therapy can actually achieve. Moreover, I too must decide whether I want to treat the couple. For me the determining factor is whether, after the first therapy session, I feel that my talking with the couple could actually start their relationship moving. Of course this is largely a matter of personal discretion. The diagnosis I have formulated while observing the couple offers some indication as to treatment, although it is difficult to answer all one's questions on the basis of a single session. Often it is especially difficult to clarify questions of motivation, which frequently develop only during the therapy process. Tests that clarify indications for treatment (for example the Joint Rorschach Test developed by *Willi*, 1973) can substantially refine diagnosis. But I think that the crucial factor is always my personal impression of the couple, because the relationship that develops between us is of the utmost importance. But my diagnosis of the structure of the couple's relationship cannot, by itself, tell me whether or not to involve myself with them, and in part this decision remains a "partner choice" on the part of the therapist.

When the signs are right the partners feel encouraged to enter therapy, seeing it as an opportunity to talk about their conflicts in the context of a sober and businesslike atmosphere where unproductive behavior, manipulation and intrigue are not allowed. An important goal of the first interview is to convey to the couple the realization that their problems are mutual. To a great extent the success of treatment will depend on the partners' ability to get something out of the talks and interpretations, and on their readiness to fathom the underlying meaning of the crisis and to work on changing their behavior as a result of what they have learned.

If possible, at the close of the first interview I try, together with the couple, to reach a decision about what is to happen next. A difficult problem for the therapist is knowing what to say if he has the impression that he cannot help the couple further. As a rule therapists in this situation plead lack of time in their schedule and recommend that the couple seek out another therapist. If a therapist chooses to tell the couple directly that he does not feel he could work with them, he must phrase the statement tactfully, for otherwise the couple may feel shattered and condemned. For example, he might say, "Unfortunately, from what we've talked about together today, I don't see how I can help you with the methods I use.

What would make it really difficult for me to treat you is that I don't feel sufficient readiness on your part to . . . Certain conditions must be met for me to be able to do my work." I consider statements like this useful if one wants to give the couple a realistic chance to change their approach and make another attempt at therapy.

Some General Points of View Regarding the First Interview

Psychoanalysts and psychotherapists will probably feel that my conduct of this first interview is quite highly structured. But a therapist has good cause for maintaining a fairly active posture, for as a rule the couple are very anxious when they arrive at the session, and one partner may hope that the therapy setting will provide him with an arena where he can confront the other partner, and where the latter will have no chance to wriggle out of his grasp. The partner who did not telephone the therapist may attend the session with great reluctance, trying to keep open an avenue of escape. If all the avenues are cut off, he often becomes aggressive in an attempt to defend himself. Frequently the couple may have avoided talking for years, having been discouraged by their attempts to discuss their problems. Now they are entering therapy, thus placing themselves in a situation where they will be forced to talk with each other. This releases anxiety that the dam will burst and emit torrents of rage, hate, abuse and humiliation. By structuring the conversation I keep it from getting completely out of hand, for it is important, both for the couple and for the therapist, that this first talk should not end in a sense of failure. Analysts have repeatedly told me that they cannot do couples therapy because they feel discouraged after the initial visits. They simply could not bear, they said, to sit there watching a couple abuse each other hour after hour; they could not tolerate this degree of chaotic destructiveness and uncontrolled aggressivity. I believe that like family therapy, couples therapy demands that therapists do more than simply look on passively while partners tear each other apart, hoping meanwhile that at some point they will wear themselves out and admit that things cannot go on this way. As a rule the therapist will be disappointed if he believes that he need only let the couple go on fighting until they become so bewildered that finally they turn to him/her and are willing to listen to reason. On the contrary, passive behavior in a therapist gives the couple the impression that in therapy things happen just as they do at home, and they feel overwhelmed with resignation and hopelessness. If the first interview misfires, it may discourage the couple from committing themselves to therapy (*Greene*). I believe that, particularly in the beginning, the therapist must establish a clear-cut therapy framework and actively show the couple that he can be trusted and can manage the therapeutic process so that it does not degenerate into chaos. I try to steer a middle course between structured and nondirective therapy. To be sure, I do not think that it is necessary to structure couples therapy as tightly as many communications- and behavior-oriented therapists do; or at least that it is not necessary if one attributes any importance to the unconscious dynamics of the couple's problems. These unconscious dynamics can most readily develop and express themselves if the partners are given enough freedom so that they can co-manage the shape of their sessions.

As a rule the partners are afraid that the therapist will be biassed. I believe that during the first session the therapist should show that he is fair—as well as sympathetic and committed—in his efforts to confront the conflict, and that he will not ally himself with one partner against the other. This is easier said than done. Frequently the couple enmesh the therapist in the conflict so completely that he is quickly able to empathize with the problems of one partner, and therefore does not see how the other partner is affected by them. Or one partner may need help so desperately that he claims all the therapist's attention for himself, and the therapist finds it hard to perceive the other partner's need for therapy. It is a good rule of thumb to assume that each partner is contributing fifty per cent to the couple's troubles. I convey to the couple my view that neither partner is "the only one to blame" or "the only one who is sick," but that both are contributing more or less equally to the crisis. Although we may not yet have adequate scientific verification of this assertion, and although it may not be true in every case, it is nevertheless an effective working hypothesis in couples therapy.

3

INDICATIVE CRITERIA FOR THERAPY AND THE CHOICE OF THERAPY METHOD

The Purpose of Diagnostic Indications

The practice of arriving at a specific diagnostic indication for therapy derives from somatic, scientific medicine. Ideally, arriving at a specific diagnosis determines the cause of the illness, and eliminates it by some clearly defined method. The more drastic the therapy method, the clearer must be the criteria indicating its use. Its anticipated curative effects must be carefully weighed against the undesirable side-effects. The ideal models are the infectious diseases. For example, if a patient has fever, headache, vomiting and a stiff neck, a lumbar puncture is indicated to clarify the diagnosis. If the cerebrospinal fluid is found to contain pus, the diagnosis is meningitis, which can, for example, be caused by the bacterium *haemophilus influenzae Pfeiffer*. If the illness goes untreated there is a high probability that death or severe brain damage will result, but the administering of an antibiotic such as chloromycetin will destroy the pathogenic agent. Of course the chloromycetin may cause agranulocytosis (the destruction of white blood corpuscles), which may result in death. But the chance of a cure far outweighs the risk of the side-effect, so that the administering of chloromycetin is medically indicated. This type of medical model was transferred to the practice of psychiatry and psycho-therapy, despite the fact that the possibility of clearly defining diagnostic indications is quite limited both with respect to the diagnosis of patients, and with respect to the effectiveness of the therapy method. *Rapaport* (1959) claims that the basic method of psychotherapy is the relationship between two people, so that in addition to the variable of the patient and the variable of the therapist, there is the variable of the relationship that develops between them (*F. Heigl*, 1976). The course and effect of a psychotherapy are largely dependent on the specific configuration of the patient's relationship with the therapist. Thus it is only minimally possible to define a general indication for a particular therapy method. The specific "pharmacological effect" of the "doctor drug" (*M. Balint*, 1957) can less readily be objectified than the therapy method and yet as a rule is more significant than the method and often as important as the patient's personality.

The last few years have seen increasing criticism of the attempt to define diagnostic indications. *Minsel* (1974) states, "The more specific the method, the more prominent the institution, and the more specialized the training of the psychotherapist, the less flexibility there is in the application of the method and the more clients are turned away." There is a clear tendency to attach too much importance to psychotherapeutic indications, which in effect contravenes the possibility of therapy. Therapists who belong to a particular school are particularly inclined to expect patients to adapt to a therapy method rather than to adapt the method to the patient. During a conference *Watzlawick* stated that there are no incurable patients, only incompetent therapists (v. *Praxis der Psychotherapie*, 1977).

No doubt it is perfectly valid to question whether indications and contraindications can be said to exist for the treatment of marital conflict. *Sager* (1966) states that in couples therapy the only real contraindication is the therapist's inability to prevent one spouse from using the sessions to behave destructively towards his partner. *Kaufmann* believes that there is no such thing as a true contraindication, because no properly conducted family therapy could cause damage; the only thing that might conceivably be called a contraindication would be a situation in which family therapy has no effect. Very likely the same thing applies to couples therapy. But even if the therapist regards the treatment as ineffective, the patients often find it meaningful and regret neither the time nor the expense. So what is the point of arriving at diagnostic indications in the first place? Whose interests are they intended to serve? *I believe that often they do less to protect the patient from inappropriate therapies than to preserve the mental health of the therapist!* Psychotherapy is a difficult profession. Understandably, psychotherapists must take certain measures to keep their own psychological balance as they enter the often chaotic world of the patient. Diagnostic thinking helps the therapist to hold on to his sense of direction, and to subject himself to the prescribed doses of stress without overtaxing his strength. Thus diagnostics directly serves the patient's interests and is by no means—as people opposed to psychiatry often claim—a mere labelling process that degrades the patient and creates distance between patient and therapist. As a rule an ineffective therapy is not without its effects on the therapist, who has invested his own hopes in it and who is running the risk that a disappointment might decrease his motivation and commitment to further therapies. In this sense an ineffective therapy harms the therapist more than the patient. Diagnostic indications help the therapist arrive at a more realistic evaluation of the possibilities of a therapy. To be sure, often the therapist has recourse to them only after the fact, when reviewing a therapy whose results have disappointed him. He explains the outcome of the therapy by telling himself that the patient did not meet the requirements for the method used. By thus objectifying and detaching himself from the situation, he is able to alleviate his sense of personal failure.

Diagnostic indications make it possible for the therapist to discuss with the couple the prerequisites for a particular therapy method so that the factors advantageous and disadvantageous to therapy can be more clearly evaluated.

The following factors must be considered in evaluating the possibilities of couples therapy:

(a) The couple: The structure of their relationship, their marital situation and their conflict

(b) The psychotherapy method: Its limitations and potentials

(c) The therapist: His professional competence, his methodological preferences, his personal attitudes about marital conflicts, and his specific relationship with the patient couple

The Couple and Their Marital Situation as an Indicational Criterion

Psychiatric literature already contains a great deal of data—some of it conflicting—about indications for couples therapy. Initially one might assume that the criteria are the same as those applicable to analytic focal therapy (*Beck* 1974, *Malan* 1965, *Meerwein* 1967, *Bellak and Small* 1972, et al.). As applied to couples therapy, this would mean that the ideal patients would be those who present a clearly delimited conflict of which the couple are more or less conscious, but which at the same time causes them considerable suffering so that they are motivated to work at therapy, and who have fairly strong egos (among other things this presupposes that they function well professionally and socially), so that they can meet the demands of therapy and of building a working therapeutic alliance. I believe that *Richter* is right to emphasize that many patients can be treated in the couples therapy setting who would be neither willing nor able to carry through a successful individual therapy—for example, clients who suffer from so-called lack of insight into their illness or a general incapacity for introspection, i.e. "handicapped patients."

Specific criteria indicating couples therapy can be found in the literature (*Grunebaum, Christ and Neiberg* 1969, *Greene* 1970, *Hollender* 1971, *Richter* 1973, *Lief* 1976, *Christ* 1976, *Skynner* 1976, et al.).

—Both partners should basically want to continue their marriage and should feel an approximately equal degree of commitment to it (*Lief*). I believe that if this condition is met it does augur well for the therapy, but it must not be applied too rigorously. Therapy, as a clarification of the relationship, should from the very beginning assume the possibility that in the end the couple may decide to split up.

—The couple should have a well-established relationship of several years' duration that has led to a more or less firmly fixed interactional conflict (*Richter, Christ*). Couples therapy places both partners under great stress. Their relationship must be sufficiently valuable to them that they are prepared to tolerate this stress. Thus as a rule their relationship should be more than a fleeting encounter, and should contain areas that are intact, gratifying and conflict-free, which can give the couple the support they need to work at solving their problem.

—The crisis should have lasted long enough to motivate the couple to deal with it in depth, but not so long that they have grown resigned and lost faith that their problem can be solved, and not so long that their inappropriate behavior has become an integral, ego-enhancing and ego-stabilizing part of their relationship. Ideal in this respect are marriages that have been satisfying over a comparatively long period and then suffered a relatively acute crisis (*Christ*, 1976).

—The couple should be capable of entering into a therapeutic alliance. That is, they should be able to feel allied to the therapist's observing ego so that they can achieve a certain understanding of their conflicts (*Smith and Grunebaum*, 1976). The two partners are hurting each other for the most part unintentionally. But while they are in therapy they must decide, despite any disappointments they may suffer, to work at coming to some understanding (*Richter*, 1973). Couples have little aptitude to join in a therapeutic alliance as long as they are forming an unconscious coalition to resist all change, so that no therapeutic intervention makes any impression on them. But partners who choose to use therapy sessions in a purely projective way, to reproach their spouse and put him in the wrong, are hard to reach with a therapy technique based on fostering insight.

The following cases have been cited as contraindicative for couples therapy:

—If the partner who takes the initiative towards therapy does so only under pressure from the other partner (*Hollender*), for example to seek help with his impotence after he has been threatened with divorce.

—If the psychiatrist is simply being asked to bestow his blessing on a divorce that the couple have already decided upon, and therapy would only serve as an alibi for divorce.

—If the therapy situation will be used by the initiating partner to ferret out the other partner's secrets, for example to find out about extramarital affairs (*Christ*, 1976).

—If the couple intend, even in their joint sessions, to hold on to their mutual dependency and are not willing to tolerate anything they do not share.

—If one or both members of the couple claim that they are no longer capable of feeling anything for their partner (*Hollender*). As I show in a detailed example, it seems to me that one must be very cautious about accepting the claim that one partner feels nothing for the other. Often one partner tries to defend himself against unfulfillable demands by asserting that his love for the other partner is dead. The therapist must carefully evaluate whether there is still something to the relationship.

Unlike many American therapists who have written on the subject, I do not favor the drawing up of therapy contracts as a means to the rigorous clarification of the requirements of treatment (*Sager, Greene* et al.); for I have often observed that during treatment the partners' attitudes to therapy—and especially the attitude of the progressive partner—may undergo positive change, and that the agreements of a contract may boomerang and place the therapist at a disadvantage. At the start of therapy many partners cannot admit their desire to stay married and the fact that they still love each other, for they feel that this admission would place them under an obligation. Ambivalence and skepticism are not necessarily unfavorable signs in therapy. If the therapist measures the couple's motivation by overly rigorous standards, he will frighten many of them off and burden them with guilt for having failed to qualify for the therapy that would have "saved" them. Yet many of these partners would be quite capable of undergoing therapy if the therapist simply recognized the parallel between a person's hesitancy to commit himself to a therapeutic relationship and his hesitancy to commit himself to the marital relationship, and saw that this parallel could in fact form the focus of treatment.

All the above indications and counterindications should be interpreted as difficulties in carrying out a therapy and should be discussed with the patients. The therapeutic discussion of these criteria can make a major contribution towards clarifying for the patients the limitations and possible results of couples therapy, and can elucidate for them the kind of motivation that will be required. The therapist should be able to recognize inauthentic motivations and should find an appropriate way to discuss them with the couple so as, if possible, to improve the outlook for therapy. The classification of motives seems to me important in ensuring that the therapist and his methods will not be misused but will harmonize with the therapeutic goal enunciated by both patient and therapist.

The partners' expectations of therapy can be quite contradictory: The wife says that she wants her husband to give up his mistress and come back to her exclusively; the husband says that he will take part in the therapy only if it does not involve his mistress. I believe that the therapist might say something like this, "You have already tried all sorts of things to resolve this crisis and you haven't yet had the results you want. I believe that it's a positive sign that now you would like to try working on your problems with a third party. This work will put a strain on both of you and of course it presupposes that your relationship means enough to you that you are in fact willing to go to all this trouble." I also suggest that the mistress might play an important part in hindering any therapeutic progress, though I could not say that for sure. My experience has shown that it is easier if contact with the mistress is stopped during the term of therapy. This statement places the husband in a therapeutic double-bind. If he wants to continue his contacts with his mistress he must prove that this relationship does not sabotage any progress made in therapy.

I will briefly discuss a few types of inauthentic motivation, which ought to be clarified with the couple but which do not automatically rule out the possibility of couples therapy.

—*"Anyone who takes the initiative to obtain couples therapy is genuinely motivated for therapy."* In this case one must ask: How does the person who has made the initiative towards therapy intend to use therapy and the therapist? Does he hope, above all, that the therapist will use his authority to pressure the other partner into returning to the initial definition of their marriage, to give up extramarital relationships, and to be more sympathetic and obliging? Or does he hope that the therapist will tell him that he is right and back him up against his partner? Or is he primarily interested in using therapy to get the partner to change? Does he believe that he can change his partner through couples therapy after he failed to motivate the partner to undergo individual therapy? Often the partner who takes the initiative towards therapy is less receptive than the other partner to the question: "What could you contribute towards improving your relationship?"

—*"When people are in a lot of pain, they are highly motivated for therapy."* As a rule people who are motivated to undergo therapy are people in a lot of pain, but people in a lot of pain do not automatically become people who are motivated to undergo therapy. Many couples suffer from particularly dramatic conflicts and suffer particularly severe pain. When the marriage is in crisis they may attempt suicide, develop severe depressions, psychosomatic diseases like stomach ulcers, hypertension and biliary colic. The partners appear to be in hell, the wife is beaten and humiliated, the husband has started drinking and lost his job, and so on. One would expect them to do everything in their power to get out of this state. One may easily overlook the fact that a symptom is not exclusively distressing but that it can also draw a couple together. (Cf. Chapter 5 on resistance in couples therapy.)

At the beginning of therapy the therapist faces the tricky question: Can the couple change their relationship, and do they want to? Do the symptoms they have developed represent a compromise that is the best among a number of bad solutions? Does their disease symptom constitute such an effective method of neutralizing their conflict that to give it up would release intolerable anxieties to which the partners are not yet prepared to expose themselves? Are there so few conflict-free areas and stabilizing resources in the relationship that the partners quite rightly feel their collusion is the thing that is really keeping them together, so that in fact they cannot give it up? One must find out to what extent the couple really want to change the relationship. Has their suffering and complaining become an integral part of their relationship? Have the couple accommodated themselves to their conflicts? In this case too we must ask: How do the couple want to use therapy and the therapist? Do they mean the therapist to serve as just another clever gambit in their game of mutual torment? There are some couples for whom the continual invention of brilliant new devices for oppressing and abusing each other has a stimulating and intriguing aspect, so that it is almost impossible for therapy to effect any change.

—*"High expectations of the therapist and the effectiveness of his methods are the expressions of particular trust."* The therapist is prematurely heralded as a saviour and is stimulated by the patients' gargantuan faith in his magical and omnipotent powers to try to heal the marriage by simply waving his wand, without asking the patients to do any of the work. The couple abandon themselves to the therapist like children, demanding advice and instructions on how to behave. The more uncritically the patients accept such advice, the greater the danger that they will follow it in an absolutely literal way, thus contravening the therapist's true intention.

Indications for a Specific Methodology

In choosing a therapy method the therapist must decide

(a) the nature of the therapeutic setting; for example, couples therapy or individual therapy.

(b) the particular method of couples therapy, which varies with different theoretical concepts. For example, some methods are designed to work on conflicts, and others aim at behavior modification.

There is nothing homogeneous about marital therapy either in form or in method. Forms of treatment for marital conflict include individual therapy, group therapy, couples therapy, group couples therapy, and so on. There are also many subforms (v. *Greene*, 1970 and *Grunebaum and Christ*, 1969/1976).

—*Collaborative therapy,* in which each partner is treated by a different therapist. The therapists then exchange their findings, perhaps under joint supervision.

—*Concurrent therapy,* in which both partners undergo individual therapy with the same therapist at the same time.

There are also combinations of the above: The four partners involved in a *collaborative therapy* may all meet together in joint sessions, or the therapist conducting a *concurrent therapy* alternates individual with joint sessions. Some therapists consider the combination of the various settings, or the change of methods, a particularly productive technique (*Berman and Lief* 1976, *Skynner* 1976), whereas others take the view that a therapist should decide on one particular method and adhere to it (e.g. *Hollender*, 1971). Which of these settings is chosen depends largely on the training and preferences of the therapist, but it is important to differentiate between the therapeutic possibilities inherent in various settings. Once again, the point is not so much to work out specific indications for a particular setting or a particular therapy technique as to look at the dynamics promoted by the various methods.

Couples Therapy or Individual Therapy?

Couples therapy sessions have the advantage that neither partner is partly or completely excluded from therapy. Both participate to an approximately equal degree, whereas if the partners are offered nothing but individual therapy, as a rule only one of them makes use of it. It often happens that someone incapable of undergoing any other kind of therapy *is* capable of couples therapy (*Richter*, 1973). The therapist's task is easiest if he can point out the interdependence of the partners' behaviors while both partners are present. The couple interact in his presence, which limits the degree to which they can get away with non-objective accusations, and makes the therapist more conscious of his tendency to join them in acting out their conflicts. It is in the couples therapy setting that the therapist can show, in the most credible and spontaneous way, that he does not intend to identify with one partner against the other but will try to look at every phenomenon from both sides and search for the common roots. And it is in this setting that the therapist can best keep under control his temptation to ally himself with one partner against the other, or to engage in a destructive rivalry with the progressive partner (v. *Couples in Collusion*). In couples therapy neither partner can confide secrets that the therapist must not repeat to the other, and thus the therapist can operate freely with all the information he is given in therapy. And in this setting it is easiest for him to keep treatment focused on the relationship between the couple (*Greene*, 1970). Changes produced by the therapy have to prove that they can stand up to the test of reality, whereas individual therapy is often accused of confining itself to the unrealistic world of the treatment room. In individual therapy, which exposes the therapist to the subjective views of one partner, it is often virtually impossible for him to detect the nature of a collusion, which is a subtle interplay between both partners. Nor is the collusion always reflected in an individual patient's transference-countertransference relationship with the therapist, for the therapist's behavior can be very different from that of the spouse. Thus in individual therapy there is a risk that the partner not undergoing treatment may upset all the therapist's calculations. *Michael Balint* (1970) comments that the assumption that phenomena observed in the course of a psychoanalytic treatment can be taken as representative of the whole human development is in fact invalid; for first, not everything that the analysand has experienced in his development is repeated in the psychoanalytic situation, and second, what *is* repeated is highly distorted by the specific conditions of psychoanalysis.

But individual sessions also have advantages over couples therapy. They provide better protection against hurtful remarks. A partner with low self-esteem is overtaxed by a couples therapy if he is called on to reveal vulnerable sides of his personality which in the past he has always carefully shielded, and if the other partner takes advantage of the opportunity to inflict on him the very injuries he fears. Individual therapy can also be used as a preparation for couples therapy if one partner or both partners find it very difficult to become aware of their feelings and show them to the other partner. Moreover, because of the overpowering sense of rivalry and the pronounced envy and jealousy that arise in a couples therapy, it may lead to nothing but a destructive acting-out designed to win the therapist's favor. In individual therapy the therapist can build his relationship with the patient more peacefully, show him more empathy and bolster his self-esteem. Occasionally a patient may also find individual therapy more challenging because in couples therapy he remains overly involved with his partner and has too little sense of himself. Individual therapy sends him back to himself.

The particular advantage of individual therapy is that it makes it possible to probe more deeply the ramifications, for one individual, of certain disorders and problems. Thus it is especially recommended for the treatment of disorders that preexisted the marriage or that, during the marriage, are felt to be relatively independent of the relationship with the partner.

One particularly important difference between the two therapies lies in the fact that individual therapy permits a much greater degree of therapeutic regression, for it concentrates completely on the patient's subjective experience and takes relatively little notice of the objective realities of therapy. As a "playground of transference" it makes it possible for the patient to test his behavior and to free-associate, saying things that would never get past the strict barriers of shame, guilt or anxiety if the situation were taken to be real. Couples therapy permits this kind of regression only within narrow limits because it unfolds within the social reality of a marital relationship in which anything either partner says can lead to real, irrevocable effects that are in no way confined to the frame of the therapy session.

Example 1:

A woman arrived for marriage counselling, which she claimed was a last-ditch attempt to save her marriage. She stated that she was determined to get a divorce if her husband's behavior towards her did not undergo fundamental change, as she was no longer willing to put up with his oppression. He was in his fifties, more than ten years older than she. He gave the impression of being a staid, patriarchal businessman, solid and immovable as a rock, who did not turn a hair in response to the violent accusations of his wife. The wife looked attractive and youthful, but seemed to identify in an exaggerated way with the concerns of the women's movement. She placed the entire blame for her past neglect of her personal development squarely on her husband's authoritarian behavior. To begin with she had found security and protection with this man. But now she wanted to stand on her own feet. Under threat of divorce the husband had said he was willing to do anything his wife wanted, even enter into therapy, although he did not show any personal motivation to do so. Instead, like his wife he expected me to achieve miracles. He said, "I wouldn't have come here if I didn't believe you can help us. Now I'm here. What else should I do?"

My efforts to find out how he intended to use the therapy sessions, what he could contribute to the therapy, and what he would like to communicate to his wife met with no response whatever. Once he intimated that he thought it was a good idea to have a therapist present because then the couple would be on their best behavior and would hurt each other less. At this point I managed to get through to him by addressing the topic of his vulnerability, which he himself had just raised. His face suddenly acquired some animation when he reported that he was very sensitive and was convinced that if he showed his feelings here, they might be used against him. As a man he felt compelled to put up with the woman's offensive remarks without showing any sign of distress. Instead of rewarding him for his confession, which he had to overcome a great deal of anxiety to make, she at once attacked him with aggression and scorn. I had the impression that couples therapy would be too much for them. This man had never confided his feelings to anyone in his life and for more than fifty years had lived with the belief that he had to deal with all his problems on his own. It seemed to me that only individual therapy (if indeed even that) would offer this man the haven he needed to reveal more of himself without having to fear being hurt or exploited. Individual therapy seemed to me more appropriate in the wife's case too.

In cases like this couples therapy involves the risk that a person who has missed out on the opportunity for personal development may continue to put all the blame on the partner—in this case the husband. The husband's behavior is in fact authoritarian and repressive, in part of course to hide his feelings of insecurity and sensitivity from his wife and shield himself from her provocative behavior. In individual therapy the patient must concentrate on himself. Of course he can complain about his partner, but individual therapy demands that he come to grip with his own problems. In this case I advised the partners to go into separate individual therapy with different therapists, advice that they both followed.

Example 2:

A highly successful manager has been married for more than thirty years. His wife requests couples therapy. The husband comes to the first meeting against his will. Their reason for coming is conflict over an extramarital relationship the husband is having. He openly admits that he finds it hard to grow old and that he keeps himself young with sports cars and liaisons with younger women. He expects his wife to understand this, all the more so because he feels that life has passed him by because he devoted himself too much to his work. He says he would feel too much was being asked of him if he had to break off his extramarital relationship, and afterwards he would feel resentful towards his wife. For more than five years now he has had no physical relationship with his wife. In his view they ought to leave each other free and lead separate lives. He could not stand it if she were simply to sit around the house feeling depressed and bitter, waiting for him to come home. She has always been such a maternal and sensible woman, he cannot understand why she is making such a fuss now. The wife says that she is fed up with always having to be strong, and for once she too would like to make some demands, after having played second fiddle her whole life. The husband is prepared to come to further sessions, but shows no motivation to make any effort to understand his wife's situation better. Instead he expects the therapy to bolster up his wife so that she will learn not to be depressed and reproachful, and will let him have a girlfriend. He does not like his wife's reproachful attitude. Earlier, when his girlfriend said that she wanted to marry him and he had considered getting a divorce, his reaction had been to develop an acute duodenal ulcer.

During our talk I received the impression that this man was still deeply attached to his wife and that divorce was not the solution. But because of his problem in accepting that he was growing old, he did not at the moment show the slightest motivation to work on the relationship in order to make it more satisfying for both of them. Instead he wanted to make up for the time he had lost and wanted to use the therapy to get his wife to sanction this wish. In this case too I recommended individual therapy for the husband so that he could deal with the problems of aging, and for the wife so that she could work at finding other sources of fulfillment and not be wholly dependent on her husband to make her happy.

The choice of therapy depends on the diagnostic indications. If one partner, because of more severe symptoms, comes to psychiatric treatment, individual therapy may be continued until it becomes apparent that the marital conflict is playing a significant role; then the partner ought to move to couples therapy. In such cases I would, as a rule, bring the other partner into therapy if he lets me know, either directly or via the primary patient, that he is troubled by the way the therapy is going or that he feels excluded and would like the therapist to inform him about the therapy. The transition from individual to couples therapy poses certain problems for all concerned, but these are not insurmountable if the therapist gets everyone to talk about them. The primary patient, who up to now has been in individual therapy, now has to share the therapist with his partner, which he may experience as a loss of his privileged position. The newly arrived partner may feel that the therapist is already prejudiced by the one-sided information he has received and has allied himself with the partner he treated first. As a rule he will also find it more difficult to accept the patient role. The therapist too may regret having to give up the intimacy of a two-way therapy and bring the second partner into the therapy; all the more so if the second partner tends to compete with the therapist in the attempt to aid the primary patient. The therapist can also run the risk of overcompensation, of being overly indulgent and supportive of the newcomer in order to avoid giving him the feeling that he is not fully accepted in the therapy.

Another indication for couples therapy is a marital conflict already stated when the caller first makes his appointment. In these cases I customarily conduct the treatment exclusively in the form of couples therapy. If it does become necessary to introduce individual sessions I will not undertake them until both partners have formed a secure, trusting relationship with me, and neither fears that the other could use the individual sessions against him. In the individual setting I refuse to talk about the absent partner and maintain the focus on each individual's part in the troubled relationship. But occasionally after the first few sessions I get the impression that individual therapy could help the partners more than couples therapy. In this case it is recommended that the consideration of couples therapy be postponed and that for now the partners be put into individual therapy.

Unlike other psychiatrists, I find that couples therapy can readily be combined with individual therapy with another therapist, as long as the patient refrains from playing off the two therapists and therapies against each other. Opinions are divided regarding preference for either couples or individual therapy, or a combination of the two. I believe that marital problems can be worked on in any of these therapies, even in individual therapy with only one partner. The most important thing is that the therapist should be clearly aware of what he is doing and what emotional dynamics are being developed in the therapeutic triangle of man-wife-therapist.

Couples Therapy Reflecting Different Concepts of Therapy

Today couples therapy is already being conducted using various methods reflecting different concepts of therapy. Couples therapy methods fall into two basic categories:
    —Growth-oriented techniques that work on conflict,
    —and problem-oriented, systems and communications techniques.

Therapy techniques that work on conflict and insight are designed to help the partners achieve a better understanding of their own and their partner's behavior, and to recognize more clearly its genesis and ramifications. The expectation is that the process of becoming conscious of hitherto repressed urges will effect a powerful change in experience and behavior, and that increased communication about the partner's feelings and fantasies will promote self-acceptance as well as acceptance of the partner, and encourage personality growth in the relationship. The attitude of a therapist using this approach tends to be nondirective, sympathetic and indulgent. An analytic technique presupposes the patients' ability to make use of what therapy offers to become better acquainted with themselves and each other, and to expand the foundation of mutual understanding. Partners whose socialization has not accustomed them to perceive and express their own fantasies, ideas and feelings and who find it easier to interact socially or to behave in accordance with the rules of their environment have more trouble making use of analytic therapy. There is a risk that they may use the greater openness achieved in the therapy sessions in a destructive way, to attack each other or pressure each other to reveal secrets. Also less suited for this method are couples who are strongly inclined to rationalization and who acquire insight and understanding on a purely intellectual level, without establishing a link to their experience and behavior.

Behavior-modification techniques are less concerned with the origin and ramifications of intrapsychic conflicts and instead set out to directly modify behavior and communication in accordance with a concrete model for the resolution of conflict. Their emphasis is on learning by doing; that is, they are based on the assumption that positive behavior and constructive communication exercise a positive effect on the deeper layers of experience. An active posture is adopted by the therapist in the attempt to restructure the relationship and modify behavior. Sessions are often highly structured and consist to a large extent in exercises that enable the partners to test and learn new ways of behavior. Frequently the therapist's behavior is overtly manipulative, pedagogical, and structured so as to offer suggestions. This attitude is effective primarily in cases in which destructive marital behavior has been turned into a ritual—for example in cases where husband and wife are engaged in a power struggle, or in psychosomatic collusions (*Willi*, 1976), in which the couple are so trapped in acting-out that there are no longer any valencies free for a therapy aimed at promoting insight. Behavior-modification methods are also to be recommended when the partners are not making progress by endlessly rehashing their problems verbally and ought to be doing something to solve them instead (e.g. sex therapy à la *Masters and Johnson* or *Helene Kaplan*). But when the partners need to perceive their conflicts in a more differentiated way and come to an understanding about them, these exercises in behavior are felt to be too pragmatic.

Indications for the Use of a Specific Therapist

The therapy method depends not only on the suitability of the patient but also on the preferences and aptitudes of the therapist. Personally I am most at home with an analytic workstyle, although in many cases I also use structuring methods. Structured techniques involving the use of exercises have the advantage (which perhaps is also a risk) that the clarity of their underlying concept makes them easier to learn. The use of exercises enables the therapist to cut through the extremely complex psychodynamics of marital conflicts, giving him the feeling that he is on solid ground and working to bring about concrete change.

Formulation of a Collusion Focus

In behavior-modification and systems-oriented couples therapy it is very important to define the couple's problem exactly. The same is true in dynamic couples therapy, where a focus of therapy must be clearly defined as well. To avoid being caught up in the surface fireworks of a partner conflict, it is recommended that the therapist formulate the focus for the therapy, if possible, during his first interview with the couple, and definitely in the course of the first few therapy sessions. The focus defines the direction and inner guideline of the therapy work. According to *Beck* (1974), the lack of an overall focus in short-term therapy generally leads to breaking off the treatment prematurely. Failure to understand the psychodynamic processes at work arouses in both therapist and patient feelings of disappointment, resignation and lack of motivation to go on working together. It is impossible to conduct an analytically oriented short-term therapy without a rough notion of the patient's disorder. The focus is intended to make comprehensible the unconscious meaning of the symptoms. In therapy the patient is supposed to resolve the basic, unconscious conflict to which his major symptom and his difficulties are related. Thus the focus serves as an intellectual orientation point for the treatment.

I consider it essential in couples therapy that, to avoid getting lost in the patients' jungle of accusations and counteraccusations, the therapist be able to reduce the material presented to him to its common denominator, to the unconscious formula underlying it. In couples therapy the symptom or disease is the faulty behavior of both partners. Often they themselves cannot understand this behavior and so experience it as something imposed on them from outside, which they cannot escape. The formulation of a formula that embraces the faulty behavior of both partners is an integrative act that the therapist must perform to avoid being drowned in the endless sea of details that streams from the patients. This formula is a hypothesis by the therapist, derived from observation of the couple's inappropriate behavior, which initially he keeps to himself. The therapy process must determine the extent to which he can express the formula, either step by step or all at once. The basic formula of a couples therapy should be drawn up as soon as possible and should be supplemented and defined more exactly as the therapy unfolds. *Balint* et al. (1973) state that the focus enables the therapist to work with "selective attention" or, as the case may be, "selective inattention."

I suggest the following guidelines for formulation of the focus in couples therapy:

1. The focus should be a formula applicable, in the I-form, to each partner separately, and in the we-form to the couple, so that it points up the analogous disorders in the two partners' way of relating.

2. The formula should consist of an introductory sentence that relates to a basic need that both partners have in common, that has always been frustrated in the past, that the couple had hoped to satisfy through their relationship, and that is obviously still present.

3. The concluding statement should allude to the *present-day defensive behavior* of the partners relative to their basic frustration and in terms applying to both partners.

The formulation of the focus should be so specific that it relates to the partners' manifest behavior, but should remain open enough so that it can integrate a broad spectrum of their unconscious experience and so can be deepened and expanded in the course of therapy.

A few examples:

> "We have to protect ourselves from our longing to become one by continually hurting each other so we can both keep our distance."

This formulation describes a narcissistic collusion and relates to the example portrayed in detail in Chapter 12.

> "The need to keep my most intimate feelings to myself is borne out by the way my partner tries to hurt me."

In this case the husband had great difficulty showing his feelings. When he made tentative efforts to express his feelings in therapy, his wife, immediately feeling hurt, attacked him and once again charged him with being egotistical and unfeeling. His wife's attempts to get under his skin had for a long time concealed her own dread of showing her feelings.

> "We are safe from the danger of being engulfed by each other as long as our relationship is counterbalanced by relationships with other partners."

In this last example both partners had extramarital relationships that were not making them happy but rather served to protect them from closeness and dependency.

> "As long as we have to depend on each other because we are ill, we don't have to worry about being abandoned by each other."

This was a case of oral collusion in which the wife was afraid to give up her depression because then her husband would no longer have to be concerned about her. The husband had similar fears about the wife.

> "Our mutual dependency is assured as long as neither of
> us feels capable of living without the other."

In this anal-sadistic collusion the wife did not dare to become
liberated because she felt any change would cause her husband great
insecurity and because she would have regretted their loss of mutual
dependency.

> "The fact that it is more important to the husband to
> have his wife's approval than to gratify his instincts is shown
> by his willingness to allow her to govern his potency."

The childish way in which the husband wanted his wife's approval
because he regarded her as a substitute mother made her contemptuous of
his lack of masculinity, although on the other hand, she was also afraid of
any partner who seemed to be stronger than she.

> "My partner will be unable to exploit my desire to be
> dependent as long as I remain stronger than he is."

The symmetrical form of this relationship led to a power struggle
between husband and wife.

> "Our relationship will not break down from boredom as
> long as we use fighting and jealousy to keep it exciting."

This attitude describes the exhibitionistic needs of the partners in a
hysterical marriage, needs that are designed to compensate for low self-
esteem.

The formulation of the focus should apply to both partners, in
accordance with their contributions to the formation of the collusion. Thus
the focus guards against one of the principal dangers of couples therapy,
namely the possibility that it may turn into an individual therapy for just
one of the partners, with the other partner serving as cotherapist. But if
the therapist keeps in mind his formulation of the focus, it is easier for him
to involve himself for a few hours with the problems of a single partner
without being compelled to restore the balance immediately. The formulation of a focus is the best technique for preventing a couples therapy from
getting bogged down in those problems of the partners as individuals
which have little to do with their relationship. Even if a collusion is
dissolved in the course of therapy this does not mean that all the problems
have been mastered, but by then it will be clearer whether the therapist
should recommend individual therapy, which might achieve further
progress at a deeper level.

Individual therapy, as a follow-up to couples therapy, will have a less destructive effect on the dynamics of the couple's relationship if the partner not involved in the individual therapy is already well-informed about the underlying causes that necessitate the therapy.

I share *Richter's* view (1973) that in dynamic couples therapy it is not possible to work on that portion of the individuals' symptoms that is not directly linked with the couple's problem. The therapist must guard against the temptation to behave as he does in individual therapy and must refrain from probing too deeply into the individual problems of each partner. Instead he should deliberately concentrate on that part of an individual's problem that feeds into the therapy with the other partner and thus can be looked at and worked on by both partners. Couples therapy is a supplement, not an alternative, to individual therapy. A couples therapy can form a meaningful follow-up to an individual therapy. It can also serve as a preparation for individual therapy in cases in which a patient first needs relief from the pressure of a serious marital problem before he can begin work on his own emotional problems. Yet couples therapy can also serve as "indirect individual therapy" because it can affect those individual symptoms characterized primarily by their "dialogue function," that is, symptoms that are nourished by the dynamics of an interactional conflict.

Summarizing Guidelines for the Evaluation of Requisites for Therapy

1. Diagnostic Evaluation of the Couple's Problem

—What do I see as the basic conflict between the partners and the personal and social background of this conflict? Where can I see interdependent polarizations and fixed, interlinked interactional circles? If possible, I must formulate a collusion focus.

—In what form has the couple attempted to resolve or neutralize this conflict (for example through illness or the involvement of third parties, especially children)? Do pseudo-solutions, apart from their disadvantages, also furnish appreciable advantages to both partners? Have the couple already made other attempts at therapy, and what were the results?

—How great is the partners' inner flexibility and willingness to give up their present compromise solution, challenge their ideal of marriage, and restructure their relationship? What is likely to happen if the progressive partner begins to reveal his hitherto hidden sensitivities and anxieties? Will the regressive partner use the progressive partner's admissions to hurt him and thus once again confirm the latter's belief that he must keep his feelings to himself and deal with his problems on his own? What is likely to happen if the regressive partner begins to assume responsibility for himself and no longer chooses to be dependent on the protection and help of the progressive partner? Will the progressive partner feel threatened by this bid for autonomy and forestall every effort in that direction, or threaten the regressive partner with the withdrawal of his love?

—What external circumstances limit the scope of therapy (e.g. the wife's lack of professional training, the wife's financial dependence on her husband, obligations to parents or children, joint ownership of property, appreciable differences in the partners' age, education, level of individuation, sociocultural norms and values)? What would be the probable consequences for the partners personally and for their families if their marriage were to break up? Is progress in the couples therapy linked to intolerable disadvantages for other people to whom the couple are close?

—What satisfying, conflict-free areas in the couple's relationship, and what resources in their common past and their life together, can act as stabilizing factors? What common tasks and goals confer a strong motivation to continue the relationship despite all the couple's problems?

—What stress-reducing gratifications are available to the couple outside their relationship?

—What do the partners expect from therapy?

2. Goal-Setting

—*What is the ideal goal of a couples therapy?* Increased ability to integrate the claims of self-development, the partnership and the environment. The break-up of the collusion and the relaxation of the rigid, confined interactional personalities. The opening up, or the clear definition, of the couple's relationship to the outside world.

—*What is the concrete goal of the therapy?* As focal therapy, couples therapy is a short-term treatment that as a rule does not allow the couple to do more than begin to move towards the ideal goal. One goal that is of practical importance in an ongoing marital relationship is the renunciation (as far as possible) of inauthentic solutions (the neutralization of conflict through illness or the involvement of third parties), along with acceptance of the limitations of one's own capabilities and the partner's capabilities in a relationship; and the recognition by the partners of their need to relieve the excessive demands made on a marital relationship by finding other means of gratification. If, after the partners have achieved a clear picture of the situation, it seems impossible for them to build a satisfying relationship, one practical goal of therapy is to give them the courage to separate, assuming that they have the chance to begin again and that they have not shared their lives for so long that they cannot conceive of life apart, and that other people, especially their children, will not suffer unduly.

3. Available Therapy Methods

—Which therapy methods are actually unavailable? Is couples therapy and/or individual therapy the preferred treatment? Are the partners primarily interested in working on their personal problems or on their relationship?

—Can the partners work constructively with the therapy technique offered?

—What does the therapy setting require in terms of time and money?

4

RESISTANCE
TO COUPLES THERAPY

Resistance of the Partner Unwilling
to Undergo Treatment

Resistance of the Partner Who Consents
to Therapy

The Couple's Resistance

The Therapist's Resistance in Couples Therapy

The two mainstays of psychoanalytic treatment are transference and resistance. How is resistance expressed in couples therapy?

According to Freud the patient resists the elimination and change of his repressions. The ego tries to avoid the discomfort that would result from the release of repressed material. It wants to hold on to the secondary advantages derived from illness. Thus resistance is the correlative of repression and so arises in every therapy that treats neurosis by uncovering conflict.

41

In the literature on group therapy, concepts from psychoanalysis were transferred to the group setting. This literature speaks of the group as a single organism that is articulated through its individual members. The therapy method that reflects this conception interprets the group as a collective entity, which addresses obstacles to the progress of the whole group and thus works on the group's resistance. This analysis of resistance helps members of the group to remove obstacles so that they can get on with the principal business of analysis.

It is helpful to apply this concept of group resistance to couples therapy. As a rule the two spouses are not equally motivated to take part in therapy. Indeed, one can even say that the more strongly motivated one partner appears, the more resistant the other partner's behavior will be. If one partner refuses to come to therapy at all the therapist may work exclusively with the partner who wants treatment, but invariably it soon becomes clear that the absent partner is trying to block the progress of the therapy at every step. If only the resistant partner did not exist (the therapist and the patient think) they could really have made great strides and the patient would have become more independent, more emancipated and more capable of using his own initiative and of forming mature relationships. The therapist and the partner seeking treatment form an increasingly close alliance against the wicked partner. Soon the therapist begins to consider the divorce to which his patient could (apparently) so easily be motivated if it were not for the external factors that are forcing him to stay married: the children, the home, the family's reputation, the elderly parents who would not survive the shock, and so on. The sessions begin to turn into a joint airing of grievances, which may make life a bit easier for the patient in the short run but which unquestionably makes his marital situation worse.

But if we were to take the collusion concept as our starting-point and examine the couple—in terms of the neurotic stranglehold they have on each other—as a dyad, a single unit composed of two parts, we would have to reach the much more banal conclusion that the couple's dual resistance to treatment is being expressed through only one of the partners. This would make it clear that the couple, that is both partners, are resisting any change in their relationship and, especially, resisting awareness of their collusion, and that they refuse to give up the secondary advantages that the collusion affords them on the behavioral level.

I would now like to describe separately the resistance of the partner unwilling to undergo treatment, the partner who wishes treatment, and the therapist, so that we can get a clearer look at the destructive resistance-games in this triangle.

Resistance of the Partner Unwilling to Undergo Treatment

In around 60% of the couples I have treated, it has been the wife who has taken the initiative towards treatment. Other therapists report 80%. Thus the partners who refuse treatment are more often men than women. This fact has a direct bearing on the reasons for the resistance of the unwilling partner. Today, when men are under pressure from the women's liberation movement and are adopting a defensive posture of guilt and anxiety, it seems to me, as a therapist, important to take the attitude, "From *his own point of view* the unwilling partner has 'good' reasons not to come." One must try to understand him instead of attacking and reproaching him. Indeed, to begin with one must follow the procedure used with a patient suffering from psychosomatic symptoms and support his defensive gesture, treating it as a measure that makes sense. Understandably, many male therapists—and perhaps to an even greater extent many female therapists—still find this difficult.

Fear of the Loss of the Progressive Position
Of those couples exhibiting a progressive-regressive role polarization, the progressive role has been assumed by the man in around 75% of the cases I have treated. In my experience the progressive partner clings to his apparently superior position not only because he is anxiously trying to protect the privileges and self-validations linked to it, but also because he feels that the regressive and destructive behavior of his partner makes it necessary for him to take a firm stand and keep a clear head at all costs; for otherwise the two of them would go down together. Often one hears a progressive partner say, "After all, both of us can't be patients, one of us has to stay healthy." Progressive types fear that they do not have the strength to bear the additional burden of therapy, all the more so if, as men, they feel responsible for the support and security of their families. They feel that the confrontation with their own weaknesses might so damage their self-esteem that they would become failures even professionally. The partner in the regressive position often fails to make it clear that he would be quite capable of assuming more responsibility; for his feelings of defiance, rage and vengefulness are fixating him more and more in a destructive attempt to make himself weak, and all his efforts are directed towards exposing the progressive partner as an impotent dictator. Often the progressive partner is perfectly capable of opening up to his own weaknesses and fears if, in the therapeutic setting, he feels safe from the threat of being hurt by his regressive partner. The progressive partner

needs adequate reassurance from the regressive partner, as well as the therapist, that he is not only able to acknowledge his weaknesses but that if he does so, his relationship with his spouse will become more spontaneous and human. It is largely the behavior of the regressive partner that determines whether or not the progressive partner receives the needed reassurance.

But progressive partners often give the therapist a hard time when they distance themselves from the regressive partner by diagnosing the latter's illness. "My wife is suffering from depression," the husband says when he wants to commit a troublesome wife to the care of a doctor or therapist. In couples therapy, rather than talking about an illness called depression, it is better for the therapist to say, "Your wife seems to be really down because . . ." or "Your wife is despondent about . . . ," as this emphasizes the communicative aspect of the wife's behavior. For example, *Minuchin* (quoted by *Haley*, 1975) does not speak about a child with anorexia nervosa but of a child who does not want to eat, which also makes clear the goal of therapy: to get the child to eat again.

In couples therapy the partner who is resisting treatment can use vague medical diagnoses to free himself from any need to inquire into the real cause of the problem, for now it seems to be a medical matter that he is not competent to deal with. The despondent behavior and the reproaches of the regressive partner need no longer be taken at face value, and this enables the progressive partner to adopt the superior attitude of a "therapist." He may now be more patient and helpful towards the regressive partner, but is not forced to take him seriously, for after all, he is "sick." The progressive partner strongly resists any effort of the therapist to get him to look at this detached, superior posture, for the progressive partner fears that if he drops the diagnostician's pose that is his shield, the regressive partner will attack him with unbridled destructiveness just as he has done in the past, and exhaust him with his demands. For this reason it is not a good idea for the therapist to let himself be provoked into saying things like "Do you really want to destroy your partner completely?" or "Don't you know that it's only because of you that your partner is sick?" The hypothesis that each partner contributes about 50% to any marital conflict not only helps us to see how the progressive partner makes the regressive partner sick but also how the regressive partner fixates and exploits the attitude of the progressive partner.

Often the therapist will find it difficult to see where the progressive partner needs help because he seems so in control, so serene. He will understand the progressive partner's problems more easily if he asks why the partner who seems so on top of things has teamed up with a regressive and infantile partner who needs support and help.

For example, the therapist can ask the progressive partner, "But how are things for you when your partner is feeling so bad?" At first the progressive partner will try to justify himself. Then one might say, as a follow-up to the first question, "But it can't be easy for you, living with a partner who complains so much?" If this comment does not start the ball rolling either, the therapist can make more apparent his therapeutic view that the progressive partner is suffering from a narcissistic sensitivity, "I can see that you are making a really determined effort to be brave and not complain about the burdens imposed on you because your partner is not feeling well. It seems to me that you feel you are chiefly responsible for your marriage and that you believe you have to put up with everything that happens. I think that it's admirable of you to make this effort, but I wonder whether you don't sometimes ask too much of yourself. Maybe because of this continual strain, you have had to put on a hard shell to protect yourself from your partner's demands and expectations and to fulfill your duties to your family." I have often found that patients— especially the husbands of wives suffering from depression, symptomatic neuroses or psychosomatic disorders—seemed to be completely transformed by remarks of this kind. As soon as they saw that the therapist wanted to talk with them without any intention of hurting, accusing or judging them, they were able to open up more. They had expected the therapist to behave like their partner, showering them with reproaches, or supposed that he would think they should assume even greater burdens in their marriage. The understanding attitude of the therapist made them feel accepted, so that they were relieved of the burden of believing that they had to be personally responsible for everything that happened in the relationship.

Fear of Moral Judgment and Obligation

Partners unwilling to undergo therapy feel that their partners have called them up to appear before a judge—the therapist—to answer charges for a "breach of proper marital conduct," such as an extramarital relationship. They believe that if they were to comply with the summons to therapy, they would in effect already have pled guilty. The partner who wants therapy announces the therapy as if it were a sort of court session where it will be determined who is guilty of causing the marital strife. Often there is a fear of being manipulated by the therapy. Partners who feel this way have frequently learned, in childhood as well as marriage, that "discussions" (or the experience of "accidentally" finding a book like *Couples in Collusion* lying around!) merely represent a carefully laid trap and that a mask of frankness and understanding is intended to manipulate the victim. Often partners of this kind suffer from narcissistic disorders and are so hypersensitive to any attempt to place them under obligation that it was even difficult for them to pronounce their marriage vows. When entering therapy they must first learn to believe that they are respected as individuals in their own right. If things go well in therapy they feel sheltered while they develop in their own way and form a relationship suited to their capabilities. The therapist cannot place a reluctant partner under an obligation to enter couples therapy any more than he can permit the partner who wants therapy to use it to strengthen the marital constraints placed on the other partner. Example 3 below makes this abundantly clear.

But if it is in fact not possible to interest the resistant partner in coming to therapy, the therapist must ask the partner who wants therapy, "What do you expect from therapy now? Do you want to use it to change your partner or yourself?" Useful therapeutic work can be done with a single partner only if the partner seeking treatment really wants therapy for himself and is not looking for justification, reinforcement and added ammunition against his partner.

Example 3:

> A woman with an air of desperation requested therapy, saying that life with her husband had grown intolerable. Dissatisfied with his job, he vented his bad temper at home, demanded boundless devotion, and at the same time disparaged everything she did for him. At the same time he accused her of being too dependent and subservient, and said that he could only respect a liberated partner. He was having an extramarital relationship with a colleague at work with whom he could discuss all his feelings. The wife appeared seriously motivated to undertake therapy. She was also aware that she had learned, from her mother's example, that a woman was supposed to adjust to a man and follow his lead. However, she felt, no doubt rightly, that her husband could not bear it if she made any personal demands and developed a personality of her own. The husband resolutely refused to accompany her to talk with me, because he believed only she needed treatment.

If this woman had gone into individual therapy, the obvious course would have been to encourage her to become more independent and break free of subservience to her husband, while supporting her in standing up to him. If these efforts had succeeded, in a short time the couple would have ended up getting a divorce or, even more probably, found themselves caught in an unending power struggle.

The other therapeutic course, and the one I chose to pursue, was to clarify the woman's motivation to seek liberation. To me the crucial factor seemed to be whether she wanted to free herself simply to combat the husband, so that inwardly she was still conditioned by him and was perpetuating their collusion, or whether she wanted to work to develop herself as a result of her subtle observation of certain objective factors, especially the personal capabilities of her husband. At first I suggested she should work to liberate herself in areas that would not directly intensify her conflict with her husband. She applied herself to completing the professional training she had broken off, and also sought self-development outside the confines of her marriage. Not until she had made some progress in this direction and begun to feel more confident did she begin to work more intensively on her relationship with her husband. Therapy had already given her enough insight into her tendency to behave in a passive and docile way, so that she could stand up to her husband with calm determination, as well as with the necessary degree of self-awareness. Now she was much freer in her ability to think about whether or not she wanted to go on with the trying relationship with her husband. Her more resolute attitude enabled her to have constructive talks with her husband in which he found it possible to talk about his professional disappointments without having to treat her as if she were responsible for them, or to run her down and complain that he did not understand her. Her fifteen-year marriage, the raising of their three children, and the home they had built together meant a lot to her, so that she decided to continue living with her husband. In therapy it was important to keep her from achieving an inauthentic liberation by using her new-found freedom as a weapon to get the better of her husband. It was also important to point out to her that for the time being, the only therapeutic course she could pursue was to develop her own potential.

Resistance in the Partner Who Consents to Therapy

The Elimination of Delegated Resistance

In group therapies in which the group members did not know each other previously, the same thing happens again and again: The member of the group who puts up the strongest fight against treatment tends to become a scapegoat whom the rest of the group blame for their inability to make progress in their therapy. The group forms a consensus, agreeing that unless they succeed in eliminating the resistance of this group member, they must postpone dealing with any other therapy topic. So the resistant member becomes the representative for the group's resistance and makes it possible for the others to exempt themselves from confrontation with their own fear, weakness and defensiveness. A similar group dynamics may evolve in the triangle husband-wife-therapist. I proceed on the assumption that husband and wife share more or less equally in resistance to therapy-induced changes; so I refuse to join with the partner who wants therapy in hatching plots for luring the other partner into therapy against his will. Instead I concentrate on the question of how the willing partner and I are jointly making it hard for the other partner to enter therapy. I have repeatedly heard patients portray their absent spouse as a real monster; and then when I invited the spouse to come to a session he proved quite willing to take part in the therapy. Often a transference phenomenon occurs: The partner who wants treatment experiences a kind of sibling rivalry and wants to keep the therapist all to himself and to be the favorite child who complains to his parents about a wicked sibling and receives approval and comfort. If the therapist himself has a preference for individual therapy, the partner who is resisting therapy is quite right in feeling that he only serves as a scapegoat. If the therapist suspects that the partner who wants therapy will summon the reluctant partner to therapy in such a provocative way that the latter will not come, the therapist himself can telephone to invite him for a talk, saying something like this: "The problem or illness of your partner seems to be closely connected with the relationship between the two of you, and so I think it's important for you and me to have a talk so that I can hear what you think about it." I would not, as is sometimes recommended to therapists, try to entice the partner into therapy by offering him a post as cotherapist: "I am counting on your help in treating your wife (or your husband)."

It is often assumed that the partner who initiates couples therapy is motivated to receive treatment and so will resist it less. This assumption is false. If the therapist succeeds in getting the unwilling partner into therapy, the partner who initially wanted therapy often feels insecure, or feels that he is getting less support from the therapist, and may even feel pressured, for he has lost all the advantages that went along with having initiated the therapy. Often he will behave provocatively in an attempt to rekindle the formerly uncooperative partner's resistance, insinuating that his mate's new-found willingness to undergo therapy is sheer hypocrisy, a lip-service paid to the therapist, the falsity of which is attested to by many incidents that allegedly occurred outside the therapy sessions. In situations like this I say something like: "For me as a therapist it isn't possible to get an idea of what happens outside our sessions. The important thing to me is what happens *during* our sessions, so it seems to me that the best thing is for us to concentrate on what we can learn right here. For the moment I'd just like to note that you (the unwilling partner) are willing to join in our talks, and naturally this is one of the basic requirements for a couples therapy." If the wife has initiated therapy and the therapist is a man, the loss of the special alliance between the wife and the therapist against the husband is not always an easy problem to overcome, for it intensifies the woman's already-existing fear that the two men might gang up against her. Thus the therapist must show both partners a nonpartisan sympathy and, whenever possible, behave as if they were both more or less equally resistant to treatment.

Resistance to Loss of the Inappropriate Behavior and to Elimination of the Symptoms

As I described in detail in *Couples in Collusion*, the couple's mutual marital misbehavior is not only an agonizing strain on both that drives a wedge between them, it is also the means by which they keep a stranglehold on each other that makes their relationship almost indissoluble. As long as the partners maintain their collusion, their behaviors are so inextricably linked that soon no communication takes place between them that does not represent a reaction to each other's behavior. Once the couple have seen through their collusion it is harder to maintain, and each partner—especially the partner who "wants treatment"—begins to fear that the other could use his new-won freedom to move away from him. This is by no means true only of the progressive partner, who fears the loss of his position of power and privilege, but also of the regressive partner, who feels he has lost the advantages deriving from his position as plaintiff and challenger, and as the oppressed and disadvantaged one. Sharing one's life with someone is a good deal more difficult if one cannot simply let oneself go and behave in the old provocative way, blaming one's partner for everything, but instead must accept responsibility for one's behavior and come to grips with one's own contribution to the troubled relationship. Many therapies grind to a halt at this point because the couple cannot or will not give up their inappropriate behavior. In marital power struggles, strife and accusation not only represent unsatisfactory, inauthentic solutions, they also exert a stabilizing and stimulating effect.

Resistance to any change in the relationship is even more marked in a case involving psychosomatic or neurotic symptoms. Again and again in couples therapy I have seen couples who, when faced with the prospect of giving up a symptom, were terrified that once there was no compelling reason for them to stay together, their relationship would fall apart, for each partner feared that the other partner would no longer need him or have any interest in him. Often a couple cherish and care for a symptom as if it were their child, for it is the inexhaustible theme that unites them. But it also comes between the partners and prevents them from getting close and dealing with their marital conflicts. The loss of a symptom can release depressive reactions, and often demands that the couple work through their grief as if their child had died.

The Couple's Resistance

Resistance to the Disintegration of an Idealized Image of Marriage
This resistance is especially hard to overcome. Most couples who resist the destruction of their ideal of marriage have strictly banned any argument and difference of opinion, and their marriages are like little islands of paradisiac peace in a world full of discord. As a rule the partners in these idealized marriages consult a doctor or psychotherapist only with the greatest reluctance because of a severe psychosomatic illness or sexual dysfunction. Often the couple exhibit something akin to panic because of their fear that their relationship will fall apart if the model of marriage to which they initially pledged themselves is challenged by therapy. In this case it is important to make certain that they understand what therapy is like. Their illness, I say to them, is a sign that there are some unspoken problems in their relationship. As a therapist I feel that we would have to work on these unresolved tensions by talking about them, for otherwise there is a danger that the illness might get worse. Obviously, I say, expressing deep-lying tensions is something they are not used to and at first it will be quite a strain; they will also have to realize that many things in their relationship will change, and at first this will cause anxiety. Often this kind of couple can profit more from group couples therapy, for here they may see how other couples quarrel without feeling they have to run away. But certain couples become especially anxious in group therapy because up to this time they have hermetically sealed themselves off from the outside world and have not wanted anyone to know anything about their private affairs. I have repeatedly observed that these idealized relationships ended in divorce once both partners were able to speak more openly about their feelings and attitudes. The breakdown of the relationship during therapy can leave one or both of the partners bitterly disappointed in the therapist, whom they view as having destroyed their marriage. No one wants to rob them of their utopian happiness; but the presence of psychosomatic symptoms indicated that there was something about the relationship that did not work.

Joint Resistance Reflecting the Marital Power Struggle

The marital power struggle represents a confusing situation for the therapist (v. *Couples in Collusion*). Both partners seem to be suffering greatly from their continual combat and to be making an appeal for the therapist's help. But nothing whatever will happen in therapy as long as the therapist confines himself to analytic interpretation or works to establish therapeutic empathy. The sessions are unproductive, for the partners spend their time incessantly reproaching each other for trivial offenses committed in the last few days, and turn dogmatic and pedantic, dredging up incidents out of the remote past to prove their points. Their joint resistance is revealed by the fact that they give the therapist no possibility whatever of intervening. Often this situation can be remedied by the formation of a therapeutic collusion (v. Chapter 6 on countertransference and therapeutic collusion). That is, when the therapist feels helpless, he lets himself get into an open quarrel and power struggle with one of the partners. In doing so the tension is transferred to the therapist who now serves as a model of the couple conflict and can thus demonstrate how to resolve it.

Nonneurotic Resistance

The analytically oriented therapist is inclined to interpret as neurotic resistance everything that patients do to impede the progress of the therapy process, without questioning whether in some cases a patient might not be healthier than we therapists are, and whether it is not the therapist's notion that should be considered "neurotic." The literature of psychotherapy has from the beginning been overburdened with absurd theories that tell us much more about the psychological makeup of therapists than about patients. Every therapist aligns himself with a particular theory and its concomitant method of treatment. But it is essential that every therapist should also recognize the relativity of his theory in light of the complexity of the human situation, and when confronting obstacles in therapy ask himself whether these really represent resistance on the part of the patient, which must be analyzed and interpreted, or whether the resistance might be more on his part, calling for self-analysis. This applies in particular to concepts in couples therapy that are vulnerable to upheavals in the social milieu. One of the attitudes most essential for a good therapist to maintain is respect for the patients' view of therapy, for the things the couple have learned in their relationship, and for what they have built and gone through together.

The Therapist's Resistance in Couples Therapy

In *Couples in Collusion* I went into some detail about the professional and personal resistance of the therapist in the treatment of couple problems. Often psychoanalysts, whose theoretical concept of therapy derives from Freud, are not willing to do therapy work with their patients' families. Until recently even marriage counsellors worked, for the most part, only with one spouse. They did not positively exclude the other spouse from therapy, but usually they were a little too quick to accept the idea that it would be hard to motivate him to undertake therapy. I find that it is almost always possible to bring the second partner into therapy sooner or later if one views his resistance as a problem of resistance on the part of all three participants (husband-wife-therapist). Often it is hard to understand the clumsy and unfeeling way in which well-trained therapists treat their patients' families. In fact one frequently gets the impression that the more empathy they show towards their patients, the more dismissive will be their attitude towards the families. The therapist's will to help is most readily roused by people who are weak, regressive, anxious and depressed, and who turn to him for help. (Cf. *Beckmann*, 1974.) We therapists are quick to feel offended or uninvolved when someone tries to deal with his problems himself, without our help. From my observations, the chances of doing successful therapy with regressive patients are no better than with progressive ones. Of course the regressive patients are more open to their feelings and more willing to give their trust to the therapist, but this same tendency to wait passively for the therapist to do all the work actually makes it harder to work with them. It is more difficult for the progressive patients to work up trust in the therapeutic dialogue, but once they have actually become involved in therapy, they are often more willing to use their own initiative in working on their problems. The following example shows how difficult it can be for the therapist not to identify too closely with the patient who has come for help.

Example 4:

A husband arranges for his acutely depressed, suicidal wife to be hospitalized in a psychiatric clinic. At the clinic he tells the female doctor handling the case that he will not allow his wife to come home until she is completely well again, and that until this happens he wants nothing to do with her. The doctor responds in fury: "You're probably just trying to get out of dealing with your wife's crisis, without even asking whether you might not be to blame for her depression.

Obviously you're interested in your wife only when she's at her best." After that the husband refused to take part in the couples therapy recommended by this female physician. The wife was released when her condition was slightly improved, and then sent to another therapist, this time male, who said he would treat her only if her husband was willing to attend at least their first meeting. The male therapist said something like this to the husband: "From what you said at the clinic I gather you feel your wife's depression is putting such a strain on you that you can hardly go on yourself. You may have been hoping that the clinic would take the responsibility off your shoulders and return your wife to you in a better frame of mind. But I think that neither you nor I can help your wife by himself. Instead all three of us should try together." Then the husband explained in great detail all the things he had already gone through in the course of his wife's depression and how hard he had to struggle not to be overcome by depression himself. Clearly he was relieved not to be met with the same old accusations, and instead to be given a chance to talk about his concerns and his own past difficulties. He explained how deeply hurt he felt by his wife's passive resistance when, for example, she refused to look after the house, left everything lying around, and withdrew from him sexually. His wife's depression had been a great drain on him, for in addition to his responsibilities at work he had had to take over most of the running of the household and to look after the children. So he felt he had been left to cope on his own. To his wife's surprise he then talked about some of his own fears and sensitive spots, things he had never told her before.

5

DYNAMICS OF THE RELATIONSHIPS IN A THERAPEUTIC TRIANGLE

Possible Forms of Transference in the
Therapeutic Triangle

Transference in Individual Therapy and
in Couples Therapy

Specific Work on Transference in Couples Therapy

Freud described as transference the fact that, according to his observations, the analysand (patient) does not see the analyst as he really is but in a distorted way, tending to project onto the analyst the image of some person who was important to him in the past, like his father or mother, and attempts to pattern the relationship with the analyst in such a way that it repeats this earlier pathogenic relationship. In psychoanalysis one part of the ego regresses and thus part of the relationship with the analyst also regresses and, to a great extent, takes on the qualities of a relationship between an adult and a young child. The transference relationship repeats the essential traits of the conflict a person experienced in childhood, so that the conflict can be directly, concretely worked on in the transference itself.

Later it became clear that not only the relationship with the analyst but in fact all deeply felt human relationships reflect childhood experiences, frustrations and fixations, and thus exhibit many aspects of transference. More than any other adult relationship, marriage displays the traits of transference, especially certain elements of the parent-child relationship (v. *Couples in Collusion*). The marital relationship arouses fantasies and memories of earlier experiences and causes a spouse to transfer to his partner expectations, fears, notions and fantasies that he has had about other people he was close to, and to pattern the marriage along the lines of these same experiences and fantasies.

Possible Forms of Transference in the Therapeutic Triangle

The situation in couples therapy is especially complex because *the two people to whom a person can form the most intensive transferences are both present at the same time: the spouse and the therapist.* These circumstances permit the development of many different kinds of transferences.

Uniform Transference to the Spouse and the Therapist
For example, a wife may offer both her husband and the therapist the same kind of relationship she had with her father. She treats both the husband and the therapist (male) as a father.

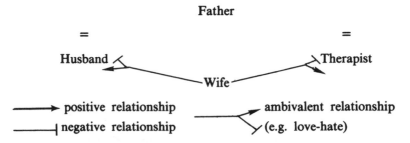

Thus the wife may be tempted to build with the therapist the same kind of disturbed relationship she has with her husband. For example, she may perceive him as cold, despotic, indifferent, and so on, and behave in the same frustrated and demanding way she does towards her husband. In this case she may elicit the same reaction from the therapist as from the husband, and the therapist is in danger of identifying with the husband. He may find that rather than responding directly to the wife's transference, he is using her husband as a mouthpiece for his own reactions; or he may serve as the husband's delegate if the husband is struggling to stand up to his wife.

Example 5:

> A woman of so-called hysterical character manages to keep all the members of a couples therapy group breathless with suspense for long periods by continually demanding support from the group—just as she does from her husband—and then invariably complaining that what they have done is not enough, so that the group develops a feeling of impotence and failure. Commenting on the couple's sexual problems, I tell the wife, "You're making us all impotent." She is very hurt by this remark and over a period of months stages violent quarrels with me during which she showers me with hatred and abuse; but in the process she loses her depressive helplessness, while at the same time her husband regains his potency.

Split Transference to the Spouse and the Therapist
The wife may split up her childhood feelings about an important parental figure by behaving differently towards the therapist than she does towards her husband, transferring to her husband the negative aspects of her relationship with her father—her rage, disappointment and hatred—while she transfers its idealized aspects to her therapist.

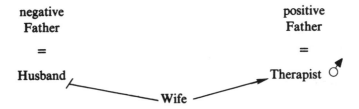

The therapist can get into a really tricky situation here. He can identify with the wife's "projections" and agree with her that in contrast to her husband, he is a positive figure. He may be insufficiently aware that the wife idealizes him just as she did her husband when she fell in love with him. Without realizing it the therapist can end up as the husband's rival. Or the wife may have married her husband in the first place because he was *not* like her father. This phenomenon occurs primarily in so-called hysterical marriages (*Willi*, 1970, 1971). Fearing that the man she marries may turn out to be tyrannical, frightening and brutal like her father, she marries a man who is especially gentle. But women of this kind are often quite high-spirited, so that this type of husband may not give her the response she needs. In couples therapy she hopes to find in the therapist the idealized aspect of her father. The following example shows the difficulties that can arise in a situation of this kind:

Example 6:

> A colleague calls me in for consultation and asks me to sit in with him on one session to help him decide whether he ought to continue couples therapy or terminate it and begin individual therapy with the wife. Initially the patient was the wife, who had come to a psychiatric clinic to be treated for migraine and withdrawal from addiction to painkillers. There she began psychotherapy, which was later carried on by the same doctor on an outpatient basis. Among other things, the therapy revealed that for eight years she had had a lover without her husband's becoming aware of it. The wife secretly mocked him for not noticing. In therapy she gave up her extramarital relationship in order to "get our family affairs in order." She told her husband about the relationship, whereupon her migraines disappeared. Her husband's reaction was to fall into a severe depression, so that the therapy was continued in the form of couples therapy. After a period of apparent improvement, the wife had a relapse, developed migraine again, and once again became addicted to painkillers. So the therapist was forced to prescribe tranquilizers for her again. Up to this point the husband's role in the therapy had been more that of a cotherapist, and he had not talked about his own problems.

During the session that I attended as consultant the wife struck me as vigorous and passionate, whereas the husband, on the other hand, seemed pallid, frail and joyless. The wife said that her relationship with her husband was that of a mother to a child, which did not suit her. Basically she would prefer to be married to a father-figure. She had, she said, a lot of deprivation to make up for where fathers were concerned, as her father had been an uncontrollable, brutal drunkard whom she had always feared. One of the main reasons she had chosen to marry her husband was that she wanted to be sure she would not end up with a man like her father.

Both my colleague's reports and my own impressions led me to conclude that the wife looked to her therapist to be an idealized father and preferred having him to herself in her sessions rather than having to share him with her husband. Her husband was participating in the therapy only to a marginal degree anyhow, and so the therapist was considering working on the wife's idealized-father transference in an ongoing individual therapy. I regarded this projected change in the basic structure of the therapy as problematic because the therapy would then, in externals, fixate the wife's neurotic tendency; for she wanted a relationship with two men, one of whom she could despise while idealizing the second with whom she would have a relationship involving fewer obligations (first the lover, now the therapist).

Naturally the idealized-father transference could have been treated in an individual therapy. But although idealized relationships of this kind can be discussed, often their actual character does not change because the gratification derived from being able to discuss one's most intimate problems with the idealized-father substitute is often stronger than the pressure to really work through the relationship in order to free oneself from it.

Homoerotic-Competitive Transference to the Therapist

Whereas uniform and split transference is found primarily in the partner of the opposite sex from the therapist, the form I will discuss now is found chiefly in the partner of the same sex as the therapist. The sparse literature on the triangle relationship in couples therapy jumps to the conclusion that an Oedipal situation is involved. But how are we to understand this Oedipal situation? Oedipus killed his father and married his mother. In psychoanalysis the term Oedipus complex means that the son competes with the father for the mother's love. But couples therapy is not equipped to treat fantasies of this kind, for the therapist is most readily experienced as father or mother, and perhaps as rival or lover. The husband in the therapeutic triangle is not in the situation of an Oedipus who would like to take his mother away from the therapist as the fantasy father-figure.

The situation in couples therapy is much closer to post-Oedipal conflict. Freud and psychoanalysis view a boy's development, culminating in his overcoming of the Oedipus complex, as follows: If it is made clear to a boy that he cannot marry his mother and displace his father, this frustration will aid his development, causing him to look for a partner of his own age. But I do not believe that the Oedipus complex is resolved by this development; instead it continues to exist in an altered form. Often a young man who has just married will feel that he has to prove himself to his father and his father-in-law. He wants to prove to them that he is a real man, and if possible surpass them in virility. Often the father and father-in-law have a critical, competitive attitude towards the son or son-in-law, and even make erotic overtures to the daughter or daughter-in-law. This can lead to jealousy between the son and his father or father-in-law. The son may be afraid that the father will take away his wife if he does not prove himself as a man.

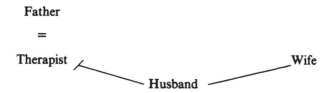

This pattern is meaningful in couples therapy. Often we see men who are clearly ashamed to reveal to the therapist the failure of their manhood and who find it acutely embarrassing to be described by their wives as domineering, egotistical, weak and impotent. So they begin to compete with the therapist. They need to have their masculinity confirmed: "Am I successful as a man?" "Are you more of a man than I am?" They want to discover that the therapist is also a failure as a husband, so that they will not feel humiliated in his presence. For example, a man remarked at a group couples therapy session held one evening, "Of course it's easy for Willi to have a peaceful marriage. There can't be any fights when he's never at home."

The Partners' Joint Transference to the Therapist
Generally too little attention is paid to this form of transference because we are used to thinking of transference as a phenomenon found only in individuals. Often the conflict between the partners is so all-consuming that the therapist overlooks their joint transference.

The nature of this transference can be perceived in the atmosphere and in the emotional reactions of the therapist, that is in his counter-transference, more readily than it is seen in the partners' behavior. For example, when two partners engaged in a marital power struggle incessantly try to run each other down and keep calling on the therapist to act as arbiter, it soon becomes clear that they are quarrelling like two children in front of their parents and that it is very important to them which of them the father says is right. Marital power struggles conform primarily to the anal-sadistic model of collusion. As a rule at least one of the partners is still very much tied to his parents, leaving the other feeling shut out and slighted. The strong dependency on the parents is generally

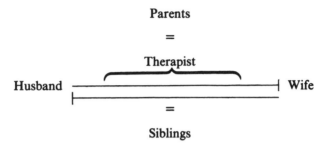

transferred to the therapist. Two siblings fight and compete in his presence. Their acting-out is so intense that in the beginning it is completely impossible for them to do any insight-based therapy work because each of them dreads that the other might be judged right and draw the father onto his side. As a rule the therapist must accept the exaggerated authority that the couple confer on him if he is to structure the situation actively and impartially, the way a father has to do at the dinner table when two children get into a loud quarrel and neither will quieten down because each thinks that if he does not yell loudly enough he will lose out to the other, and so each one tries to use all the means at his disposal to keep the parents from paying any attention to the other.

But sibling rivalry is revealed not only in the anal power struggle, in which as a rule the couple's current dependency on their parents is transferred to the therapist, but also in their highly idealized relationship of both partners with the therapist.

Example 7:

A couple who had been married for more than twenty years began treatment after the wife had several times undergone psychiatric hospitalization for alcoholism. To the amazement of the female therapist, who at this time was still in training, the woman suddenly stopped drinking after the first few sessions, apparently without the slightest effort. Her symptom was cured. Neither partner had resisted going into therapy. But the tapes of the sessions clearly revealed that both partners regarded the therapist as a mother with whom they wanted a close relationship, and that they were involved in a sibling rivalry. The therapist's self-esteem was boosted by the great trust they showed in her, and quite understandably she was happy with the therapy. But it seemed to me important that she make the couple's dependency on her a theme of the therapy, especially as both partners were still very dependent on their parents. The man had trapped the wife into marriage to free her from her parents' influence. Thereupon the wife had become devoted to her mother-in-law and was very close to her, just as the husband was. Thus in therapy they had to work on their idealized relationship to their ideal mother and the hidden rivalry that it entailed.

Another form of joint transference is the voicing of complaints about the failure of therapy to achieve any effect. Both partners express their conviction that the therapist could make the therapy more productive by giving useful advice. The therapist is called on to create an ideal marriage. The couple are furious, defiant and vengeful because the therapist has not only failed to fulfill their expectations but has even made it impossible for them to continue their collusion, their neurotic way of interacting, which has secretly been a source of gratification. Often the partners behave like two baby birds, greedily opening their beaks wide and asking the therapist to feed them. There is a danger that the therapist may get caught up in these expectations and feel remorseful because he is unable to fulfill the couple's demands. This can lead to an oppressive atmosphere in which the therapist does not dare to terminate therapy before all the couple's expectations have been fulfilled. If the therapist does not dare to confront the situation and treat the couple's overblown expectations as a problem in therapy, an unfortunate situation can result. The therapist thinks that he must go on making even better, shrewder, more accurate interpretations, or devote even more time to the case. Or he reacts counterphobically and tends to curtly dismiss the couple when they are not expecting it so that they leave feeling hurt. The best approach is for the therapist to show by his attitude to the couple that he can set clear limits, and to bring home to them that he cannot do the work of therapy all by himself. Perhaps he may also have the opportunity to indicate to the couple how they had fantasized the relationship with the therapist as an all-powerful means of wish-fulfillment, just as they had imagined their marriage to be.

Transference in Individual Therapy and in Couples Therapy

The literature reveals that so far not much work has been done on transference and countertransference in couples and family therapy. *Berman and Lief* (1976) state that the couples therapy setting is less suited to working through problems of transference neurosis, so that elements of transference tend to go unexamined. The majority of family therapists believe that the transference concept is not central to family therapy, because in this setting the therapist works primarily with the relationship within the family and transference to the therapist becomes less important. *Stierlin* (1977) has devoted a special study to the processes of transfamilial and intrafamilial transference. In couples therapy the two people to whom, as a rule, the most intense transferences are formed are present at the same time: the spouse and the therapist. The relationship with the spouse already exhibits all the traits of an established transference, whereas the transference to the therapist has yet to be formed—in analysis often a time-consuming process. A number of psychiatric authors find that the special advantages of couples therapy lie in this very fact that the transference can be dealt with much more directly in terms of the relationship between the partners than in the relationship with the therapist (*Sager*, 1967).

The spouse is considered to be the number-one transference figure, and the therapist serves as a sort of secondary transference figure. This may be a disadvantage for psychotherapists who get particular satisfaction from their work on transference. The therapist and the relationship with the therapist are considered to play a less central role in couples and family therapy than in individual therapy. The therapist is seen as a kind of director who tries to keep things going on the stage without himself playing the major role. At first I believed that as long as I concentrated on the dynamics of the couple's relationship, the couple would not develop any noticeable transference to me; but later I saw that a clear correlation existed between the failure of many of my therapies and unresolved problems in the relationship between me and my patients, so I began to pay increasing attention to transference. But in many cases I was unable to separate transference and countertransference because transference problems became of central importance precisely when the couple and I had formed a collusion in which the patient's contribution could not be distinguished from my own. (On didactic grounds I still adhere to the traditional distinction between transference and countertransference.)

I see two principal reasons why transference is often less evident in couples therapy than in individual therapy:

Limited Possibilities of Regression in Couples Therapy
As a rule partners who go into therapy already have a regressive relationship. Their reactions are irrational, affective and projective, often senseless and out of control. Generally the therapist must not promote regression, but rather must support the healthy part of the patients' egos as a prerequisite for establishing a working therapeutic alliance. By doing so

he also curbs the formation of the transference, which usually goes hand in hand with regression. Many therapists, and especially those with a leaning towards behavioral therapy, actively structure the therapy by entering into a contract with the couple which both partners must live up to. Or therapists assign the couple "homework," which generally requires constructive and controlled activity by both partners. Often it is impossible to do therapy work if the therapist allows the dynamics of the couple relationship to disintegrate to an acute regression of the level of primary process thinking (*Balint,* 1970). There are couples who try to outdo each other in regression, each trying to show the therapist that he is even more helpless and needs even more attention than the other. In other cases, if one partner wants to regress during therapy, the other has to place himself under a strain to compensate for it. In such cases I often try to forestall regression in the first partner and get him to accept his share of responsibility for our work, because if this does not happen a couples therapy will turn into an individual therapy for the regressed partner, with the progressive partner serving as cotherapist.

Limited Openness in Couples Therapy

There is limited space in couples therapy compared to individual therapy for therapeutic regression; there is also limited space for the development of openness. I.e., the presence of the other partner blocks the development of a "private world" between patient and therapist (*Leslie,* 1964). It is particularly difficult for all concerned when feelings of love for the therapist are expressed in the other spouse's presence. There is a risk that a positive transference to the therapist may be expressed in a negative form, as rage and anger instead of as feelings of love. Psychiatric authors like *Giovacchini* continue to prefer the classic individual therapy in the treatment of marital problems because transference neurosis is considered not to be resolvable in couples therapy. I cannot agree with this view. I believe that in couples therapy transference problems can be resolved in a different manner than in individual therapy.

Specific Work on Transference in Couples Therapy

As a rule transference to the spouse is closely related to transference to the therapist, so that if possible the transference to the therapist should not be treated as an isolated phenomenon from which the spouse is excluded.

One way of working on transference is to trace the transference to the spouse and to work on it in terms of the dynamics of the marital relationship. This method is applicable primarily to cases involving an idealized transference to the therapist but a negative transference to the spouse. In most cases the transference to the therapist corresponds to the idealized transference to the spouse at the time of partner selection. Pointing out that there is a connection between father, husband and therapist will prevent the therapeutically undesirable polarization (in the eyes of the wife) of the husband and the therapist. The wife's transference now becomes a productive element in the treatment of the marital relationship. Thus if possible the transference to the therapist should be treated as secondary to the relationship so that therapy may remain focused on the couple's relationship.

A different approach to transference must be used in cases where transference to the therapist is so all-consuming that it cannot be referred back to the transference to the spouse. If in this case transference is not treated directly, the therapy threatens to bog down. At times when I have failed to establish a constructive working relationship with the couple, therapy was broken off at the instigation of the partner who had a strained relationship with me. Often the partner in question was a wife who was especially dependent on my approval but whose needs I had dismissed as extortionate, or a husband who felt competitive with me and felt that he had not received sufficient confirmation of his manhood from me. As I gained experience, I saw that in these cases the therapist could not remain aloof towards the relationship but had to engage in a concrete confrontation with the patient manifesting the transference. My fear that the other partner might feel excluded if I did this proved unfounded. Often the other partner actually feels relieved if the therapist takes from him some of the burden of his spouse's transference and directs it to himself.

When the therapist does choose to actively deal with one partner's transference, his way of doing so must serve as a model for the other partner in dealing with his spouse's transference to him. This can be an extremely valuable learning experience for the second partner and can greatly intensify the therapeutic process. All this will be discussed in more detail in Chapter 6.

6

THE THERAPIST'S INVOLVEMENT WITH THE MARITAL PARTNERS VIEWED AS THERAPEUTIC COLLUSION

Achieving a Therapeutic Attitude of
"Universal Bias"

The Failure of "Universal Bias" in the
Face of Countertransference

Therapeutic Collusion as an Attempt to Make
Countertransference into a Therapeutic Tool

Achieving a Therapeutic Attitude of
"Universal Bias" (*Stierlin*)

The concept of collusion as I have described it in *Couples in Collusion* (1982) is designed to give the therapist a theoretical foundation from which to observe and treat marital conflicts as a whole. Many therapists shy away from doing couples therapy because they perceive that they are unable to devote equal sympathy to two patients at the same time, and that again and again they fall into the trap of allying themselves with one partner and against the other. The collusion concept is intended to make it possible for the therapist to keep his attention and empathy divided equally between both partners.

The principal studies of the problems of bias in family therapy have been done by Boszormenyi-Nagy and Stierlin. *Boszormenyi-Nagy* (1972) talks about the family therapist's "multidirectional partiality"—a partiality that is directed to each individual family member but applies to all (v. *Stierlin*, 1975).

Stierlin talks about universal bias. The therapist is supposed to try to win the trust of every member of the family. He should enter into, empathize with and understand the feelings of each one, and yet be fair to all. This does not mean he must compulsively analyze whether or not he is devoting exactly the same amount of attention to each one, but that basically he must give all the family members the feeling that they are understood and respected.

In couples therapy it is even more difficult to preserve this universal bias, perhaps because generally psychotherapists have not resolved the conflicts in their own marriages.

The Failure of "Universal Bias" in the Face of Countertransference

Despite the collusion concept, by which I believed I was protecting myself from the risk of partiality in couples therapy, the video tapes showed me that under certain circumstances I failed to behave in a neutral and impartial way during therapy. Frequently my conduct makes it all too evident that I like one partner a good deal better than the other and that I feel more empathy and understanding for one than for the other. At first I found this realization disturbing and doubted my ability to do couples therapy. Then I tried to work out which kinds of behavior I had particular trouble in dealing with. For example, I get into difficulties with women who seem to me to make exorbitant demands that I should take their side and who strike me as having an insatiable need for acceptance, support and comfort. In time I observed that I could easily lapse into treating them just as their husbands did. The more unapproachable I became, the more the wives resorted to destructive, uncontrolled weeping and complaining. But the same women were able to calm down and work constructively at therapy when I managed to convey feelings of warmth, sympathy and genuine understanding. But what was I to do when I could not feel genuine sympathy, when in fact the women got on my nerves so that I was barely capable of doing my job as a therapist, which was to search into the underlying cause of their behavior?

Freud had little to say about how countertransference can be used as a tool in therapy. He viewed countertransference as a kind of analyst's "blind spot," which represents an obstacle to perception and thus an obstacle to treatment. He recommended that it be overcome in a teaching analysis. *Paula Heimann* (1950) was among the first analysts to see countertransference as a meaningful tool for understanding the hidden value of patient communications. The truly novel aspect of this idea was that the analyst's own feelings and fantasies about the patient represented a sensitive instrument with which to measure the processes taking place within the patient. If the analyst observes his own mental associations while he is listening to the patient, he discovers a secret sympathy between the patient's unconscious and his own. According to Paula Heimann, the analyst's unconscious understands the patient's. This deep-lying relationship is manifested on the surface in the form of feelings that the analyst notes are his reactions to his patient—his countertransference.

It was not until the last few years that the countertransference reaction has also been studied as a *behavior* of the analyst, building on the view of countertransference as an intrapsychic diagnostic process within the analyst. *Sandler et al.* (1973) state that the person to whom the manipulations and provocations of a transference are directed either conveys the idea that he will not accept this role or, if he has an unconscious urge to comply, the idea that in fact he does accept it and is prepared to act accordingly. In terms of the collusion concept this means that the person who is the object of a transference is free to refuse or agree to enter into a collusion, that is to interact in accordance with the terms of the collusion. *Sandler et al.* claim that in addition to the analyst's free-floating attention he also evinces a free-floating responsiveness. Although the literature often portrays the analyst as a machine that, with absolute self-control, takes in impressions and emits interpretations, the analyst's actual behavior, according to *Sandler et al.* (1976), is quite different, for the analyst speaks with and greets the patient, may joke with him, and permits his reactions to deviate to some degree from the classical norm of psychoanalysis; and both in his overt behavior and in his thoughts and feelings the analyst may show a more or less pronounced willingness to take over the role assigned him. I believe that even when he thinks he is conforming to the classic model of the analyst's behavior, he conveys his emotional reactions to the patient. *Watzlawick et al.* (1969) claim that by definition we cannot "not behave" in a human relationship. If a female patient confesses to the analyst that she loves him, the analyst can simply accept her statement without saying a word. In terms of their relationship this tells the patient that she is free to offer him her love again if she chooses but that he does not intend to take her up on her proposals. In this case the patient may feel that her feelings are not appreciated and tend to keep them to herself. Or the analyst can encourage the patient to communicate her feelings even more clearly. From this she may infer that he is interested in her feelings. A third possibility is for the analyst to interpret her declaration of love as a transference of her feelings of love for her father. From this the patient will probably conclude that the analyst is shifting the responsibility of responding to her offer of love onto other people and so avoiding the issue. It can be especially disastrous if the analyst reveals to the patient any discrepancy between what he says and the way he actually relates to her: that is, if he interprets her offer of love as transference but reveals by his tone of voice and his interest in her remarks that he is pleased by her invitation. He may get his comeuppance when his interpretations are greeted with remarks like: "Oh, Doctor, I can't ever listen properly to what you're saying, I'm so happy when I just hear the sound of your voice." No matter what the analyst does or does not do, he is responding to the patient's offer of love, and his behavior in turn elicits reactions from the analysand. To be sure, in classical psychoanalysis the analyst can conceal his own emotional reactions to such a point that at least at the beginning of the analysis the patient is uncertain what is happening inside the analyst. In couples therapy, in which the therapist plays a considerably more active role and must meet the eyes of his patients, who are no longer lying on a couch, it is an illusion for him to try to hide his attitudes, feelings and reactions.

Freud (1911) required the physician to recognize his countertransference and to overcome it. Every psychoanalyst, Freud believed, could get only as far as his own complexes and inner resistances permitted. This is why he has to undergo self-analysis, and if he cannot manage that then he does not have the ability to treat patients in analysis. According to *Rogers* (1973), the psychotherapist's attitude is the most essential requirement for an effective therapy. Rogers claims that on the one hand the therapist must be genuine, whereas on the other he must show the patient unconditional positive caring, unreserved responsiveness. Commenting on what he has learned from his own experience, he says that in his relationships he has found that in the long run it is not useful to pretend to be calm and friendly when he really feels angry and full of qualms, to be amiable when he is actually feeling hostile, to seem self-assured when he actually feels anxious and insecure. Indeed, Rogers says, he attributes most of the mistakes he has made in his personal relationships and most of his failures to help people to a defensiveness that caused him to behave just the opposite of the way he really felt.

But what is the therapist to do if the demand for sincerity conflicts with the demand for unreserved positive acceptance of the patient? What is the analytic therapist to do if despite his own analysis and other personal experience in therapy, he is forced to admit that he cannot achieve a free-floating responsiveness and universal bias, but is in danger of giving way to his emotional reactions to his patients?

Therapeutic Collusion as an Attempt to Make Countertransference into a Therapeutic Tool

Gradually I learned to make a virtue of necessity and to use my inability to achieve universal bias and unreserved acceptance of both partners as a tool in therapy.

A psychotherapist's competence is not measured by his success in avoiding any interaction with the patient but by the degree to which he can make conscious use of his personal idiosyncrasies, his reactive tendencies, and even the remains of his neurosis as a therapeutic tool.

It is less important that the therapist achieve an unattainable impartiality than that he set up no pretensions between himself and his patients. The feelings the patient stirs in him are by no means simply reactions to the patient's transference, but to a large degree represent the therapist's neurotic transference to the patient, that is, the infantile attitudes of the therapist to his patients (*v. Beckmann* 1974, *Moeller* 1977).

As a rule the tendencies to transference on the part of the therapist are initially only latent. They do not surface until they are mobilized by the patient, at which point patient and therapist form a genuine collusion. By sharing with the patient the same basic fantasy, the therapist engages in a conflict in which his behavior is largely determined by the behavior of his patient, and he in turn reinforces the patient's behavior. At this point, when the therapist's behavior is intermeshed with his patient's, his personal limitations with respect to universal bias will become especially evident to him. But he will try to convince the patient that he is making a sincere effort to resolve fairly the conflict that has arisen between them. He will not deny his antipathies and tensions, but on the contrary will face the conflict head on, and face it as himself, with all his personal limitations. In this way the effort to resolve the conflict between patient and therapist will serve as a model for the patient couple in dealing with their own relationship. Thus when the therapist lays himself open to a partner-adversary relationship with one of the patient couple, he enters into a collusion. This, however, becomes a therapeutic collusion if the therapist is able to work therapeutically on the conflict with all three parties involved.

Therapeutic collusion refers to the following process: Using his own urges to form a certain kind of relationship—urges of which he is not himself conscious at the outset—the therapist involves himself in a collusion with one of the patients. His behavior and that of the patient become increasingly interdependent and, as a rule, increasingly polarized. After this process has gone on escalating for a while, there comes a point when the therapist becomes aware of his predicament and is able to regain his perspective. Now he works therapeutically on the collusion by interpreting it as a process between two partners. The work on the collusion between the therapist and one of the partners then serves as a model for resolving the marital collusion.

The therapist must use his emotional reactions (i.e. his countertransference as well as his "neurotic" transferences) as more than just a diagnostic instrument. While trying not to reveal his feelings, he must at the same time accept them and do nothing to avoid genuine conflict with the patient, trusting that sooner or later he will find a way of resolving it. Of course it is essential that he not be completely or permanently caught up in the conflict, and this can most easily be ensured if he does not try to repress it. Part of him should retain a sense of perspective about what is going on, or at least be capable of regaining perspective. The therapist's involvement in a collusion becomes the central focus in treatment for some time. This sets in motion a process that is highly significant for all three parties.

—The patient who acts as the therapist's partner can learn how the therapist, who began in a neutral position, has entered with him into a conflict quite similar to the one he is having with his spouse. Thus he confronts the question of whether he may not continually be experiencing the same conflicts in his personal relationships.

—It is important for the emotional health of the therapist that he is not forced to dam up his own feelings during therapy but can enter fully into an emotional process, trusting that a solution satisfactory to both parties can be found. Thus the therapist learns about himself in his work, learns things important to him personally.

—The process is also important to the partner who initially is not involved in the conflict. At first, one may assume that he will feel a certain satisfaction at seeing his partner get into the same difficulties with the therapist as with himself: for clearly the therapist is colliding with the same behavior patterns in his partner that he does. Then a second, contrary feeling arises: The spouse may feel guilty for leaving his partner all alone to fight it out with the therapist. He also feels left out of the intensive confrontation between the therapist and his partner-adversary. If this confrontation leads to a breakup of the therapist-patient collusion, the resolution of the conflict serves as a model for dealing with the marital collusion. Both partners experience the therapist's open, fair-minded efforts to understand himself and his partner-adversary, and his efforts to accept both the patient's limitations and his own. This challenges the other partner to confront the marital collusion, which, it now appears, can generally be resolved. The experience of the therapeutic collusion gives both partners a certain detachment from the marital collusion, and so they can devote themselves to resolving it with greater efficiency. So far I have never seen the other partner, on a long-term basis, try to derive any personal advantage from the conflict between the therapist and his partner-adversary. The therapist's obvious effort to arrive at a fair solution is transferred to the spouse. Above all, the couple discover that it is worthwhile to experience conflict, that conflict brings people closer and enables them to find solutions together. Thus therapeutic collusion is a corrective emotional experience for all three parties (v. *F. Alexander*).

Limitations and Risks of Therapeutic Collusion

I work on my relationship with the marital partners only when it becomes a problem in the therapy process. I believe it would be disastrous for a therapist to deliberately try to create therapeutic collusions, thinking that this demonstrating of his readiness to enter a collusion might intensify the therapeutic process. Generally this simply is not true. Couples with narcissistic disorders, as well as couples who feel great anxiety about entering therapy, look to the therapist, first and foremost, to be stable, impartial and imperturbable. If the therapist were to admit straightaway that he finds one of the partners personally disturbing and that he would like to clarify their relationship, it would only cause anxiety and confusion. After all, couples go into therapy to work on their *own* relationship, and they are better able to do this in the presence of a third party who remains *neutral*. In general, they would find it disturbing if this third party dragged his own problems into their conflict. In fact they would feel it was really

asking too much of them to have to worry about the therapist's personal
feelings as well as their own. Patients can become furious if they are not
able to idealize the therapist and view him as capable of enduring
unlimited stress. Many couples therapies run their course in a calm,
benevolent atmosphere, with no problems at all arising between patients
and therapist. The couple cling to the relationship with the therapist,
treating it as sacrosanct, because it gives them solid ground to stand on so
that they have the courage to confront each other while the therapy
process runs its course. After termination of the therapy many patients
have told me, in response to my questions, that it had been important to
them that I was never perturbed and could remain neutral even when they
could see that this was not easy for me. I believe that a therapeutic
collusion should become a topic of therapy only if it has actually become a
problem for all concerned. But if this does happen, the therapist should
not try to avoid conflict, nor should he interpret it one-sidedly as a
problem for the patient alone, but should get involved as an interested
party, saying, "I feel some tension between us. I see that I'm having
trouble in relating to you, and I imagine that you're feeling the same about
me. I'd be glad if we could get a clearer idea of what's going on between us
now . . . I feel that right now I'm annoyed with you because . . . But it's
very important to me to understand your reactions and my own . . ." (v.
the detailed sample therapy in Chapter 12). Careful attention should be
paid to the phrasing of this statement. The therapist must communicate
clearly to his partner-adversary that he himself is affected by the conflict
and is genuinely concerned to clarify and resolve it, which means that he
must be prepared to adopt a self-critical attitude. It would not benefit
therapy if the concept of therapeutic collusion were misunderstood to
mean that the therapist should express his feelings "spontaneously," that is
thoughtlessly, which could easily lead him to say things like, "If I had to
be married to someone like you, I would have run off long ago. Really, no
one could put up with your behavior." This formulation expresses a
disparaging and condemnatory attitude, which would tend to make the
partner-adversary break off the therapy. But by using the formulation I
have outlined, I try to involve the partner-adversary in a confrontation
that is harder for him to escape from because he feels he is being treated as
an equal partner in a "collusion."

For me therapeutic collusion does not mean the same thing as the
therapeutic technique that *Zuk* (1975) describes as triadic family therapy,
in which the therapist, having deliberately striven to attain a position of
power, actively takes sides in order to disrupt the balance of the system
and thus make it possible for new relationships to be formed. Zuk
describes the therapist as one who takes sides and casts the weight of his

authority on the side of family members or takes stands about family conflicts in order to structure relationships as he deems appropriate. The therapist brings himself into the family system as go-between and tries to develop a conflict through partisanship. He can use various skills and therapeutic gambits such as confrontation, reflection, advice, rejection, or evasion, Zuk claims, in order to preserve or reinforce his influence as therapist. Whereas a number of systems-therapists work to gain power, my concept of therapeutic collusion derives rather from my recognition of my impotence as a therapist.

A further question is whether, in his role as partner-adversary, the patient is not in such a disadvantaged position that the therapist-patient confrontation can place him under too much stress. I do not feel that there is much risk of this happening as long as the therapeutic collusion arises out of the therapy process itself. As a rule the therapeutic relationship has become reasonably stable by the time the conflict arises. The partner-adversary must be able to feel that the therapist is genuinely interested in resolving the conflict and is not abusing his position as therapist to beat the patient down with one-sided interpretations.

As a male therapist I often think it is important to express my own emotional involvement, because a female patient with whom I am interacting can easily experience my therapist's neutrality as closely akin to the unfeeling behavior of her husband. Open expression of the conflict developing between us does of course assume the patient's ability to endure stress. The patient may also experience it as a positive achievement because, although he sees that it is possible for him to disturb the therapist's equanimity, he also sees that the therapist does not deny the conflict but confronts it until the tension can be relieved.

As a rule work on a therapeutic collusion greatly improves the relationship between the therapist and his partner-adversary. But what are the effects *on the partner not involved in the conflict?* The therapist should now devote special attention to this other partner, who may feel excluded and, in particular, is afraid that now the therapist has a special sympathy with his former adversary, which puts the left-out partner at a disadvantage. He may also feel that it is easy for the therapist to set an example for solving marital problems because, after all, the therapist does not have to live and deal with the other spouse outside their sessions. *Thus in couples therapy it is essential to substitute the principle of equalized bias for the principle of impartiality or neutrality.*

Should the Therapist Discuss Personal Problems with His Patients?

In my view the therapist's behavior towards his patients ought to be sincere, but he should not ask their help in treating his own problems.

Patients have frequently told me about therapists wanted to discuss their personal problems. The reactions of the patients were totally negative, generally disappointment, scorn and contempt: "He's got even more problems than I do. In the beginning we talked about my problems, but later we talked only of his. I was his therapist more than he was mine, but I was the one who had to foot the bill." To be sure, the therapist ought not to pretend to the patient that he is beyond having any problems, but he should make his professional position clear and then stick to it: He is treating someone who wants help and who is paying him for the work he does. Patients need a therapist who sets aside his personal needs in order to enter into their feelings, and who shows himself to be stable and capable of tolerating stress. Thus the therapeutic collusion should remain strictly within the bounds of the therapeutic working alliance. To be sure, the therapist should remain open to the feelings he is having at the moment, but he should not make his personal problems and needs a topic of therapy as whole. Therapeutic collusion involves a deliberate interaction between the therapist and his patients in which the therapist is not only aware of his countertransference but also behaves in a way appropriate to his emotional situation at the moment.

7

SEX-DETERMINED LIMITATIONS OF THE COUPLES THERAPIST

The Flirtatious Female Patient and
the Male Therapist

The Relationship Between the Male Patient and
the Male Therapist

The literature of the various schools of psychotherapy, including the literature on family and couples therapy, hardly ever mentions the fact that the therapist is not of neuter gender but is a man or a woman. In analytic literature, for example, the relationship between patient and therapist is treated almost exclusively in terms of transference and countertransference, that is, as a relationship distorted by infantile fixations. Thus in psychotherapeutic jargon the term "transference" has often been substituted for "relationship," especially with reference to the "love relationship" between patient and analyst. This practice is not justified by the facts; for naturally the relationship of analysand to analyst does not consist purely of disturbed emotions, fantasies and perceptions transferred by the analysand from the parent to the analyst, but is in fact also a genuine and realistic love for a person who is willing to listen without judgment and with compassion. Thus the concept of transference should be expanded to mean relationship. This is also true of the psychotherapist's emotional reception of the patient in his attempts to rationalize the patient's idealizations and erotic claims.

Only through my work in couples therapy did I become aware of the great significance of the therapist's sex in shaping the therapy process. This connection became particularly evident in couples therapy groups in which I worked as cotherapist with *Margrit Rotach-Fuchs*, and also during course discussion of video tapes in which I was repeatedly struck by the fact that the female therapists reacted quite differently than I did to the couple under discussion. Thus it is essential that cotherapy be included in therapist training so that therapists may have a chance to learn more about their own sex-determined emotional reactions. However, I do not consider cotherapy economically feasible except for the training period of the analyst, and thus in this book I concentrate on couples therapy with a single therapist.

In couples therapy there is a triangle: Two partners are of the same sex and one of the opposite.

The sexual complications that arise in couples therapy are the same as those that we normally find in heterosexual triangles. By their very nature triangles are more tension-charged than twosomes or relationships between members of larger groups. Most significantly, they are bound to turn into relationships of two against one. Their stability lies in this 2:1 ratio (v. *M. Bowen*). Another reason why the therapeutic triangle is subject to the same parameters as a heterosexual triangle is that often the therapist is, in realistic terms, of an age that makes it impossible to view him as ineligible for a sexual involvement. It would be almost impossible to find any therapist who is not personally involved in sex-determined conflicts and who is not himself suffering from unresolved sex-role problems. Hence it would be virtually impossible for a therapist to open himself up to his patients' marital conflict without being personally affected by it.

To give an example: If a wife tears into her husband in a so-called hysterical way, I am inclined to identify with the man. Only gradually have I learned to view the wife's acting-out not merely as a theatrical put-on but as a reaction to the imperturbable attitude of her husband and me, as a genuine and desperate attempt to make some emotional contact with us. I found it difficult to avoid becoming defensive about the wife's emotional explosion, and instead to understand it as behavior that was meaningful in terms of the present situation. The wife's acting-out is often a protest against a self-righteous, pseudo-superior attitude of the male. But another thing that made it hard for me to understand this behavior on the part of many women was the fact that they would label themselves "hysterical," "sick," "unstable," and so on; and then, having established themselves as "patients," claimed all my attention for themselves.

But I am by no means always inclined to side with the husband against the wife. In fact I almost as frequently encounter situations in which I tend to ally myself with the wife. These are usually situations in which the man strikes me as so unresponsive, boring and tiresome that I feel sorry for the wife. In such cases I have often asked myself how the wife can stand living with him. Only with time have I learned to ask why the woman chose this man as her partner in the first place, and whether his unassuming, gentle and reliable nature was—and still is—of great importance to her. Moreover, it is not by chance that these particular men ended up with wives a good deal more vivacious than themselves; actually they hoped that the women's high spirits would be infectious. In therapy they often become more animated, especially if they learn to trust their feelings and, most importantly, to express them. In the course of therapy the therapist's sympathy often swings back and forth. In the beginning it is frequently easier for me to understand the partner of the opposite sex, and later the one of the same sex. *Cartwright and Leuner* (1963) report that at the beginning of therapy, counsellors have more difficulty relating to clients of the same sex, whereas in the course of therapy this tendency changes and sympathy for the partner of the same sex significantly increases.

The Flirtatious Female Patient and the Male Therapist

Christ (1976) claims that the therapist becomes an object of identification for the partner of the same sex, and an object of sexual attraction for the partner of the opposite sex. But what happens to a therapist when the woman flirts with him and he also likes her, when she tries to catch his eye to create an unspoken agreement between them that her husband is really impossible? At first the therapist may go along with this subtle exchange of glances and cherish the unconfessed notion that basically he would make the better husband. When he becomes aware of his fantasy, his behavior may tend to change abruptly. His professional ethics urge him to make it clear to both the woman and the man that he does not intend to play any erotic games with them. I have repeatedly noticed, both in relation to myself and to other (male) therapists, that we tolerate anger and aggression from patients much better than tenders of love. Tenders of love make us feel much more insecure or threatened, and we often try to get rid of them by behaving very curtly and brusquely. Whereas I (probably like most male therapists) find it easier to express what disturbs or makes me tense in a relationship, it is more difficult for me to say what delights me.

The behavior of female therapists, on the other hand, is often just the opposite.

In couples therapy, flirting often has a deeper meaning. It is easy to understand why, at the beginning of a relationship, each partner tries to get the therapist on his side, to join in an alliance against the other partner. As a rule the wife soon notices that her husband "speaks the same language" as the therapist, that the two men can communicate more easily. If, because of her past experiences, the woman has come to regard men as powerful and women as inferior, she will find the situation in couples therapy especially threatening, for she risks having to stand alone against superior male odds. Often her flirtation with the therapist stems not so much from the fact that she finds him especially attractive as that she is very afraid of not being accepted and understood by him. She tries to establish a special alliance with him because she fears she may be crushed and rendered absolutely defenseless. She would like to get the situation under control by using means that have proven effective in the past. If, in her effort to find protection, she is rebuffed by the therapist, who reveals her maneuvers and strikes the weapon from her hand, she may easily become panic-stricken. In one situation like this a woman directly accused the two men of having entered into a homosexual conspiracy against her. The therapist should try to accept the woman's flirtatiousness in this light and attempt, in a way that does not hurt or shame her, to address the fear that underlies it.

If he accepts the wife's flirting, the therapist has to be concerned that he might make the husband jealous and be accused of breaking the pledge of impartiality. Often this concern turns out to be unjustified, for frequently the husband is proud if he feels that the therapist fancies his wife. Then the husband and the therapist become homoerotic pals on the grounds of their agreement that this woman is really quite attractive. The best course is for the therapist to maintain a firm, clear-cut attitude of acceptance and convey to the couple that he regards the wife's displays of affection as an important, productive element in building a good, therapeutic working relationship with her.

The Relationship Between the Male Patient and the Male Therapist

Probably the therapist has the easiest time if the husband slightly idealizes him and attempts to identify with him. This facilitates the therapist's entering into a relationship with the wife which can serve as a model for the husband. But often a strong rivalry can develop, especially with phallically structured men. Such men find it embarrassing having to play the role of patient in front of their wives while the therapist, in his professional role, seems to float above them safely out of reach. This feeling can lead a husband to try to pull the therapist down off his high horse and point out the therapist's own faults to him. Other husbands try to depreciate the therapist's interpretations or to impress him with their professional accomplishments. I found that this situation was often relieved when I expressed my feelings directly: "I have the impression that a really tense atmosphere has developed between us, a kind of rivalry, as if you had to be inferior because you are in therapy or I had to be superior because it is my function here to be the therapist. You came here to get help with your problems. For me therapy is a professional responsibility that I am trying to meet as well as possible, just as you do your best in your profession. I have a wife and children at home, and we have our problems and difficulties like every other couple and every family." Naturally in analytic terms this rivalry could also be related to the husband's relationship with his father. But as a rule I have better results if my refusal to allow the husband to provoke me into competing with him enables him to experience directly what may be new and unexpected emotions.

Analogous problems arise for female therapists in their relationships with female and male patients. The following example shows the great extent to which the therapist's perceptions can be determined by his personal emotional attitude:

Example 8:

A female therapist had been treating a woman for some time and then involved her husband in their work. The therapist referred the couple to me for joint treatment. She described the husband as a brutal, dangerous despot, quick to lash out at people and incapable of empathizing with others. His brutal behavior and surges of ill-temper were, she said, the expression of a brain-localized, epileptic psychosyndrome, the result of skull damage. She had tried in vain to get him to take psychopharmacological drugs. Quite by chance we had access to a case history on the wife in which the same man had been described several years earlier, by a male therapist, in completely different terms, as weak, infantile and strongly attached to his mother. My impression was that this man had allowed himself to be provoked into acts of violence because he felt that he had been shut out of his family by his wife, who had allied herself with the children against him, and that he was trying, by his violent acts, to hold onto his position as father in the family. But his authoritarian brutality, which had intensified during the wife's individual therapy, had simply resulted in his becoming more isolated. During the couples therapy, which went on for more than six months, he never displayed any fits of rage or acts of violence. In our therapy sessions he exhibited no clinical evidence of brain damage. An open discussion with the self-critical female therapist revealed that in her own marriage she was suffering from the same kinds of problems that she perceived in this patient couple.

8

COUPLES THERAPY CONDUCTED BY A THERAPIST COUPLE (COTHERAPY)

Different Dynamics of the Therapeutic Triangle
and the Therapeutic Quadrangle

The Cotherapist Couple

At this stage the reader might be wondering why we are carrying on so about the complex, problematical area of the therapist's sex when there is such an obvious solution to the problem of sex-determined limitations—namely, that a male and female therapist should conduct a couples therapy together.

Masters and Johnson (1973) point out that a male therapist can never completely understand the sexual functions or dysfunctions of a woman, for he never experiences an orgasm as a woman does. If he has the least claim to objectivity, he can never trust completely in his notions about women. The same thing is true of a female therapist with reference to the sexual functions of a man. For example, if a couple with sexual difficulties come to a male therapist, even if the therapist has learned to define himself in terms of his own sexual role and to deal with the sex-specific dynamics of the relationships within the therapeutic triangle, who is supposed to interpret or explain to the woman those things that are clearly related to female sexuality?

Economic factors also play a role in determining whether cotherapy is indicated. The need for marriage counselling and couples therapy is so overwhelming that we could not afford to use two therapists in couples therapy unless it had been clearly established that this form of therapy achieves substantially more efficient results. However, I consider cotherapy—here understood as therapy involving a male-female therapist team—important in therapist training.

Different Dynamics of the Therapeutic Triangle and the Therapeutic Quadrangle

In many respects the therapeutic quadrangle, consisting of a patient couple and a therapist couple, exhibits a different dynamics from the therapeutic triangle.

—The sexes are equally represented: There are two women and two men. The fear of being overpowered by one of the sexes, which all parties concerned may experience in the therapeutic triangle, is diminished.

—As many therapists are present as patients. Each patient can, potentially, have "his" therapist. The competition for the one therapist and the fear that he/she will side with the other partner is diminished. At the same time the therapist feels freer about the degree of attention he/she devotes to each partner and feels less pressure to continually distribute his/her attention equally. Because balance can be restored by the cotherapist after every intervention, it matters less what conclusions the couple draw from the intervention concerning themselves and their marital relationship. An experienced cotherapist team can divide their roles efficiently, and can achieve productive results by addressing every phenomenon in the couples therapy from two different angles. But the holding of different viewpoints presupposes that the therapist couple are capable of a high level of cooperation. This cooperation is not achieved if severe unspoken conflicts between the therapists are acted out via similar conflicts experienced by the client couple. The patient couple experience the relationship with the two therapists quite differently from the way they experience a relationship with a single therapist. As a rule they view the therapists as a couple. It is more difficult for a female patient to flirt and try to gain the erotic attentions of the male therapist in the presence of the female therapist. The female patient may also feel less threatened by the two men because there is another woman present, and thus may find it easier to renounce erotic behavior. The patient couple are much more concerned with their fantasies about the relationship between the therapists than with any attempt to build a special relationship with one or the other of the therapists. In this sense the therapeutic quadrangle is less charged with tension than the triangle. The patients experience it as more stable, more peaceful, and also more clearly divided into therapist couple and patient couple. This can have a calming effect on chaotic marital crises involving a strong tendency to act out. On the other hand, tensions and conflicts in the cotherapists' relationship often create problems.

The Cotherapist Couple

I find the greatest advantage of cotherapy lies in the possibility of experiencing the degree to which the therapist's perceptions and interventions are dependent on his or her sex. Everyone can feel the extent to which he remains trapped in his own sexuality and can only approximate the experience of the other sex. This has never been as clear to me as when I was doing cotherapy in a couples therapy group in which my female colleague, Margrit Rotach-Fuchs, often interpreted the same patient data in terms diametrically opposite to mine.

The structure of the relationship between the cotherapist couple involves three closely related aspects:

—The cotherapists may be married or friends, or they may have no personal relationship at all outside their professional activities.

—The cotherapists may have received the same level of training and have the same professional status, or their training and status may be different.

—The cotherapists may deliberately assume different roles in the therapy, or they may do so unintentionally.

The Cotherapist Couple Is a Married Couple

All the married cotherapist couples I know have emphasized that their cotherapy practice has greatly enriched their marriage, though it also caused considerable turmoil and stress. Many couples were actually motivated to do cotherapy in the hope that working together on the problems of other couples might help them make progress in dealing with problems in their own relationship. Often they felt that the experience had been similar to an encounter group, which can be disadvantageous if the cotherapy arouses such turmoil in the cotherapist couple that they are barely able to hold on to their primary task as therapists. Supervision is especially essential in such cases. Cotherapy should not be practiced if the therapists are themselves in an acute crisis, or if there is a risk that a long-term crisis has been brewing that the therapists would be addressing for the first time via the cotherapy.

Many married therapist couples who work together very harmoni-ously report that they find it easier to deal with differences of opinion that arise within the therapy setting than other, unmarried therapist teams do. They experience less anxiety when they disagree in the presence of patients, for their relationship can support more stress. Other unmarried cotherapists claim they find cotherapy easier to practice with a profession-al colleague than with their spouse, because with their colleague they have a more clearly defined work relationship, and a difference of opinion between them does not immediately take on a personal and dogmatic character. Patient couples are often able to achieve an intimate relation-ship with the therapists more quickly if the therapists are married, and especially if they have children. The patients then assume that the therapist couple also have unresolved conflicts, and are interested to know how they deal with them. In this way the therapist couple can serve as a model with whom the clients can identify; but this involves the risk that the therapist couple may feel under pressure to have a perfect marriage.

Married therapist couples can be motivated to work together in order to have more time together, which is sometimes a problematic move. They should ensure that a large part of their married lives remains untouched by their activities as therapists, and a sizable portion of the professional life of each partner should be kept independent of the professional life of the other.

The Unmarried Therapist Couple

The unmarried therapist couple will appear less like a couple, often for purely external reasons: The unmarried therapists may be of different ages and may in other ways seem less personally attuned to each other. Whenever possible the selection of a therapy partner should be discussed in a supervised session before the two partners start work together. As a rule external factors will greatly limit the choice of partners, but even in cases in which the therapists have a limited range of choice, they will have both positive and negative expectations about the work they will do together. The motives behind their positive expectations should be examined just as in the case of a married couple. For example, a male therapist may wish to work with a female therapist because he believes that he will not have to compete for the right to be in charge of the therapy, and the female therapist may think that she can lean on the male therapist and avoid having to assume total responsibility for the therapy.

The most important factor in the success of a cotherapy is the relationship between the therapists (*Peters, Belleville*). To put it simply, the cotherapists should like each other. They should feel free to discuss openly any rivalry or other difficulties that arise in their work together. It is not necessary that their concept of the therapy be identical, but their therapeutic attitudes should be compatible.

Even if the cotherapist couple are not married, their joint work will actualize many problems in their personal relationship. Often these problems involve the most personal, intimate sphere of their lives. In discussing a therapy session the cotherapists will communicate to each other many things that they may never have been able to discuss openly with anyone else, not even with their own spouse. The other therapist can easily become a confidant to whom each therapist confesses unresolved marital problems. This in turn can cause problems in a cotherapist's marriage. It might be important that the spouse not involved in the therapy know the other cotherapist and feel satisfied that the relationship between the cotherapist and his/her spouse is confined to their work.

Cotherapists of Different Educational Standing

In group therapy, as well as in couples and family therapy, it is recommended that for training purposes cotherapy be conducted by a teacher-student couple. In couples therapy this combination can involve problems because the clients often view the therapist couple as a model couple. If the more expert therapist is a man and the trainee a woman, the therapists will present the clients with an image of the man as the more competent, and the woman as the docile pupil. On the other hand, if the status of the therapists is different—if, for example, the woman is a psychiatrist and the man a social worker—then despite the fact that they may be equal in professional competence, the male therapist may find the situation difficult. The therapist couple can see that their clients view them not only as a working couple but also as a man and a woman. As such the therapist couple should not present the clients with a model of confinement within traditional role structures, but neither should they overtax themselves by undertaking too extreme a role reversal. In general I believe that the rule of parity is as applicable to the cotherapist couple as to any other couple relationship: The self-esteem of both therapists ought to be as equal as possible within the therapy situation. If they cannot achieve a sense of parity, their difference in status ought to be clearly defined to the patients. This allows both therapists freedom of movement.

The relationship of the two therapists to the couple is also variable. Often a four-party couples therapy will follow an individual therapy held by one of the therapists with one of the patients. Thus the relationship to one therapist is already established, and the other therapist may feel left out. But if the patients have applied for help specifically to deal with marital problems, and if the therapists have made plans for a cotherapy, it is best if the first interview is conducted with all four parties present, or at least if each of the two therapists has an introductory interview with the couple.

Role Differentiation in the Therapist Couple

Like any couple, the therapist couple have a tendency to differentiate and to polarize their positions, for example to polarize them into an "evil" and a "good," an "active" and a "passive," a "confrontational partner" and a "supportive partner." In itself this role differentiation is beneficial to the therapy because it creates a richer field for transference. Cotherapists may deliberately adopt polarized roles. One assumes the role of an evil, frightening father and the other the role of the kind mother who supplies security. The question is whether the therapist couple may not place themselves under too much stress by doing this, and by denying the rivalries between them. The female therapist may be allowed to express her social timidity by trying to make herself loved and pawning off all the unpleasant duties onto the male therapist. The male therapist may go along with this because of his own insecurity, which leads him to enjoy this opportunity to appear strong and show that he can put up with anything. The defensive character of both these attitudes, however, casts doubt on their appropriateness for therapy.

On the other hand, problems often arise when therapists try to deny the differences between them. There is often a real difference in professional competence even when the same level of training has been achieved, and patients will perceive this. In order not to let the obvious differences surface, therapists are often driven to try to adapt to each other, thereby creating an atmosphere of constraint: The more competent partner forcibly pulls back in order not to upstage his less competent partner, who in turn feels that he is under pressure to perform up to the other's standard. Whenever the less competent therapist speaks, he feels he must say something especially pertinent, and as a result his interpretations are addressed more to the cotherapist than to the patients. If possible neither cotherapist should have to place himself under too much strain. In making efforts to remain attuned to each other, most cotherapists tend to become too dependent on each other.

Example 9:

Serious difficulties had arisen in a cotherapy conducted by a married therapist couple. The female therapist felt that her husband was dominating the therapy, so she became more and more passive and withdrawn. The male therapist, on the other hand, thought that his wife was depreciating all his interpretations, so he felt provoked into offering increasingly complex and intellectual interventions. Both therapists were finding it more and more difficult to focus attention on their work with the patient couple. Their behavior as therapists was increasingly aimed at their own relationship. In fact things had become so bad that the therapists were competing for the patients' approval.

It was interesting to note the differences in the way the therapist couple perceived the patients. The male therapist viewed the male patient as a rather compulsive person who nevertheless had made good progress in expressing his feelings. The female therapist, on the other hand, dismissed the male patient's progress as inauthentic and confined to an intellectual plane. The female patient rejected all the male therapist's interpretations and corrected his interventions, whereas she clearly got along well with the female therapist. A situation had developed in which the female patient acted as a representative for the female therapist by confronting and competing with the male therapist. The conflict of the patient couple coincided more and more with the conflict of the therapist couple.

Under therapeutic supervision the two therapists sought to learn how to remain more separate from each other during therapy; that is, to relate to each other in their work together, but not to allow their behavior to be determined by each other. It was evident to the therapists that they could help the patient couple only to the degree that they made progress at solving their own difficulties, which paralleled those of the patients.

9

OTHER METHODOLOGICAL
FACTORS

The Methodological Basis: System and Behavior-
Modification Therapy, or
Conflict-Oriented Therapy?

Dynamics-Oriented Couples Therapy
as Systems Therapy

Reframing Progressive and Regressive Behavior

It is impossible for me, in a single book, to examine all aspects of couples therapy that deserve comment. Instead I will try to select a few points that seem to me of particular importance. In this chapter I would like to comment on certain theoretical and practical aspects of "collusion therapy." This will involve the repetition and elaboration of ideas already mentioned in the preceding chapters, but which here are viewed somewhat differently.

The Methodological Basis:
Systems and Behavior-Modification
Therapy, or Conflict-Oriented Therapy

Although I ascribe general significance to the collusion concept as I described it in *Couples in Collusion*—without of course claiming that it covers all the facets of couple conflict—my therapeutic practice is strongly determined by my personal way of working with patients. I do not believe that there is any one correct therapy method as such, but that some psychotherapists, depending on their inclination and aptitude, feel more attracted to certain methods than to others, and also that some patients can benefit more from certain methods than from others. Although a therapist's personal choice of the therapy method may not depend on criteria like right and wrong, it still seems to me important to think about one's own work method and to compare it with others.

As I have already mentioned, in the area of couples and family therapy we can distinguish between the systems and behavior-modification methods, and methods that work on conflict. Common to these two approaches is the fact that they view, as the center of the conflict, systems of force that the family therapist must learn to recognize and to influence. But there are various views on the nature of the interventions necessary to achieve this end. The aim is for the family therapist to break through deeply entrenched behavior patterns by means of massive interventions and in accordance with his own "structural model." The therapist may manipulate the seating order, the style of discourse, and the time allotted to family members to talk; he may assign tasks, break up existing alliances, intervene in family role structures, and interfere with the balance of closeness and separateness maintained by the family members.

In strategic therapy the therapist behaves almost like an animal-trainer, stage director or chess-player, and directs the partners in the direction that he thinks is healthy.

In behavioral therapy the therapist's work is more that of an educator. The attempt is made to shape behavior through "operant conditioning," the deliberate reinforcement of desirable behavior patterns and the elimination of undesirable behavior. Stuart claims that to improve disturbed marital interaction it is essential to stimulate both partners so that they learn to reinforce each other's behavior more often and more intensively. Behavioral therapists claim that individuals feel more attracted to each other when they succeed in getting each other to comply with each other's wishes. Conflicts as such are not worked on, and thus behavioral therapy proceeds on the assumption that both partners must clearly commit themselves to their partnership, for otherwise they would not choose to accept all the exercises and homework imposed on them.

There are many couples incapable of defining their marital conflicts clearly. Also, they think it is useless to isolate and solve just one concrete problem, because their main problem is that their conflicts are indefinable: when, for example, they are not quite sure whether or not they want to stay together, do not quite understand why they love each other and at the same time hate each other, why they seek intimacy and yet at the same time cannot tolerate it, and at first find it impossible to clearly express what they really want and what they are afraid of. If a husband says to his wife, "Become liberated, don't be so dependent on me," his share in the marital conflict may consist of the fact that he cannot make this statement without ambivalence, because his feelings are themselves ambivalent, and his wife feels that she cannot liberate herself because her husband would not like it. In therapy I would try to clarify what is going on inside the husband when he makes this ambivalent remark, rather than simply demand that he express himself more clearly. The same thing applies to a wife who tells her husband, "Be more active" and at the same time ridicules every effort he makes to do so.

Stuart says that the therapist defines his role as that of an educator who works along with the family. He will not designate any of the family members as sick and burden them with the moral recrimination that attaches to patients in psychoanalytic concepts of therapy. It is not necessary, Stuart says, for family members to confess their "weakness" or their irrationality; for insight per se is not regarded as essential to life. I believe that in psychotherapy one cannot and should not spare the patient the necessity of confronting guilt, weakness, irrationality and illness, because I view a crisis in a relationship as invariably involving an opportunity for growth, as an occasion to come to terms with the deepest aspects of human existence. In a therapy whose focus is work on conflict, asking questions about the meaning and goal of the couple's life together will be of central concern. The aim is not for the therapy to simply make a crisis disappear, but to enable the couple to grow through the crisis.

Dynamics-Oriented Couples Therapy as Systems Therapy

It seems to me less important to *distinguish* systems and behavior-modification concepts from concepts involving work on conflict than it is to *integrate* them. Even if one is an analytically oriented therapist, or a therapist whose work centers on talking with patients, one who refrains from deliberately trying to acquire a position of power in the family or couple system, and even if one does not claim to manipulate or educate one's clients, nevertheless every behavior of the therapist inevitably helps to shape the communications system of the therapeutic triangle. After all, the therapist "cannot 'not behave'" (*Watzlawick,* 1969). Hence the analytic therapist must not deny his influence on the therapeutic system but rather must ponder it. *The observation of therapist behavior in couples therapy shows clearly that the therapist does not give equal attention to both partners but tends to concern himself far more with one than with the other.* In this connection the most important thing to keep in mind is the progressive-regressive role-polarization of the partners. The regressive partner is more frequently the one who shows the symptoms, the one who is manifestly suffering. He openly complains about his partner, he acts out, cries, hurls abuse, threatens to run off, to break off therapy, to get a divorce, and so on. All this attracts the therapist's attention and lures him into devoting more care to this partner than to the progressive partner, who appears more rational. As a rule the progressive partner does not express any need for help and voluntarily tends to fall in with the idea that the regressive partner is the one who needs treatment. In this situation the couples therapist must not passively go along with his clients' representations but must resist his own spontaneous tendency to devote more attention to the regressive partner. Often he will find this difficult, because the behavior of the progressive partner, who rejects help, is less compatible with someone in the role of therapist. The therapist regards the patient's expression of suffering as a prerequisite for his behaving conformably with the patient's role. He waits for the patient to evince some need for help before building a therapeutic relationship. It is not easy to get a progressive partner to do this. Instead the therapist must actively work to secure the progressive partner's trust by showing him that he does not mean to hurt him and that he respects the progressive partner's great vulnerability.

The reactions of the regressive partner also make it hard for the therapist to devote care to the progressive partner. The regressive partner, who is used to being the exclusive object of other people's attention and care, readily feels jealous and abandoned when the therapist devotes care to the other partner.

Thus dynamic couples therapy must incorporate certain fundamental elements of systems-modification therapy.

Reframing Progressive and Regressive Behavior

Every behavior presented in couples therapy can be interpreted in various ways, depending on the attitude of the therapist. If the therapist takes the view that therapy ought to break down the progressive-regressive polarization, he can attempt, in his interpretations, to point out the regressive behavior. If, for example, in a therapy situation the regressive partner suddenly starts threatening to apply for divorce, the therapist might say, "It seems to me that this plan of yours expresses a wish to separate yourself more clearly from your partner and to stand on your own feet." Or if the regressive partner threatens to run out of the therapy session, the therapist can say, "I think that you'd like to give your partner a chance to get more out of therapy on his own." Or if the regressive partner gets sick or depressed because of his marital problems, the therapist can say, "I see that you're a lot more open to recognizing what's wrong with your relationship and to express the suffering it causes you."

I use these interpretations to try to address the progressive potential of the regressive partner. His acting-out is not interpreted as an expression of weakness but as an uncompromising, responsible way to behave in light of the fact that the partnership has gone awry.

It is also possible to address the regressive aspect of progressive behavior. For example, when the progressive partner behaves in a controlled and impassive way in the face of the other partner's depressive reproaches, the therapist can say, "I imagine that you need to work hard to control yourself in order to protect yourself from your own tendencies to get depressed." Or if the progressive partner refrains from complaining as the regressive partner is doing, and expects no help from the therapist, the therapist could remark: "Apparently you have never in your life been allowed to complain about anything or to express your own needs. So you've fallen into the habit of dealing with your problems all by yourself."

Watzlawick (1974) begins a chapter on "The Gentle Art of Reframing" with the joke: "Question: What is the difference between an optimist and a pessimist? Answer: The optimist says of a glass that it is half full; the pessimist says of the same glass that it is half empty.— Anonymous." Watzlawick defines reframing as changing the conceptual and/or emotional setting or viewpoint in relation to which a situation is experienced, to place it in another frame that fits the "facts" of the concrete situation equally well or even better, thus changing its whole meaning. "Reality" has to do with "opinions," the meaning and value attributed to phenomena. But the actual definitions of reality are legion. What *is* real is what a sufficiently large number of people have agreed to *call* real. This definition, founded on consensus, is then reified so that it is experienced as objective reality. Adherence to this view of reality is then taken not only to be a sign of normality but also adjudged "sincere, honest, authentic" and so on. Thus Watzlawick mocks those therapists who "are playing the game of not playing a game." (V. p. 92ff. of the American edition of *Change: Principles of Problem Formation and Problem Resolution,* New York: W.W. Norton, 1974). Although I find systems-oriented psychotherapists intriguing because of their clever tricks and find their ingenious and elegant gambits both stimulating and amusing, these gambits often seem to me to rely too heavily on manipulation, and the idea of beating one's "opponent" too controlled by the political aim of overcoming a foe by "willpower." In my work as a therapist I like to say nothing that I do not really mean and feel. This may be rather boring and lacking in wit and flair. Undoubtedly Watzlawick is right when he points out the relativity of the concepts of reality, objectivity and therapeutic morality. But even if we take these concepts as only subjectively valid, it seems to me important that the therapist, with all his personal limitations, should show patients that he is sincere, comprehensible, and trustworthy, for by doing so he gives patients a clear orientation in their relationship with him. Watzlawick, on the other hand, compares his problem-solving technique to judo, in which an opponent's blow is not met with a counterblow, but rather one gives way before the blow, thus intensifying the other's attack. The opponent is caught unaware by this cooperative behavior because it does not obey the rules of the game he has staged. This form of therapy is not intended to promote insight but only to teach a different game, or make it impossible to continue playing the old game. According to Watzlawick it is the goal of treatment to break this feedback cycle rather than to try to realize a philosophical abstraction of what a human being should be. I feel that this approach ascribes little validity to the client's subjective experiences and gives him little opportunity to grow through personal insight and responsibility. This kind of therapy may meet the real needs of some couples in conflict, but surely there are many whose needs it does not meet.

Even reframing must be viewed in terms of the dynamics of the therapeutic triangle. If the behavior of Partner A is reframed, the therapist assigns this behavior a different meaning. Thus he does not react in the way that A expects and that B customarily chooses, but may show just the opposite reaction. The therapist emphasizes the progressive aspect of regressive behavior, the regressive aspect of progressive behavior; the hidden love in expressions of hate; the desire to shield one's own vulnerability expressed by hurting one's partner, and so on. Reframing makes it hard for Partner A to continue behaving in the routine way, and often makes room for a new and different behavior. Under the therapist's protection Partner A can reveal more of the feelings and sensitivities he has been carefully shielding up to now, or can work in a more responsible and committed way to developing the relationship. Partner B may feel disoriented by this because now he too must behave differently. But often at the next session B will come out with the remark that A's behavior is changed only when they are with the therapist and that when the two of them are at home A behaves in the same way as before, which of course proves that A's new behavior is not sincere. In reality the fact that A behaves differently in the therapy situation than he does at home does not necessarily mean that his behavior is not sincere, but rather may simply indicate that for the time being Partner A is capable of behaving differently only under the protection of the therapy situation. One of the therapist's principal concerns is in fact to keep the two warring partners apart; to make himself a go-between and give both of them room to change their behavior and to express feelings they have always kept hidden. This is why it is not advisable for the partners to talk about the things they discuss in a therapy session after the session is over, for as a rule they will not make any progress on their own, but instead tend to destroy the progress they have begun to achieve.

10

PROBLEMS OF VALUE
IN COUPLES THERAPY

The Attempt to Maintain a Nonjudgmental
Attitude in Psychotherapy

Goal-Setting in Couples Therapy as an Expression of
Attitudes Towards Values

The Difficulty of Refraining from Making Value
Judgments in Therapy

Should the Therapist Reveal His Own
Norms and Values?

The Attempt to Maintain a
Nonjudgmental Attitude in Psychotherapy

The nonjudgmental attitude of the therapist is a basic assumption in virtually all schools of psychotherapy, and consequently is hardly ever challenged. It is assumed that the client liberated by therapy will be capable of discovering appropriate values for himself, and it is viewed almost as a technical error if a therapist succumbs to the temptation of instructing his patients about values and norms. The therapist tries to accept his patient fully and completely regardless of whether the patient's norms and values are compatible with his own. The patient himself is the standard with respect to his own values. In therapy, universally binding social values are regarded only as internal or external data with which the patient must learn to come to terms. According to *Redlich* (1959) analysis is incompatible with the attempt to suggest to the patient values other than those that, consciously or unconsciously, are his own, or that he decides to strive for or to discard. In therapy, value systems that limit the patient's ego-strength, self-realization, discovery of identity and independence are challenged. These days many therapists still believe that their attitude is value-free, and may neglect to consider more deeply the subtle influence of their own values. Yet the external setting of therapy is already a very concrete expression of certain values. If we offer an individual 300–400 hours of therapy, from which his spouse and family are excluded, we clearly admit by doing so that the development of the individual is the supreme value of therapy. In family and couples therapy a higher rank is assigned to the existing social community, and the individual is treated more concretely in terms of his relatedness to his group.

Boszormenyi-Nagy (1973) called attention to certain ethical aspects of family therapy when he showed what a dubious procedure it is to investigate that period of crisis when adolescents must separate from their parents exclusively in terms of infantile dependency. Often a far more central factor is the conflict of loyalties that the adolescent experiences between his struggles for emancipation and what he feels are the just claims of his parents in the light of all they have done for him, which do not permit him to simply walk off and abandon them. Boszormenyi-Nagy and *Stierlin* believe that essentially this separation process involves reconciling various contradictory urges and finding a compromise that is tolerable for all concerned, including the parents.

But even in family and couples therapy there is a risk that the groups of people under treatment may be viewed in too isolated terms, without sufficient regard to the outside world, to the rest of society. It is also a clear-cut definition of value when a therapist refuses to bring a third party, an extramarital lover, into a couples therapy, for by doing so he conveys to the extramarital partner that he will allow him no opportunity to directly influence the course of the therapy.

Research shows that one of the major effects of psychotherapy is the change in the patient's attitudes. Other studies show that in the course of therapy the patient's values come to match those of the therapist (*Rosenthal*, 1955). According to *H. Bolgar* (quoted in *Charlotte Buehler*, 1962), much of what the therapist interprets as signs of growth in the patient stems from the patient's adoption of the therapist's values, and much of what the therapist views as resistance to therapy represents a rejection of the analyst's values. *Buehler* challenges the therapist to acknowledge the dubious nature of the satisfaction he feels when the patient moves in the direction of the therapist's own values.

Spiegel points out that the therapist's value system provides the frame of reference within which he works; yet he might not necessarily be clear in his own mind about how his values influence his procedure and affect the patient. Wittingly or unwittingly, the therapist always transmits to the patient something of his own attitudes, values and norms. *M. Patterson* (1959) warns against the mistaken notion that the counsellor and the therapist are neutral with respect to values, when in reality both express their own views either directly or indirectly. The therapist ought to make it clear that his values and opinions are his own, and should make the patient feel free to choose.

Every human communication is, among other things, an exchange of values, and psychotherapy is no exception. If psychotherapists refuse to perceive the nature of their values, psychotherapy could turn into a dangerous method of indoctrination—dangerous because it is unconscious.

Goal-Setting in Couples Therapy as an Expression of Attitudes Towards Values

Many misunderstandings arise throughout the field of marriage counselling and couples therapy because the standards of value that determine how a marriage is to be discussed and treated have not been clearly defined. Definition of the goals of therapy is intimately bound with the therapist's notion of the criteria that should be used in judging the condition of a marriage.

Confusion often arises concerning the following three value systems for marriage:

1. The Ethical Value System: The Good Marriage Versus the Bad Marriage

In the past the Christian churches were traditionally and almost exclusively responsible for marriage counselling in the Western world, and they still play a major role in counselling today. But despite the fact that the churches' values are also in a state of upheaval, marriage counsellors as well as couples seeking help depict marital crises in terms of moral standards. The law too evaluates marital behavior in relation to norms that are formulated in great detail. In the ethical value system people speak about marriages as good or bad. As a rule the indissolubility of marriage is regarded as a positive value, divorce as a negative one. Marital fidelity is an absolute value, infidelity is sinful and inimical to marriage. Unselfishness, tolerance, a conciliatory nature, self-sacrifice and a sense of duty are reckoned to be good qualities in marital partners, whereas quarrelsomeness, selfishness, wilfulness and a demanding nature are bad qualities. Many couples seek out a counsellor or therapist with the notion that he will act as a judge or a clergyman, evaluate the marital crisis by moral standards, pronounce one partner right and the other wrong, and devise means to save the marriage.

Many couples are disappointed or overtaxed when the therapist does not fulfill their moral expectations about therapy. They look to the therapist to serve as a fatherly authority figure who will put their disturbed relationship back onto the right track, the track of traditional norms.

2. The Medical Value System: The Healthy Marriage Versus the Sick Marriage

This value system centers around the concept of health as a positive value and sickness as a negative value. A healthy marriage is one that, both on a physical and an emotional plane, functions efficiently, tolerates stress, and is relaxed. A sick marriage is subject to tension and stress, leads to symptoms of physical or emotional illness, and cuts down efficiency.

Many troubled marriages first come to a doctor's attention in the form of an emotional or physical illness. Often the patients expect nothing more than to have the doctor rid them of their symptoms, and do not feel that they either need or are prepared for any in-depth work on the crisis in their relationship. The goal of treatment is to get the marriage working again. The typical example is sex therapy, which as a short-term therapy generally focuses directly on sexual dysfunctions, which it ideally can eliminate in a short time. A psychiatrist would diagnose the marital problem in terms of the psychopathology of the partners. The ideal goal of therapy would be a marriage in which the relationship is not determined, on either side, by neurotic fixations or defensive behavior.

3. The Emancipatory Value System: The Growth-Oriented Marriage Versus the Stagnant Marriage

This ideal is a socio-cultural product of the Western industrialized societies of the past twenty to thirty years. No one has had much time to try it out yet, and it is probably best-suited to the ideals of the educated classes. But most therapists of today identify with this ideal. In fact often they are so overidentified with it that in therapy they cannot help guiding the couple towards the goals offered by this model. In terms of the model a couple relationship is evaluated as positive if it promotes rather than limits the self-realization of the partners. A relationship of this kind is growth-oriented, creative, and allows both partners an attitude of independence, free of constraints and obligations. Relationships of this kind are expected to afford a high level of satisfaction, pleasure, vitality, ability to communicate, gratification of needs, and mutual validation. A negative marriage is one that is stagnating, bogged down in routine, motionless; the partners show no readiness for change and continual learning, but simply stay together out of habit, anxiety, compulsion and constraint. A lot of experimentation is being done on this model today. The awareness of problems in partnership is heightened today, and often is exaggerated. The analysis of the psychopathology of a marriage and the diagnosis of partnership dynamics are dismissed as irrelevant labels that have no relation to the dynamics of the actual relationship. Severe crises and symptoms are regarded as having only relative significance, or at times even accepted and welcomed as crises in a continual learning process. The criteria for a successful therapy are growth-oriented: "We have made progress in the treatment," "The couple have profited from therapy," "They have put in good, solid work on their relationship." Deviations from the social norm are encouraged as possibilities for acquiring new experiences. The partners are not given the right to expect anything of each other, which would place them under an obligation. Divorce is treated as one of various creative possibilities. The view of marriage underlying this value system is often diametrically opposed to the traditional moral value system in its evaluation of extramarital relationships, divorce, marital conflict, and so on. A representative figure of this line of thought is *Carl Rogers (cf. Becoming Partners* New York: Delacorte, 1972).

In couples therapy a therapist can find himself involved in difficult—for me sometimes almost insoluble—conflicts between these various value systems:

—A couple have been married for over twenty-five years. The husband has built a successful career, the wife has raised three children who are now independent and have left home. Confronting the prospect of old age, the husband suddenly decides that while he was busy working, life passed him by. He begins to have extramarital relationships with much younger partners. Whereas he had been committed to a strict moral code regarding marriage while he was growing up and throughout his married life, he now identifies with the emancipatory model of relationships and pleads for a liberated, open marriage that would allow him to involve himself in extramarital relationships. One can understand the man's feelings. Until the approach of old age he has remained under the sway of his strict parents and now would like to strike out more on his own and develop his own personality. His wife's resistance to his extramarital relationships is equally understandable from her point of view: She has spent her life working for her marriage and her family, and now she feels betrayed because her husband wants to destroy the common foundation on which they built their lives. His reproach that she has always overadapted to his wishes, and that now it is time for her too to develop herself, seems to her totally unrealistic, because on her own she neither has any chance of becoming involved in extramarital relationships nor of making a career for herself. Thus here the ethical value system confronts the emancipatory system. A great deal of tact is required for the therapist (if he personally identifies more with the emancipatory model) to do justice to this wife in therapy.

—A similar problem often arises in marriages between persons of different nationalities. I repeatedly saw conflicts in which the husband was Italian or Hungarian and thus came from a culture in which the family is the supreme value. He regarded it as among his highest and most inviolable obligations to show his mother respect and gratitude as long as she lived. He took it for granted that during his holidays he would visit her, or would have her come to Switzerland to stay with his own family for three months of the year. His wife, being Swiss, found this expectation unacceptable. The therapist, also Swiss, was sorely tempted to try to work on the man's relationship with his mother, treating it as an infantile dependency or an Oedipal conflict and thus having insufficient regard for the fact that in this man's value system the continuation of a close relationship with one's mother is a sign of a healthy loyalty and maturity. Here too the ethical system is opposed to the emancipatory system.

—An artist becomes severely depressed because his live model, who was his companion for many years, wants to separate from him so that she can develop more independently. She feels that he is demanding that she sacrifice herself completely for him and his work. But he considers it the supreme expression of love if two people place themselves together in the service of the art, and each, in his or her own way, subordinates himself to this work. Deprived of the possibility to work alongside his life's companion, he feels deprived of all strength and is no longer able to work.

—In psychotherapy work, with couples suffering from anxiety neurosis, I observed again and again that as a partner suffering phobic symptoms (agoraphobia, cardiac phobia, etc.) grew healthier, his relationship with his partner grew increasingly strained. For years both partners had defined their relationship as an intimate, exclusive unity which was to exclude everything that might separate them. When the patient begins to see himself more clearly and to stand up to his partner and voice his own opinions, as a rule there is an intensive power struggle that often ends in divorce or in the other partner's getting sick. Even if the attempt is made from the very beginning to bring the second partner in on therapy, this outcome cannot always be avoided. Often the therapist must confront the conflict between health-plus-divorce on the one hand, and sickness-plus-staying-married on the other, i.e. the medical value system versus the traditional ethical system.

Every couples therapy calls the ideal of the marriage into question and generally modifies it. But often one of the partners is not prepared to participate in modifying his ideal. This can lead to special problems if, in his unwillingness to cooperate, he opposes the therapist's ideals. A high percentage of the unsolved problems encountered in couples therapy involves such conflicts of value between the therapist and at least one of his patients. Most therapists have a harder time accepting a patient-partner who has a traditional view of marriage than one who wants to realize the emancipatory ideal. It is important for the therapist to remain aware of the relativity of his own values, of their dependency on a particular time and culture, and to recognize that other people, on the basis of their own experience, can arrive at different conclusions just as valid as his own. If the patients feel the therapist's genuine respect for their values, they will be more open to adopting a more flexible attitude and more prepared to compromise.

The Difficulty of Refraining from Making Value Judgments in Therapy

In couples therapy the therapist also has special difficulties in refraining from judgmental interventions because he himself is personally affected by contemporary upheavals in ideas about marriage, and as a rule is involved in unresolved personal and marital conflicts relating to values. This can lead to problems if the therapist is not able to observe and correct the effects of his particular bias.

> In couples therapy the partners often represent values in a polarized form. To enable the reader to test his own attitudes, I cite on the following pages several pairs of assertions frequently heard in couples therapy, and invite you to test yourself to see which of each pair provokes particularly strong reactions in you.

1A

I want to know where I'm at. You've been keeping me in suspense long enough. Now either you have to make up your mind you want to be married or we'll split up. Your constant evasions show me that you really don't want to, or can't, commit yourself to me and that you are evading any kind of obligation and responsibility.

2A

You simply will not understand that I can't get well as long as you neglect me so. If you're not with me on the weekend I get scared and can't stand it alone in that empty apartment.

3A

Since you were unfaithful to me I can't feel anything but disgust when you try to get close to me. Something inside me died. I used to love you so much.

4A

For me love is something absolute. Open marriage is an illusion. By its very nature deep love is intended to be exclusive. I can't and I won't share my spouse with other partners.

1B

The institution of marriage destroys love. Part of real love is that I am free to love. I only know what exists now, and I can't promise I'll still love you ten years from now. For me love is something very personal that society doesn't have any right to intrude on. Your constant suspicion makes me wonder whether your love for me is genuine.

2B

You only complain for the sake of complaining. You don't really have any reason to complain. I work myself to death all week and I have a right to some free time. No matter what I do, you're never satisfied.

3B

For years you've been frustrating me sexually. But if you can't respond to me anymore, you have no right to complain if I go with other partners.

4B

Your jealousy shows that you have the wrong attitude to marriage. You still think one can own a partner and obligate him to stay with you. For me relationships with other partners are an important personal experience, from which, in the end, our relationship may benefit. If you want to give up the chance of having such experiences, that's your business. But you can't lay down the law to me about it.

5A

This modern consumer world no longer sees any point in suffering and sacrifice. Anyone who has children has to be able to accept some limitations on his personal development. Now this development is at the service of the community, to which everyone has to contribute, the man as a husband and the woman as a wife.

5B

I let you put pressure on me for far too long. But now I know: We have to find the courage to get a divorce, and not let marriage get in the way of our personal development.

6A

I think that the drop in the birth rate nowadays and the campaign for abortion is an alarming sign that women are getting farther and farther away from what nature intended. A marriage in which people don't have a family is missing its most important dimension. If you knew before we were married that we weren't going to have any children, you shouldn't have married.

6B

Stop talking all this rubbish about motherhood. Today everyone knows that women are told motherhood is just to keep them feeling dependent and guilty. Today a woman doesn't need to have any children to prove she's a woman.

Now I would like to ask you, when reading each pair of statements, to picture the battling couple who are speaking them. Then decide which partner in each couple needs treatment more than the other, that is, which one you feel is more neurotic.

Given your detached and enlightened vantage point as a reader, you may feel able to question both sides of each pair of statements. But few therapists are capable of doing this when they are actually involved in a course of therapy. I have handed out this questionnaire in many training institutions and asked those taking part to mark the two statements that irritated them the most. As a rule there were distinct differences between the responses of the female and male participants, and also between those under and over thirty-five years old. Yet the actual results varied. At some institutions women clearly tended to take the progressive side and men the conservative side. At other times the results were just the opposite. Occasionally the older group were obviously making an effort to prove that they were progressive.

Despite all this data, many therapists still maintain that they cannot remember ever having made judgmental remarks during therapy; it was their duty to clarify the patients' values. But in couples therapy (unlike individual therapy) the therapist's values can be deduced from his statement of which of the above pairs of statements he is especially moved to question. Let's take a look at the first statement: A's reproach that his partner will not commit himself to a binding relationship could be the expression of a neurotic lack of trust or a neurotic fear of being abandoned. B's rejection of the institution of marriage, on the other hand, could be the expression of a neurotic fear of attachment. But neither attitude need necessarily stem from neurosis. To a great extent it is up to the individual therapist to decide whether he wishes to examine the attitude of A or the attitude of B more closely.

Example 10 (From a Couples Group Therapy):

A married couple suffering from anxiety neurosis had a close, stifling relationship. While the wife was away on vacation, the husband told the therapy group that a few days earlier he had begun an extramarital relationship. He did not want to tell his wife, because it would be too hard on her. In any case he intended to break off the extramarital relationship as soon as his wife returned. I interpreted this as a positive sign of budding independence—that he was beginning to strike out on his own in certain areas that he did not share with his wife. But the female therapist with whom I was working questioned why the husband was doing things, or not refraining from doing things, that he could not own up to in his wife's presence, when he knew quite well that they would hurt her. Both therapists intervened in a way that was clearly determined by their values.

Example 11:

The wife in a couple who were undergoing couples therapy with me attended a group-dynamics training session without telling me about it beforehand. She came to our next therapy session beaming, with all flags flying and behaving as if she had just been reborn, and said that completely new dimensions of life had been opened for her during the training week. In a marriage, she said, one had to stand up for one's needs; the partners had to be completely open with each other; it was absurd to suppress needs for relationships with other partners or to hypocritically carry them out in secret. Filled with initiative she began a relationship with a male acquaintance, with the full knowledge of his wife and her husband. I was resentful of her ecstatic enthusiasm. I felt hurt that she had not acquired these insights in therapy with me but in the training session, and thought her behavior uncritical and naïve. I felt a need to get her feet back down on the ground and to tell her in an authoritarian tone that of course this kind of free marriage was a lovely dream, but could hardly be realized without the suffering of her partner. I was also annoyed by the woman's provocative, defiant, self-confident smile. Her soaring flight lasted only a few weeks, until her lover's wife, who felt that too much was being asked of her, had a violent reaction. My patient's husband, who up until now had maintained an imperturbable calm, was also upset by his wife's extramarital fling and was acting up. The wife abruptly fell back to earth and became depressed. At first I noticed that I felt a certain sense of triumph, for after all, I had foreseen this debacle. But then I began to wonder whether this was not a case of self-fulfilling prophecy in which patients in a therapy are compelled to behave in such a way that they will confirm the personal experiences and expectations of the therapist (v. *Couples in Collusion*). When I had calmed down a bit I realized how close I had come to misunderstanding an important process. Until now the wife had remained strongly attached to her parents and had looked to her husband, and then to me, to be a protective parental figure who would give her guidance. Her escape from therapy into a group dynamics or encounter group, and her resultant escape from the fixed norms of her marriage, was a first step—still somewhat forced—towards growing up and acting on her own responsibility. The failure of this attempt could easily convince her that she would never be able to live an independent life and that from now on she needed the strict guidance of authority figures to get along in life. Her action also produced some therapeutic results in the sense that for the first time her husband had been stirred up a bit and had expressed his own feelings. We therapists are always in danger of thinking that patients can develop positively only if they stick to the norms we set for them. But often their potential for development consists precisely in their ability to resist our interpretations and suggestions.

Should the Therapist Reveal
His Own Norms and Values?

If the therapist's values indirectly influence patients in any case, would it, we wonder, not be more honest and positive if the therapist were to state his values openly at the beginning of therapy? I would concur with *Charlotte Buehler,* who has said that she favors, at certain specific moments, informative statements as well as statements of values; for we are living in a time of momentous upheaval of values, in which the rapid advances in science are exercising an ever-increasing influence on our interpretations of the meaning and purpose of life. Buehler believes that occasionally the analyst can give the patient a brief survey of the trends of our time in order to point out the changes occurring in values and world-views, and in order to advise the patient about various possible solutions to his difficulties, and the results of these solutions, thus making it easier for the patient to make his own choice. The idea that everyone ought to decide for himself what he wants to believe in, Buehler claims, reminds her a little of Jean-Jacques Rousseau's claim that every child ought to rediscover for himself all the scientific discoveries made up until the eighteenth century. She would, Buehler goes on, imagine that the limitations of this "do-it-yourself" approach are as apparent as its strong points. As far as possible, the therapist ought to present information relating to values in such a way that patients do not feel that the therapist's point of view is determining their choice of values. But even if the therapist thinks he is supplying quite objective information, he should examine his motives for doing so. *Simkin,* quoted in *Buehler,* believes that as a rule it is not a good idea for the analyst to adopt a judgmental attitude. The therapist's personal stand-point, Simkin says, is a defensive maneuver he uses when he feels threatened over a normative issue by his patient. The need to express a personal opinion is a weakness in a therapist.

On the whole I agree with Simkin. In therapy I have been moved to make statements of value primarily when I felt that the couple were misinformed about concrete societal data. But later I have been forced to admit that my statements were almost always superfluous to the therapy and had really stemmed from my feeling of being personally threatened by the "unbalanced" opinions of my patients. More important, it seems to me that the therapist's convictions about marriage, abortion, divorce, extra-marital relationships, the decision not to have children, and so on, needs continual re-examination to determine the extent to which his therapeutic interventions are determined, and limited, by his own values.

11

DIVORCE AND REMARRIAGE

Divorce—Liberation or Catastrophe?

Divorce in Couples Therapy

Second Marriages

Divorce—Liberation or Catastrophe?

In the last few years divorce statistics have skyrocketed so high in the industrialized nations that one has to wonder whether soon divorce will be the rule and life-long partnership the exception. It takes courage for a wife to get a divorce if she is financially dependent on her husband; and it is humiliating to have to accept alimony. In addition, the divorced woman meets with more social discrimination than the divorced man. Thus the woman's movement often equates the courage to get a divorce with the courage for liberation.

In West Germany *Ruth Hoeh* and *Annegret Kulms* (1976) carried out a representative survey on 639 women of all ages, and learned that three quarters of all divorces have occurred at the wife's instigation. In retrospect, 11% of the wives described their divorce as the biggest disaster of their lives, while 44% viewed their divorce as a liberation that gave their lives a new direction. The women who described their divorce as a disaster had for the most part a traditional view of marriage at the time they married and for the duration of the marriage. At the time of the survey these women averaged 47 years of age, so that they were five years older than the mean age of women in the survey as a whole. More than 80% of these older women had children, had been married for years, and had prepared themselves for the traditional woman's role of housewife, mother and spouse. Most often, the women who experienced divorce as a liberation had been married a shorter time, were childless, and had worked while they were married. They had identified less with the role of housewife and mother. The women who viewed their divorce as a disaster still clung to their former marriage and believed that the divorce could have been avoided. Quite often the breakup was caused by their husband's infidelity. These women tended to feel that the divorce represented a permanent trauma for the children. They had concentrated on their household, husband and children and tried, by adjusting and making sacrifices, to create a harmonious, conflict-free home. Now they felt that they had been betrayed because they had relied on the success of the traditional role of woman. In material terms their situation had generally worsened since the divorce and they felt personally more isolated than they had before the divorce. But the situation was quite different for the women who regarded divorce as a liberation: they believed that their personal lives had benefited from the divorce. They felt less isolated than when they were married and now often had good male friends. Their jobs and their attitude of critical detachment regarding the role of women made it easier for them to experience divorce as an opportunity to live more independent lives than would have been possible in a troubled marriage.

These findings by *Hoeh* and *Kulms* concur with my experiences as a therapist, but I regret that no similar studies have been done of the effects of divorce on men. Moreover, it seems to me dubious to conclude that the more liberated a woman, the more likely she is to experience divorce as emancipation. Those women in the survey who felt that divorce was a disaster had been married longer and had children, and no doubt these facts had a profound influence on their feelings. When the formative years of someone's life have been spent with a spouse, the traces of their life together cannot be erased later on. After the divorce, people and places continually remind both partners of the past. There is the relationship with the children, who have grown up and may now have children of their own, and the relationship with the same circle of friends, as well as with the house the couple shared, the town where they had lived together, perhaps the same place of work, and as a rule many interests and habits they had had in common. Moreover, when a marriage of long duration dissolves, questions of property rights can rarely be regulated in such a way that neither partner feels cheated. If they have been married a long time and are middle-aged, many married people find it easier to put up with unsatisfactory compromises than to follow through with radical solutions whose results they are not sure they could cope with. *Berman and Lief* (1976) write that regardless of how hard a marriage may be on both partners, most divorced people who live alone find their situation almost unbearable; many of them go through a long phase of depression that can last from several months to years, and for many couples who have been married for a long time there simply is no solution without pain; so that, difficult as it may be to continue a marriage, living alone may be even harder and the couple may have no alternative.

A divorce is not like the fading-away of a relationship but more like its death. Officially and on the surface the relationship no longer exists, but underneath it often lives on. *Reiter* claims that one never forgets a marital relationship even after a divorce. A difficult divorce often lingers, like a spell that cannot be broken. Later relationships may be markedly affected by it. In this sense it is always worthwhile to undergo couples therapy regardless of whether or not the marriage ends in divorce, for each spouse has to come to terms with the crisis one way or the other, and if he does not do so now, he will have to deal with the consequences later. *Norman Paul* claims that the process of mourning after the divorce should lead to deeper understanding, and to an acceptance of one's own role in, and one's own contribution to, the demise of the marriage; for otherwise the bitterness and anguish remain. The divorce means the death of one's dreams of a happy marriage and a happy family who go on living happily ever after. The notion that now one can begin life over suggests that the past can be erased. Many people, in a forcible attempt to destroy all memory of their past marriage, suppress their feelings, cut them off and, if they do not get support from their families, become rigid, remote, out of reach. It is a divorce counsellor's task to eliminate such "cut-offs" between the spouses and their children.

Divorce in Couples Therapy

In the past almost all marriage counselling was the province of the Church, and the odium of moralism still attaches to the practice today, so that many psychotherapists and psychiatrists refuse to do marriage counselling. But it is a mistake to believe that couples therapy is a way of warding off an impending divorce. Around one quarter of the couples I have treated in therapy ended up applying for divorce—and most probably did so *because* of therapy. Therapy is an attempt to clarify the relationship. That is, it is designed to show to what extent the partners have stayed together under pressure of irrational fears, compulsions and unjustified guilt feelings; and how much genuine spontaneous affection remains between them or can develop when these pressures are reduced. To the extent that I am aware of my attitude as a therapist, I exercise no personal influence on a couple's decision to divorce. Often any direct counselling from the therapist for or against divorce achieves just the opposite effect from what he intended. Some psychotherapists actually make deliberate use of the paradoxical effect (*Toomin*, 1972) by stipulating that couples in therapy should live apart, and observe that this measure often motivates couples to live together again. Often I personally find it difficult to have positive feelings about a couples therapy that ends in divorce. A therapist doing individual therapy finds it much easier to interpret a divorce as a therapeutic success because he sees it as freeing the patient to achieve the goals the therapist has in mind, and because as a rule he is not troubled by having to watch the effects of divorce on the absent partner.

As soon as a therapy really seems to be underway, one partner will often declare that he is fed up with these continual confrontations and has decided to apply for divorce. The danger is that the therapist might take this statement at face value and think he has to immediately go all out to get this partner to change his mind; that is, the danger is that he might set himself up as the custodian of the marriage. But often the partner who wants the divorce is talking not so much about legal divorce as about emotional divorce. Frequently, concrete intentions to divorce are abandoned if the couple can achieve an inner divorce or separation. Thus the therapist might reply to a partner who comes out with a desperate statement of his intention to apply for divorce: "I see that you're serious about your desire to feel separate and distinct from your partner. At the moment you're finding it difficult not to feel completely under his sway as long as the two of you go on living together. If you were physically separated from him, you think it would be easier to find yourself and stand on your own feet. It would make you feel freer if there were a more clearcut separation between you."

Divorces arrived at in therapy are unsatisfactory when they result not from the experience of clarification and growing maturity but from a destructive escapism. Often the partner who initiates the divorce chooses this way to act out his rage and hatred against the therapist for having failed to bring about the changes in the marriage that this partner had expected upon entering therapy. The model of marriage that the divorcing partner had expected and prepared for proves in therapy to be unattainable, and no other model seems acceptable. This kind of divorce destroys not only the marriage but also the therapy, and the therapist feels disappointed with his efforts. The anger, helplessness and sense of professional failure that I have felt about many therapies resulting in divorce intensifies my impression that the partner who petitions for divorce wants to hurt not only his partner but me as well.

On the other hand there are couples who face the alternative: either stay married and go on being sick, or get well and be divorced. If a person married mostly for security or because he needed to be rescued, the illness and social inadequacy of one partner will be closely bound up with the other's ability to function as a helper and guide. It is particularly difficult for the regressive patient, the one who manifests symptoms, to make progress in therapy if his partner begins to feel threatened the moment he stops being dependent, sick and in need of help. Moreover, often the partner who manifests symptoms finds it hard, in the other partner's presence, to resist the temptation to behave regressively, and to let himself be pampered, nursed and guided. Marriages entered into for reasons of security and to satisfy a need for help tend to break down in therapy, particularly if the couple have few healthy resources to fall back on—if, for example, there are gross differences between the partners in social background, education or age. For example, a marriage may be shipwrecked if a man marries a much younger, still quite inexperienced woman and cannot tolerate her continuing to grow and develop, or if one partner marries a refugee or an invalid to save him from a distressing situation, and the latter is forced to give his savior gratitude and lifelong devotion. If one partner owes the other a debt for a service, this frustrates his need for parity and severely hampers their chances of success in a therapy geared towards emancipation.

Neurotic marriages are quite frequent; but often in therapy a mistaken impression arises because a therapist sees only the neurotic aspects of a relationship. Not unless he takes the trouble to probe the matter will he learn that in addition to neurotic traits, the partners share many positive and pleasurable experiences, hobbies, common interests and leisure-time activities. It is often hard for the therapist to judge how unhappy and sick the partners really are in their relationship, for he only knows them within the framework of the therapeutic triangle, which by definition would not exist in the first place if the couple were not coming there to display the side of their relationship that involves conflict.

Second Marriages

In a high percentage of cases divorce does not mean the end of marriage but only a transition to another marriage. In the Western world there has never been such a high percentage of married people as there are today, which in view of the high divorce rate can be explained only by the fact that so many people remarry. These days 80% of divorced men and 70% of divorced women remarry. This suggests that divorced people do not reject the institution of marriage as such. Instead they assume that their first marriage failed because of specific incompatibilities, and hope that their second marriage will not suffer the same fate. Generally they do not continue in an uncommitted existence, free of responsibility, for very long. Statistically speaking, second marriages last a somewhat shorter time than first marriages, but the difference is not great enough to warrant the skepticism often voiced about second marriages. Frequently second marriages involve a sense of pressure, even a compulsion to succeed, which, although it may stabilize a relationship, also increases the stress.

A number of other problems can arise in a second marriage. A divorced person may escape into a second marriage in the hope of forgetting the first. Often one sees the following sequence of events: A person who has not yet freed himself of dependency on his parents tries to deal with this dependency by escaping into his first marriage. Then he tries to overcome a dependency he has not dealt with in the first marriage by entering a second. The anticipation of being able to begin all over again and the belief that he has learned from the mistakes of his first marriage can infuse the second marriage with hopes and expectations; but these same hopes and expectations can also place it under stress. Today, to be sure, many people know that in a second marriage one may make the same mistakes as in the past. But often the desperate effort to avoid these mistakes can itself drive a spouse into the same misguided behavior as before. *"Plus ça change, plus c'est la même chose."*

Often the partner who marries a divorced person does not have an easy time of it either. He harbors doubts and suspicions that the divorcé may cause this marriage to fail, as he did his first. Often the divorcé's former partner becomes a scapegoat on whom the sum total of all bad qualities is projected. The second spouse tries to show how different he is from the first, that in fact he is the opposite in every way. This can give the second marriage some solidity but can also cause trouble, especially when a relationship with the second partner was a major factor in the breakup of the first marriage. The second partner is placed in a difficult high-pressure situation in which he must continually prove that he really is a better partner than the previous spouse, and that the divorce was worthwhile. A second marriage may also come under pressure from the friends of the divorced partner and the children from the first marriage. The children often react negatively to the second marriage and have a tendency to withdraw from the new couple once the divorced spouse has remarried. So the second marriage has to work to prove itself in order to be accepted by other people.

Statistics show that in the past few years there has been a marked increase in the percentage of divorces taking place between partners with children (*Second Family Report*, 1975). Thus we must prepare ourselves for a time when complex family systems that include both parents and stepparents will be an everyday occurrence. *Haffter's* study shows that after the age of twelve girls find it very difficult to accept a stepmother. This may be related to an Oedipal situation. The girl has already come to feel that she is her divorced (or widowed) father's surrogate wife, and it is hard for her to give up this position. The girl may also feel guilty for the failure of the first marriage, as if she had taken her father away from her mother. Or she refuses to allow her father to have any lover other than her mother because she has already had to renounce the possibility of having her father as her lover. Sons go through roughly the same thing with their mothers, although here the problems are less acute.

Often adolescent children try to mediate between quarrelling parents, and may even develop into problem children so that their parents will be brought back together by the child's needs, and thus a divorce will be prevented. In a situation such as this a child may feel that he personally has failed if, despite his efforts, his parents get a divorce. If the partner of the second marriage was already on the scene at the time of the divorce the child may unload all his hatred on this second partner. The fears of a stepfather or, especially, a stepmother that the adolescent children will not accept her can create special problems in child-rearing because the stepparent is overly concerned with earning the children's acceptance and tends to be too indulgent and to spoil them. On the other hand it is painful for a father or mother who is now separated from his or her children to hear the children call their former spouse's new partner "Dad" or "Mom." Thus often relationships with the children become the focus for acting out all the unmastered hatred and unconscious feelings of attachment between the adults involved, and the children are employed as double agents by both their families.

Thus the failure of second marriages is not exclusively the result of the repetition of neurotic behavior patterns but often has immediate causes involving this complex pattern of family relationships. If a second marriage fails, there is a risk that a partner may decide he is incapable of being married and from then on try to avoid forming any deep attachments.

If the purpose of a second marriage is to really put a first marriage behind one, a complicated situation can arise for both partners. If there are children, they make it harder to dissolve the first marriage completely.

Example 12:

A woman initiated a couples therapy because her partner was unhappy and desperate. Continual destructive escalations were taking place in which both partners, she said, behaved irrationally. They had been living together for two years but were not officially married. The wife, Lisa, had been divorced for several years. Her two school-age children were living with her former husband, Robert, who had remarried. On the surface her problem with her present partner, Peter, was that he wanted to get married, but after the failure of her first marriage she was afraid to marry again, all the more so because her present relationship was already showing signs of great strain. Peter saw her evasiveness as proof that Lisa did not really want to make a commitment to him, and Lisa in turn accused him of trusting in love only if it had been legalized by marriage. When Peter and Lisa first met she had not yet recovered from her divorce. Her husband had become involved with another woman, which had deeply hurt and humiliated Lisa. Peter wanted to offer an absolute and unconditional love that would prove to her that her mistrust of new relationships was unjustified, so he went along with Lisa's wishes that they not tie themselves to each other by getting married. But now he felt betrayed because he felt that Lisa was exploiting his willingness to accede to her demands, and was taking advantage of him both financially and personally, without vindicating it by making a clear declaration of her love. The two had become involved in a narcissistic collusion. At first Peter had greatly idealized Lisa and wanted to fulfill her completely with his love. For the sake of this love he put his career in second place and overtaxed himself by asking himself to feel a total undemanding love. After the humiliation and insecurity Lisa had suffered as a result of the divorce, Peter's devotion boosted her self-esteem. But when they had lived together longer, Peter's idealization became a burden and placed her under constraint, so that she tried to restore some distance between them. Their tendency towards a narcissistic collusion stemmed, in both cases, from their early family relationships; but their immediate situation played at least as important a role. After moving out with the children, Robert had left his home, with all its furnishings, for Lisa's use. Peter always felt like a guest in another man's home; he had to eat out of "other people's" dishes and could not change anything about the house. To be sure, after some long-drawn-out confrontations he was given a room to fix up any way he liked, and lived in the room like a tenant. Over the weekend the children generally came to visit Lisa. Lisa devoted herself to them so that Peter felt left out and unneeded. It hurt him when the four of them would do something together and Lisa treated him, around her friends, like a casual companion rather than as the man who shared her life. He felt that Lisa was ashamed of him in front of the children and was not committed to him. Her elder son, Rolf, was afraid to sleep alone, so Lisa let him sleep with her in the bed where she had slept with her husband during their marriage, while Peter slept in the next room. The elder son quickly caught on to the situation and regarded Peter as a rival whom he knew just how to provoke with his rejecting, scornful behavior.

The initial therapy sessions showed that Lisa had not worked through her divorce from Robert but was still very much under his sway, and in fact cherished a secret fantasy that as long as she did not show the children she was clearly committed to Peter, she was saving a place for Robert's eventual return. The children became a communications link between Robert and Lisa and transmitted messages back and forth. Peter saw the children as Robert's agents. Thus he was particularly concerned to show them that now he held the first place in Lisa's affections and that Lisa and he had a happy relationship to which she felt committed.

But Robert's second marriage also had its problems. Rolf rejected his stepmother, Erika, and picked many fights with her when he was home. He made fun of her attempts at motherhood when he was with Lisa. Erika angrily called Lisa on the telephone and accused her of being a cruel and unnatural mother, of spoiling Rolf and then having nothing to do with him, leaving Robert and herself with all the unpleasant chores of raising the boy. Then Lisa called up Robert to talk with him about Erika. He complained to her about the troubles he was having in his second marriage. Thus the strained situation with the children continually fortified the alliance between the original couple.

Robert had left Lisa for Erika because he felt Lisa was neglecting him and not giving him sufficient validation. He reproached her by saying that even the children did not have a real relationship with her. After the divorce Lisa did all she could to get close to the children and to become important to them. Peter quite rightly felt that he was playing second fiddle to the children, whom he viewed as an extension of Robert. It was hard for him to look on and see how badly they were being raised because Robert and Lisa were using them to continue carrying on a secret relationship. It was also hard on Peter to have the children around so much, not only because he felt rejected by them but also because he had wanted children of his own; but Lisa did not want to have any children with him.

Lisa's failure to work through her divorce was also evidenced by the fact that in part she was avenging herself on Peter for what Robert had done to her. He had humiliated her and made her feel left out, and now she could do the same to Peter.

The clarification of these complex involvements in couples therapy led Lisa to behave with less ambivalence towards her children and her former husband, and helped Peter to understand better the impossibility of wiping out all traces of Lisa's ten-year marriage.

When the partners have been married a long time and have had a family, the history of their marriage cannot be erased. The partner in a second marriage must have a great deal of maturity to be able to accept this fact. As for a divorced partner who remarries, it is important that he understand the psychological position of his second partner and structure the situation so that this new partner feels how valuable the second relationship is to his spouse.

12

HELGA AND STANI: A COUPLE IN THERAPY

This chapter will present and discuss excerpts from videotape records of an actual couples therapy. As a rule therapists, when writing books, talk about the showpieces among their cases, especially if they are trying to demonstrate the efficacy of their theories. I chose to talk about Helga and Stani because their therapy is ideally suited to illustrate many aspects of couples therapy that I discuss in this book, and because I myself learned a lot from their therapy. Because one of my main concerns is to observe the ways in which a therapist involves himself in collusions with his patients, I chose a case in which I was especially aware of such collusions. It may be risky for me to describe a case of this kind, because it leaves me open to certain criticisms. Above all I mean it to show how difficult it was for me, as a male therapist, to be fair to both partners, especially the wife.

Naturally I could have chosen to describe a case in which my problems were less clearly apparent. But I believe that the reader can learn more from problems that I did not manage to completely overcome than from carefully manicured excerpts that show my skills at their best. Perhaps I may also succeed in showing that despite my mistakes the therapy set a constructive process in motion. The final outcome may be disillusioning. I could have selected cases that demonstrated more tangibly therapeutic effects. But I would prefer to point up the complexity of the results of a therapy, and the difficulty of documenting these results with hard facts.

The therapy consisted of thirty-one sessions held over a thirteen-month period. Both "Helga" and "Stani" consented to the publication of these individual excerpts from the records of their therapy. I discussed each passage with them because it is not easy to read about oneself in a book even if one already knows everything described. Helga and Stani were shaken by the records and commentaries that follow, but they also felt that by reading them they had lived through their therapy again, this time with a certain detachment, and thus had deepened the experience.

At times it will no doubt be tedious to read these records. They contain many repetitions and endless variations on the same theme. This is the way therapy really is. I believe that the reader should try to absorb the atmosphere in these tedious passages, for the effect of a therapy depends more on the atmosphere than on any particularly shrewd intervention by the therapist. I believe that the problems of Helga and Stani trouble many couples today and hope that the reader will also be able to learn something about himself as he participates in the experiences of this couple.

First Session, May 13: The First Interview

Synopsis
In the introductory phase *Helga and Stani introduce themselves. Helga dominates the scene with her vivacious and expansive temperament, which also finds expression in her sweeping gestures and protracted speech. Stani, on the other hand, seems to have come to our talk mostly at Helga's insistence. Helga says that their problem is her insecurity at the fact that Stani does not accept her as she is. She reacts to this by becoming more aggressive and insistent, which in turn reinforces Stani's tendency to avoid her and avoid taking any definite stand.*

The middle phase *of the session describes the relationship between the present conflict and the couple's original choice of partners. At first Stani felt attracted by those same qualities in Helga that now disturb him most, namely the direct and spontaneous way she expresses her feelings. The emotionally inhibited Stani hoped to absorb some of Helga's emotionality. But things turned out just the opposite: He felt he could not cope with her surging emotions and became even more withdrawn than before. Helga, in turn, had idealized Stani at first. She formed an image of him as a kind, understanding father with whom she could find shelter and peace. She felt disappointed because his quiet, meek behavior no longer seemed to her to represent acceptance, but rather cowardly evasion. In the beginning Stani's self-esteem was boosted by Helga's ideal image of him, but later he felt trapped by this image. The role of a tolerant father did not suit his actual feelings. But Helga reacted violently to every disappointment of her expectations, so he did not dare confront her directly but began to evade her* demands in secret, among other things by entering into extramarital relationships. The more he evaded her the more she pressured him, and the more she pressured him, the more he evaded her.

In the final phase *I try to sum up my impression in a few interpretations, at which time the partners respond positively to my attempt to show that the behavior of each is related to that of the other. But Stani is finding it difficult to commit himself to therapy at this early date, so we agree to talk again.*

Detailed Account

Helga had telephoned me to ask about the possibility of therapy. I asked her whether her husband was willing to attend our sessions from the very beginning. It seemed to me best, I told her, if she did not say anything now over the telephone, thus giving me a chance to devote equal time to both partners without forming any preconceived opinions. Helga agreed and we set a time for our first meeting.

During the first few minutes I recorded information about the couple, explained how the videotape recorder worked, and obtained their consent to my use of the tapes for this book. The names and a few superficial facts were changed on the tapes to prevent the couple from being identified.

Stani is a thirty-two-year-old engineer, Helga a thirty-three-year-old kindergarten teacher. Now she is working part-time in a children's day-care center. They have been married for seven years. They have a six-year-old son and a two-year-old son.

Helga is powerfully built, gives an impression of determination, vitality, *joie de vivre* and gregariousness. Her voice is somewhat rough and loud. Compared to her, Stani seems pale and inconspicuous. Both are casually dressed. Their appearance is that of a young modern couple.

(Th.=Therapist; W.=Wife; H.=Husband)

Th: How did you come to telephone me?

W: Well—

H: (Anticipates her) Basically it was that—we really don't quite know what we want. We thought it would be good if we got to know each other better, understand our relationship better. Some people we know gave us your name.

The couple introduce themselves.*

---

* The marginal notes alongside the spoken text provide a synopsis of the content that helps the reader get the gist of each passage.

Th: But why did you decide to do something just at this time?

W: Actually I already wanted to go to a psychiatrist three or four years ago, just to find out what's wrong. I was so insecure, didn't feel at all well, and had a really bad temper from feeling like a cooped-up housewife. But you know how it is, when one's just too sluggish to get up the energy. But I wanted to know what's wrong. We can't get anywhere on our own. I'd like to know (Turns to her husband) why you reject me the way you do, why I'm so dependent on you, why I can't get free and why I react so violently to everything you say. When someone else says things like that, I just smile. I would just like to know why I'm so dependent, and where the boundaries between us lie. I'd like you to stop rejecting me, but I'd also like to stop my own aggressive behavior, so that we can stay together.

Th: Can you give me an example of an episode when you felt very rejected, and at the same time very dependent?

W: Actually there's been less of it recently. The big crisis was really last summer. That is, it had already been going on for two years. But if you have such young children and your husband has just finished his dissertation, you suppress all that. You want to spare the children and not put too much of a strain on them. You think, maybe when they're a little bigger and all the pressure is off. You wanted to know why I feel rejected?

Th: Yes

W: He feels that I'm too big, too fat, too strong, too active, too loud, and I booze too much and— (All three laugh)

Th: (To husband) Is that true?

H: Yes, in general.

Th: Can you describe it for me?

H: I can't describe it exactly. It's more of a feeling, but in certain situations it bothers me when you (To wife) are loud, or that you're too fat or drink too much.

Th: Does it get pretty noisy around your house then?

H: When we're fighting, yes, often, but less at other times. She's too emotional.

Th: What do you do when she gets loud?

H: Then I'd like to stop. We lose our objectivity, we hurl too many personal accusations at each other. There's just no point to it any more. She gets so excited that emotionally she feels she's at the end of her rope.

The first few minutes of a session are often like the presentation of a visitor's card. How do this couple present themselves to the therapist? The way they tell the therapist their reasons for wanting therapy shows him that they already know something about psychology, and would like to clarify their relationship and their inappropriate behavior. I have the feeling that they care a lot, perhaps too much, about making a good impression on me. In any case it is striking that they do not speak at all concretely about their problems, and that their depiction of their conflicts is very detached. Whenever one of the couple is speaking, the other watches him very attentively, almost anxiously and suspiciously, as if both are trying to ensure that neither will say anything that would let the therapist see the other in a bad light. The overall atmosphere is pleasant. I like the couple. I feel that a positive relationship is developing.

W: Yes, but that's only if it involves personal things.
H: But most of the time it involves personal things.
W: Then I get very aggressive. Your reaction is simply to withdraw. You've always done that. I have always idealized you for that.
Th: The fact that he behaves so calmly.
W: Yes. Stani has rejected me and then I've felt very insecure, or he has withdrawn or said nothing at all. It disturbs him a lot when I talk so loud, but he doesn't tell me that. I simply thought, "He's a kind father, calm and benevolent." I react very strongly when something is bothering me, and I tell people about it too. I always thought, "Well, he puts up with it, he's so far—above me." I had always admired and idealized him so much for being that way, but at bottom he wasn't being tolerant at all, he just didn't say anything about it. So we got farther and farther apart.
Th: Idealized—so that you could calm down if he stayed calm?
W: Yes, that's it.
Th: (To husband) And now you simply withdraw?
H: Not so much now. Actually we rarely have fights except when we discuss something; then we often do.

Helga pictured Stani as an ideal father figure. Stani belied her expectations by being evasive.

Generally she gets aggressive, and then we break off the
discussion. Usually it ends in tears and broken dishes all
over the floor.

Th: Do you throw dishes too, or is she the only one?

H: No, she's the only one. I have shouted from time
to time.

Th: (To wife) How do you feel when he shouts?

W: Then I'm glad! Actually that's only been happening since summer, and then I feel much better. I have
something to grab hold of. Before, that never used to
happen.

Th: Then in the past he was very unapproachable?

W: Yes, I often thought, I really don't know Stani at
all. The problem grew out of the fact that Stani always
withdrew, and then out of insecurity I became more and
more aggressive. He never told me he felt I was being
aggressive, and so often I carried it to extremes, just to
get a reaction from him, because I no longer knew where
my limits were. This hurts him and drives him farther
and farther away.

Th: That made you insecure?

*Helga
reacted with
aggressivity
to her
feelings of
insecurity.*

W: Yes, and then it got worse and worse. It made me
very insecure. Then probably I reacted in completely the
wrong way and got aggressive. When I'm insecure I get
aggressive and loud, and that drove him farther and
farther away.

Th: How do you feel when you get so aggressive?

W: I think it varies, it depends on the situation. But I
think I'd feel better if I felt some resistance.

Th: You're left high and dry, you're not held in by
anything, you can't feel any limits?

W: Yes, exactly! I'm very emotional. Then I overstep
my limits. Perhaps one ought to be able to tell for oneself
when one is doing that. I don't know.

Th: You would like him to set limits for you, and then
he doesn't do it. Is it that that gives you this feeling of
dependency?

W: I don't know why I react in such a dependent way
when he says something. Probably because I don't know
whether he accepts me, that's why it gets to me so.

The partners are very different in their way of speaking and in their body language. At this moment, Stani is sitting in the armchair as if he were curled up inside himself, his arms folded. When he feels attacked by Helga, he places his hand protectively on the cheek turned towards her. He often glances at her suspiciously from the side. Helga is just the opposite in her surface behavior: She is wide open, her legs often spread wide, she gesticulates with outflung arms, makes animated faces and continually changes her sitting position. Clearly these different ways of behavior play an important role in the couple's conflict. Stani dislikes Helga's emotional eruptions. He evades her, which makes Helga feel insecure. She feels rebuffed, emotionally rejected. At the beginning of their relationship Helga thought she was being accepted by a kind, ideal father. She was deeply hurt when she felt that Stani was not like the image she had formed of him.

The couple had arrived at the following role division: Helga represents emotion, and wants to fill Stani with emotion. She wants him to serve as a kind of vessel into which she can pour herself, and by which she can feel herself limited and contained.

Now I have learned something about the couple's conflict and move on to the second phase of the interview, to the question of the *relationship between partner choice and marital conflict.*

Th:　(To the couple) Can you tell me how you met?

H:　You can tell that better than I can, you remember it much better.

W:　Well, of course, I'm not trying to get out of telling about it, but I don't want to make it look again as if you're just sitting there saying nothing the whole time while I'm trying to put something over on you.　*Partner choice.*

H:　You're the one he asked.

W:　No, he asked both of us.

H:　All right. It was while we were skiing. I don't remember the details. I don't remember any more whether I was alone or not that first Sunday when I saw her.

W:　You weren't alone, Claudia was with you.

H:　(Laughs) Okay, you remember better. I told you it would be better if you told it, I don't remember clearly any more. We'd been invited to a party, lots of people had been invited. Helga flirted with me a little. I had the feeling that she was interested. It was a spur-of-the-moment get-together. Already that first evening I wanted to be alone with her. That was the beginning. Then I came back again. I really moved fast trying to get to know her better. That right? (Husband smiles flirtatiously at his wife)

W: (Smiles back) Yes.

Stani initially was attracted by those qualities of Helga that now disturb him most.

Th: You said that you were with a girlfriend. And then you saw Helga for the first time. What was your first impression of her, what attracted you to her?

H: Strangely enough it was the same thing that bothers me now: her way of dominating everything, of being the center of everything, making an impression, everybody admiring her. That was probably what attracted me. I can't remember exactly, just off the top of my head.

Th: Was all this a contrast to this girlfriend you had then?

H: The girlfriend was more a casual thing. There were no deep ties.

Th: (To wife) Do you know what was your first impression of Stani?

Helga hoped to receive from Stani the acceptance she had wanted but not had in the past, but which Stani could not give her in their marriage because of his own problems.

W: I must say I liked you. It was a fun evening, the way it often is when you throw an impromptu party, when everyone's new to you. I liked you, but not in a special way. I simply thought it was fun and gay, and you were quiet, and we danced. I don't really know how I felt. And it wasn't clear to me for a long time. Back then I already had a boyfriend in Germany, a pretty strong tie, we were together for two years, and then I went to Switzerland and started to break away from him. And then I met you, but I still had . . . I told Stani that I had a steady boyfriend who was going to come to Switzerland too. I had a bad conscience because of this boyfriend, because I flirted with Stani all the same. But I can't say exactly what it was, why I got involved with him. I just liked him, but I don't know what was special about him.

H: I think I liked you.

W: Yes, that's a big part of it for me.

Th: You felt accepted by him?

W: Yes.

H: Admired and desired.

W: For me that probably plays the— a big role, being
accepted, I think that that's a basic requirement for me,
even the crucial thing.

When I asked how the couple met, they seemed stupefied and dazed.
Each of them tried to get the other to answer. Possibly they each wanted
the other to be the first to lay all his cards on the table and thus to be
forced into admitting how he had idealized his partner at first. It is
significant that Stani felt attracted by those very qualities in Helga that
now disturb him most, namely her way of being the life of the party and
filling up all the space. Helga can feel accepted only if she is the center of
her partner's life. The precondition of a relationship is that she must feel
admired. In the beginning Stani fully met this condition, but now Helga
feels that Stani's lack of response is leaving her with nothing solid to go on,
and she interprets this as rejection.

We see here the typical reversal of attitude in which the very
qualities that motivated the couple's choice of partners in the first place
later play a central role in their conflict: In the woman it was her
extroverted personality, her emotional expansiveness and gregariousness;
in the man it was the extraordinary degree of tolerance and acceptance
with which he responded to the woman. At first each felt that the other
made up for his own deficiencies. Clearly Stani suffers from his inability to
experience and show strong emotion, and Helga suffers from a lack of self-
esteem.

Th: How long did you go together before you got
married?
W: Fifteen months.
Th: How did you spend your time?
H: We were together only three months before we
got engaged. One reason was to shock other people,
getting engaged overnight that way.
W: I'm surprised to hear *you* say that. I thought I was
the only one who felt that way. Naturally I got a charge
out of that.
H: I was in on it too, I wanted to shock everybody
because I thought it was fun just as you did.
W: Once my boyfriend was there from Germany. He
said that there was no point in our going on, because if I
stayed in Zürich our relationship would break up. I
thought, "He's saying I should come back," but I didn't
want to come back. And I called up Stani and asked what

I ought to do. Stani came to my place and said, "Stay with me." (Wife looks at Stani) Yes, that's what you said!

H: (Smiles)

W: And then we got engaged. It was his birthday.

Th: Whom did you want to shock?

W: Shock? We didn't really want to shock anyone.

H: But we did, just a little, to shock Rolf; to do something really wild.

W: The only one who was cross was Rolf, who went out with me the night before. He was one of the guys from our group, but otherwise there was nothing between us. He was mad because I hadn't told him anything the night before. But I didn't flirt with him at all. I didn't really want to shock him, because Rolf, after all, . . .

Th: So you got engaged after three months, and then it was about a year before you got married?

H: Yes.

W: And then came the delayed explosion that has been plaguing us ever since! When was that? In May I got pregnant and got an abortion, and what really made me mad was that that very evening I said to him, "Stani, look out, it's dangerous now," and he didn't pay any attention. I really resented that, resented it very, very much, and I really started to hate him because I had this bloody mess to deal with, to put it bluntly, and besides that there was the fact that the abortion wasn't performed under very good conditions, it was in Stani's room . . .

Th: An illegal abortion?

W: Yes, an illegal abortion, by a surgeon of course, but we had to wait until everyone had gone, and I still had to rearrange everything for work the next day.

Th: That must have been very hard on you.

W: Yes, very hard, and then it was done without any anesthetic, it hurt terribly, and then I had to work the next day on top of it. I was really furious. I had already had an abortion when I was with another man; that didn't get me down so, I don't know why it was different this time. Stani said, "Come on, we'll get married," but I said, "No, you're still a student, we have no money, and there I am sitting around with a kid, it's impossible, later on we can have ten children but not under these

The relationship started playfully, but then certain events placed it under great stress and caused an imbalance in the partners' debit and credit accounts.

conditions." I'd have ended up having to put the child in a day nursery. With the other man it didn't bother me so, but it was very hard on our relationship, and then one pushes it out of one's mind and seems to forget it, but it really did make me furious.

Th: And you went on feeling that way for quite a while?

W: I don't know.

H: I'm sure it bothered you underneath.

W: Probably somehow then I stopped trusting him, I was furious for a while and then I got over it, but it was very hard on our relationship.

Th: And then you got married anyhow, that same year?

W: No, the year after.

The relationship began as a game. Clearly Stani was excited by Helga's vital personality and was stimulated to play all sorts of pranks. Then began what is termed the historical dimension of a long-term marital relationship. Fateful events occur, which create deep traumas in each partner's life and bind them together through a common history. Once done, some things cannot be undone, and they leave marks and scars. Helga's trust in Stani, whom she had pictured as an ideal father figure, was shattered by the abortion. This required that the partners make an unequal investment in the relationship. Helga had contributed more, so that Stani was forced into the position of debtor. Their life together creates unequal debit and credit accounts (terms used by *Boszormenyi-Nagy* to describe the ties of loyalty between blood relations), whose failure to balance strengthens the mutual bond but also places it under stress.

Th: And how did it happen that you went ahead and got married anyhow?

W: Yes, that's what we're wondering now. (All three laugh)

W: (To husband) Yes, why did you marry me?

H: I don't know what I told you. It was more or less that once people are engaged they ought to get married. One goes on to the next step; one doesn't go backwards. I only know I was very uncertain about it and was afraid of it, but then I blamed my fear on the fact that I was giving up bachelor life. But I thought, "This feeling won't last. It can't get any worse."

W: Naturally that made me furious when it came out. Maybe the two children and the seven years together all came out of cowardice.

Th: What did you think, why did you marry him?

W: I was under the illusion that he was marrying me because he loved me. That's what he told me and wrote me, and the whole time he made me believe he loved me. And I really said, "Stani is the ideal partner for me. I know it intuitively." I had a completely false image of Stani then. As I began to tell you earlier, he was so withdrawn that I really didn't get close enough to see what he was like. I thought he accepted me so completely because he never said anything. Every other guy would say something now and then, but he never did. Then I thought, "Yes, he's terrific, he's so mature, he accepts me," it made me feel so good. Once when I was in a bad mood he said, "That's because all you have left is me. You don't have the other guys any more." But I didn't go out with other men even though he said I could if I wanted to. I told myself, "He's so calm, he understands me, he accepts me, he likes me the way I am." He never told me any different.

Th: (To husband) Is that the way you see it too?

H: Not exactly. Sure I liked her in the beginning, her personality impressed me. After things changed—it didn't happen overnight—it bothered me. But then at the same time . . .

W: Just when was that?

H: It started before we were married.

W: Before we were married? (She is clearly hurt, her voice is hurt and piercing)

H: I was simply scared.

W: Yes, everyone's scared of getting married.

H: When I said something she didn't like somehow, no matter whether it was something critical or not, she got so aggressive that I preferred not to say anything after that. There were times when I might have started to say something about what bothered me. But I had to restrain myself because she reacted so violently. I got so used to it that I didn't even think of saying anything to her. I kept quiet about everything, kept it bottled up.

Th: Why was it that the very qualities that had attracted you at first annoyed you later on?

H: I don't know whether those qualities really attracted me from the beginning. One factor definitely was that everyone admired her so much, and I was the one who got her. That was a big factor.

Th: You felt it enhanced your self-esteem?

H: Yes, probably. I thought it was so great.

Th: You must have felt that Helga was idealizing you and looked on you as an ideal father? How did that feel?

H: On the whole it was flattering. Whenever I thought, She's not seeing me the way I am, I didn't say anything so that I wouldn't destroy her image of me.

Th: It was an image that would have fit your ideal too?

H: That's hard to say.

Th: Was that something you would basically have liked to be? A calm, peaceful man?

H: Yes, I think everyone would like that.

Stani did not want to destroy Helga's idealistic expectations, because he was afraid of disappointing her, and also because his self-esteem was boosted by her image of him.

When Helga asks Stani why he married her, his reaction is evasive: He only married her because he was afraid to withdraw his proposal and break the engagement. With this remark he strikes at Helga's most vulnerable spot. There is a clear intermeshing of their behavior: Insistent questions from Helga cause Stani to return an evasive and hurtful answer. Helga remains calm, but her gaze grows sharp. She raises one of her crossed legs as if she wanted to kick Stani. Stani's self-esteem had been enhanced by the ideal image of a big, kind, wise father, and in the beginning he had tried to behave in keeping with this image so as not to disappoint Helga. But his insecurity about his own identity tied him to this "false self" (*Laing*). Helga wants her partner to serve as a container into which she can pour herself, in which she feels welcome. Helga needs Stani as an ideal substitute father or as an aspect of her own Ideal-Self (*Richter*), as a representation of some part of her ideal self that she does not have in herself but wants to acquire indirectly through her partner. Clearly she finds it difficult to accept her own emotionality, and so wants to raise her self-esteem via her partner.

Th: So things had changed even before you got married?

H: Yes, it had started.

Th: (To wife) And you didn't notice any of this?

W: I'm not sure any more. I was afraid of getting married too. Who isn't? Everybody thinks then, now the fun's over. It doesn't matter how much you love your partner, you're always scared. Today I'm much more aware of that. But I felt that marriage was probably too much of a strain for two people, the idea that one person should fill all your needs. I was also afraid to be fixated on one person. Everyone's scared of that. But on the other hand I also thought it was beautiful.

Th: What were your fears?

W: I don't know. I wasn't very aware of them then. I've always lived very unconsciously, just went blithely ahead. I hadn't had many problems. That's why I never really faced up to it. I was never really conscious of my fears. I thought—sure, sure, it'll be all right.

Th: Looking at how things are now, would you say they turned out the way you feared?

W: Yes, I think so. Back then I'd already noticed a discrepancy between my image of Stani and how he really is. Perhaps I didn't want to see him any differently, perhaps I did see that, somehow I had already sensed that things weren't quite right. Maybe I should have written everything down. I found a letter I wrote you before we were married. Sure, it's a bit confused and immature, but that's just what it's about, the fact that I was afraid our marriage would get so dull, without any emotional charge, and so I wrote you, "Please let me be aggressive and loud just as I am." I was dreadfully afraid that Stani didn't like me the way I am and was just trying to make me over.

H: That may have been around the time when my feelings changed, because although I didn't express them, you were having such violent reactions.

W: I generally get aggressive when I'm insecure. That's how I express insecurity. I don't withdraw, I try to overact to cover up.

Th: You were afraid that he would force you to become something you're not?

W: Yes, exactly. And that's what he'd basically like to do now.

Th: Were you also afraid that you would slowly die as a person?

Helga did not want to see the obvious discrepancy between her image of Stani and the reality.

W: Yes, exactly! That's exactly what I always said, "Sure, we've survived, but we haven't lived." That's what I was really afraid of. Naturally one has to adjust and compromise. But I was afraid of having to change my whole nature, that's what I was afraid of!

Th: Did this fear sometimes make you react more emotionally than it would have been natural for you to do otherwise?

W: Yes, definitely!

Both partners show a high awareness of their problems. But so far their insights are very rational and not very integrated with their personal feelings. I return to the point where Helga had shown an emotional reaction, namely a reaction to the question of whether she had noticed a change in Stani's feelings even before they were married. Clearly Stani was already afraid of destroying the ideal image Helga had imposed on him; and Helga too felt that this image did not suit him. But she wanted to hold on to her self-deception. Thus, on the one hand, Helga was afraid that Stani might not be the way she wanted him to be, and on the other hand, she feared that Stani might demand that she be different from the way she felt she was. In her fear that in marriage she would have to give up her identity and die as a person, she reacted to Stani more emotionally and more aggressively than her own nature prompted.

W: For example, I have a boyfriend now. Stani knew that from the start; but it wasn't until later that I found out he had another relationship too. I don't mean that as an accusation, but now that we're here, we ought to talk about it. I felt so deceived when I found out about it. My initial reaction was very different from what you had expected. I didn't lay into you.

H: Yes, at first you did react the way I expected.

W: Yes, okay—I said—what did I say?—Yes, so now I have a boyfriend I get along with very well (In a long-drawn-out, provocative tone) and I'm not anywhere near so aggressive with him, but much quieter. The same thing is true about my talking so much, and being so loud . . . For example, I have a girlfriend, a child psychologist, who said, "Come on by and we'll have a drink." Then her husband joined us, we had a really good time. Then you came, just returned from America—I'll describe the way you interact in groups for a

change and not just with me—and things started to go
wrong immediately. (The husband leans back in the
chair, bored, and looks at her through half-closed lids.
The wife gesticulates more and more, leans forward,
moving her arms as if she were an orchestra conductor.)
Instead of talking about how things were in America, you
withdrew immediately. And then I talked and talked and
noticed that there was no more communication at all.
Instead of withdrawing as I really ought to have done, I
talked even more to make up for your silence.

Now the behavior Helga is describing takes place during our session:
The more active and expansive she gets, the more limp and passive Stani
becomes. And the more passive Stani gets, the more alone Helga feels, and
she reacts by increasing her torrent of words. The behavior of each partner
determines that of the other.

Now we have reached the third phase of the interview in which I try
to sort out the impressions and the information I have gathered and offer a
few trial interpretations in order to encourage the partners to express their
own points of view.

Th: (To husband) Are you almost paralyzed when
your wife gets so active?
H: No, I don't remember this incident she mentions
at all. I'm not paralyzed but I think it's a shame that she
gets so worked up. I'd rather that she just stopped.
W: Yes, but actually it's true that you withdraw more
and more and accuse me of stifling you.
Th: (To husband) At first you admired your wife for
her vitality and the fact that she can be so outgoing. Did
her vitality make you more animated too, did it spread to
you?
H: (To wife) I don't think so. What do you think? Do
you think I became more outgoing?
W: I don't know. I have the feeling that back then,
because you are more reserved than I am, you felt that I
could bring you out of yourself, carry you along, and
then you saw it wasn't working, and so you began to push
me away. I may not see that right, but I have that feeling
a little.
Th: (To husband) What do you think about that?

H: In the past, when I was with people, I didn't necessarily keep still, but I wasn't the life of the party either, I was just average, sometimes I talked, sometimes I listened. I don't think that her personality made me more outgoing. In the long run it's been more the reverse.

Th: More the reverse?

H: Back then at the beginning I'm not sure. In the long run though it's been more the reverse.

Th: How did you feel about that, the fact that it's turned out more the other way around? Didn't you realize you'd quieted down?

H: Yes, I think that happened.

At first Helga's emotional behavior stimulated Stani, but later it had more of a dampening effect.

At first Stani hoped to be carried away by Helga's vitality, get over his inhibitions and come out of his shell. In the end the results were the opposite of what he had hoped for: Instead of being stimulated by Helga, he became even more listless and withdrawn.

H: At the time we weren't aware of many of the things we're saying now. We continually try to interpret and analyze our memories.

Th: Can you say something about how you felt when that ideal image Helga had made of you—the image you identified with—collapsed? Now Helga is saying you were a coward, you weren't open with her, you withdraw—so [in her eyes] your qualities are no longer so ideal.

H: "Cowardly" means that I was afraid of her reactions. (To his wife) So you think that it was mostly cowardice?

W: Yes, that's right. You'd already been rejecting me for years. That was my fault too, the fact that I reacted so strongly, but it might never have gotten to that point if beforehand you had. . . .

H: Yes, the image you had of me crumbled. I don't know how I felt then, but now I know the image has crumbled. Inside I feel much more secure now.

Th: The fact that the image crumbled makes you feel more secure?

H: Yes. The fact that I no longer have to live up to an image.

Th: The fact that you feel more yourself?

H: Yes.

Th: And can you accept that, or do you believe that you *do* have to live up to her ideal?

H: No, I don't try any more. Recently we've deliberately tried to be more or less what we are and not what we'd like to be.

(Helga looks dubious and has to restrain herself to keep from contradicting him)

H: Naturally this led to more tension. But all the same, we're not so . . . I should say what's bothering me, but maybe I don't tell her that.

Again Stani manages to give certain apparently objective statements an emphasis such that Helga is hurt. He behaves as if he had already succeeded unequivocally in freeing himself from Helga's ideal image of him. His statement provokes Helga, but she tries to restrain herself.

The more Helga tried to pin Stani down, the more evasive he became, which in turn reinforced Helga's efforts to pin him down.

H: As for honesty, things weren't the way they should have been in that department either. I didn't exactly lie, but I kept quiet about things.

W: That's what makes me so furious, the way, when I don't ask whether you slept with so-and-so—maybe I shouldn't ask that, but I'm interested all the same—you don't tell me, and later you say that you didn't lie. But back when we were getting married we said, We'll tell each other the truth. If I'm ever going to trust you . . . If we're to find any basis, if we're to make any progress at all, if I'm ever to be able to trust you, it'll only be if we tell each other the truth, and you told me the truth all right, did you ever! All right, one shouldn't take seriously what people say at moments of crisis, but one does anyhow.

H: Yes, too seriously.

W: Yes, you told me very seriously about all the things you don't like about me. And then we said, Fine, now we'll tell each other the truth, and you didn't keep your word at all. For example, you didn't tell me anything about your girlfriends. I found out about them afterwards, and then I was so disillusioned, and I said to you, "For heavens sake, tell me the truth at last, how else can I ever trust you again." And then you said, "You know, I didn't lie, I just kept quiet." To me that's a lie too. If a person wants to know where she stands and how things really are, then the other person should take it on himself to tell how things are. I can't watch every step you take when you go to the computer center. But of course I'm interested.

H: The reason I behave like that is that she left me hardly any time of my own, and she always wanted to know what I was doing, where I was going, what I was up to.

W: No.

H: But it's true. There was always so much pressure from you that I preferred saying nothing rather than . . .

W: All right, you felt it was pressure, but I didn't mean it as pressure. For example, Peter [her boyfriend] and I tell each other everything. When two people are fond of each other it's only natural for each one to be interested in what the other is doing. I never for a moment thought that you were going with another woman.

H: Yes, but—

W: Please, let me finish talking! Maybe that's the way I came across, but I wasn't trying to spy on you. When I said that about watching you, I didn't mean anything at all by it. But of course I didn't think you were running around with another woman.

H: It's not a matter of other women. But you didn't tell me much about your feelings, you never did anything but ask what I was doing, where I was going, and so on.

The couple have gotten into a vicious circle with regard to the problem of openness: The more Helga demands that Stani account to her for his time, the more he evades her, and the more he evades her, the more she demands an accounting. Helga's whole life is determined by Stani. She cannot stand to have him feel anything that deviates from her expectations. Thus she places Stani in a double-bind, into an emotional trap (*V. Stierlin*) in which he gets caught no matter what he does: If he is open and honest, that is if he owns up to his extramarital fantasies and relationships, he disappoints her expectations relative to the ideal self that she wants to realize through him. If he says nothing and behaves as if he were thinking only of her, she pursues and supervises him until she can convict him of infidelity. Stani actively tries to destroy the ideal image in which Helga holds him captive, but he does not succeed. He also accuses her of doing nothing but interrogating him and of never talking about herself, her own feelings and experiences. Clearly Helga hardly ever has feelings that are not related to Stani.

> Th: (To husband) You felt supervised and con-
> strained?
>
> H: Yes, I realize that now. Back then it just annoyed
> me.
>
> W: And I simply told you straight out what I did, and
> I felt it was natural that people tell each other everything.
> I didn't feel that I had you under surveillance, I was just
> interested.
>
> H: You still do the same thing now. For example,
> when you go to bed, afterwards you always ask me what
> I'm going to do next. I don't do anything special, I read
> the newspaper, maybe I nip a hair out of my beard in
> front of the mirror; but always this tone of voice, so
> probing, so proprietary. I always wonder, "Hasn't a
> person got any time for himself, any time that his partner
> doesn't care about one way or the other?"
>
> W: You have so much time for yourself.
>
> H: Yeah, sure.
>
> W: Yes, it's true. I'm just interested in what you do.
> After the crisis last summer I realized that compared to
> me you have a lot of time for yourself. At the office you
> have so much time, you can go skiing all week, or if you
> get fed up in the afternoon, you go for a stroll, while I
> have practically no chance to do that, with two children
> on my hands. That's why I said you have so much more
> free time for yourself. Back when you did your disserta-
> tion, no doubt you were fed up with it, but you had all
> that time for yourself. You got to do your dissertation. I
> was sick of housekeeping, obviously, and so, on the
> weekend I said, "Now I want to go away for a change."
> Stani always felt that I was pushing him, but then he
> didn't do anything on his own initiative. Maybe I'd have
> thought it was great if he'd taken the initiative; I've
> always felt, "After all, you [Stani] have the whole week to
> yourself." So over the weekend I wanted time for myself.
>
> Th: (To husband) Do you feel obliged to reveal all
> your personal life?

H: No, I don't feel obliged, (Laughs defensively) it's simply that I'm not asked if I want to or not. In the past I even took it for granted that she had a right to keep track of me. I was never asked whether I wanted it that way. She took it for granted that she was right.

Th: Would you like to hold on to some territory you can call your own?

H: I can't stand the endless interrogation and super-vision. Now it's not quite so bad, but in the past it often bothered me. Of course I'm not talking about the last year, when she had a boyfriend and I had a girlfriend. That was the delayed explosion at the end, that was what came of all those years, it wasn't because you met Peter and I met Renate, but because for years you and I had a bad relationship and then we looked outside our marriage for what we couldn't give each other.

W: But you didn't tell me a thing about it. When I asked you [about extramarital relationships] you said, "No, no." If you want to talk about whose fault it was, you can say it was mine, because I reacted so aggressive-ly. Stani sent me off to the movies with my boyfriend, and I had a guilty conscience and thought, "Stani is so dear and nice and generous." I was really in conflict, I felt guilty, and then it turns out that he did that for his own sake, so he could go off and be free to do as he liked.

H: That's true about last year, but before that you had the same chance I did, to go out with other guys.

W: You made good use of your time and you didn't tell me anything.

Another reason that Helga feels betrayed is the role distribution in her marriage. She is tied to the house by her young children, while her husband has a job and thus can lead a comparatively unencumbered life.

Now the interview is nearing its end. I try to formulate a few interpretations in the form of personal impressions.

Th: I see that both of you have the feeling that your partner doesn't accept you as you are (Helga and Stani agree), and each of you thinks the other is forcing something on him that doesn't fit him.

W: Yes, probably that's true.

H: Mmm-hmm (Affirmatively).

| The therapist | W: | I feel that very strongly. |

The therapist
offers
interpretations
that show an
inner
connection
between the
problems the
two partners
have
expressed.

W: I feel that very strongly.

H: (To wife) Including the part about imposing something on each other? (In an incredulous tone)

W: Of course. I almost burst recently when you said, "Liberation or no liberation, the woman has to adapt more."

H: What I said was: "You have to adapt more."

W: I almost burst when you said, "You, as a woman." Often it looked as if you were sweet Stani and I was wicked Helga, I was the wicked creature who was oppressing you and castrating you and frustrating you, and so on. You're a poor man and I'm an awful woman who is forcing things on you, and I have to pack it all in. That's how it's been a lot of the time.

I try to address what the partners have in common, namely the fact that neither feels accepted by the other. In this way I also try to make my attitude clear to the couple: I will not let myself be led into siding with one partner against the other. I will look at the problem of the need to be accepted as one they have in common. In other words, I would like to establish a connection between the accusations of one partner and those of the other. I address something that the couple were not completely aware of in this form, testing to see whether they can make any sense of my trial interpretations. Stani is amazed that Helga feels she is being forced into a false image by him just as he feels he is by her. Helga expresses to the therapist her fear of always seeming to be the wicked one while Stani is the good one. In the following remarks I tell them again that I am trying to see both sides of the problem.

Th: (To wife) Probably you feel you wouldn't be like that at all if he didn't withdraw from you the way he does. The more he pulls away, the more you pursue him.

Th: (To husband) And apparently you think, "I pull away because she crowds me so."

H: Of course, if I could accept her and love her as she is, it would be a lot easier. Then she would be better able to overcome certain things.

Th: But you can't accept her because you don't feel accepted by her.

H: Yes, that may play a part, but I have very little feeling for her, and naturally she sees that, I really have to make an effort.

Th: Now we ought to think about what's going to happen next. What are your ideas about it, what would you like?

H: What I'd like—that's obvious—is for everything to be fine again. I see a problem there because the only way things between us will go well again is if I love her again, as she is. When a person loves someone, he also accepts them.

Th: And you have doubts about whether you could do that?

H: I can't tell. Sex plays a pretty big role in that . . .

Th: That isn't going well?

H: We don't know if it's going well or badly, we don't have sexual relations.

W: For me it's gone badly. When I don't feel accepted I don't have an orgasm, I feel like a prostitute. Not long ago we were on a trip to the U.S.A., and it really went very well again there. (Stani's expression shows some doubt). I don't know how you felt about it? Now I have a boyfriend I get along with very well, in every way, sexually, emotionally, I get along well with him, and he fulfills my needs, so now we [Stani and I] are having a fairly long break in the hostilities. (Helga says this with a provocative emphasis. Stani reacts with a hostile expression.) I've got more than I can handle with two men, but my needs are fulfilled. I'm ready to dissolve this relationship.

Th: Do you really want therapy?

W: I'd say yes.

H: I don't know, would that mean simultaneous therapy? By rights you ought to be the one to tell us what would be the best thing.

Th: It would seem to me that the best course would be to treat both of you in couples therapy because each of you feels that the other provokes certain of your emotional reactions, and apparently neither of you feels the same in the other's presence as he does alone. So it would be best if you could be treated at the same time.

W: I'd like us to know exactly why everything is this way. If we remain unaware of it, it will come back again. I'd like to know why I am so aggressive and why you reject me or why I stifle you.

The therapist explains the conditions and motivations required for couples therapy.

Th: I feel that the most important thing is whether you both really want therapy.

I do not pressure Stani into therapy but expect him to make a clear decision for or against therapy. Stani evades this.

Th: The point isn't that you feel your marriage must be patched up at all costs.

W: (Corroborating) Yes.

Th: Instead the question is whether you would both like to come to terms, in therapy, with what is making your life together so difficult.

W: (Corroborating) Yes.

H: I'm not sure about it, but I'm not against it.

Th: Can you say what you're not sure about?

H: Yes—a lot of effort for nothing! The only thing she wants is for me to love her.

W: No, to accept me.

H: For you that's the same thing. And if that doesn't happen, she's definitely not going to like it. I don't know if it will happen, and that's why I'm not sure whether all that effort will be wasted.

Stani is
afraid that
therapy
might
obligate him
to love
Helga and
that he
might
disappoint
Helga in this
hope.

Th: Do you think that you could be placed under an obligation to love her again?

H: It may be that I am feeling some pressure.

Th: If I may tell you what I think: I'm certain that one can't be obligated to love someone. Divorce can be a legitimate goal of therapy. But what would seem to me important is to come to terms with it. If you feel obligated by Helga or perhaps by me to love your wife again, then things will certainly turn out badly. But that would be the point we'd have to work on: the fact that you should be free to love Helga or not to love her.

H: Then I'd have to watch out that these feelings didn't develop in me.

Th: Which feelings?

H: That feeling of being obligated to love her. I'd have to watch out so that I'd notice these feelings in time if they came.

Th: You seem to feel that you are running the risk of having those feelings without noticing them.

H: Or that I might notice them too late, that's a
danger I feel, mostly because I know that she expects me
to love her.

Something has happened here that is encouraging from a therapeutic
viewpoint. Stani, who seems to be evading therapy, is not merely afraid of
being obligated by Helga or me to love Helga, but also sees in himself the
urge to commit himself to love. This makes it clear that Helga, with her
ideal of absolute love, is acting out an aspect of Stani that Stani has
delegated to her but that he resists in himself as he does in her.

W: Stani, when we've known each other for seven
years, of course I no longer expect your heart to start
pounding when you see me. It's a question of being
accepted, that you accept me for what I am.
H: To me to accept means to tolerate; to you it
means embracing with wide-open arms, really liking the
way you are.
W: Toleration isn't acceptance.
H: I'm supposed to love you, not just accept you,
that's where the problem is.
W: (Somewhat nonplussed) No, I don't really expect
so much as that, I think you're scared to express any
feelings.
H: Not long ago we were at a holiday cottage, and I
picked a little bouquet of violets, and then I was really
afraid to bring it to her, afraid of her reaction; if I
brought it to her and she was happy and thought, "He
loves me again, everything is fine again"—then I'd have
to disappoint her again.
W: No, that's not right (Straightens up in her chair), I
had stopped hoping for anything more than a little spark
much earlier. The point was more that, on the one hand,
you might want to give me some pleasure [with the
flowers], and at the same time you push me away, that's
what's so hard for me.
Th: (We have already gone beyond the allotted time) I
think the best thing would be for you to come by again in
about a week. Perhaps until then you could think a bit
more about what you really want. . . .
H: In any case we would like to come once more.
Th: Could you come one week from today, on Friday?

H: (Laughing) That would be on our anniversary.
Th: Well!
W: (Also laughs) But that doesn't matter.
H: But it does. I wouldn't like that, there could be a
reaction of some kind, I'd rather have another day.
Th: I could make it on Tuesday too.
H: Yes, I'd prefer that.
Th: Good, then let's do that.

Stani's wish not to have the next session on the day of their wedding anniversary shows his hypersensitivity about being obligated to feel love. If his relationship with Helga really meant as little to him as he is trying to pretend, he would probably forget their anniversary.

Second Session, May 20

Synopsis
On an individual level the roots of Stani's problems in relating to his wife stemmed from unmastered childhood experiences. He grew up alone with sick parents. His mother died when he was ten. This experience left him with the feeling that people whom one loves very much may die and abandon one at any time. During the discussion of Stani's childhood Helga seems like a big mother who lives out for him his pain at the severe frustration of his childhood. On the one hand, Stani enjoys being cared for this way, but on the other, the fear of self-pity and regression makes him defensive about his feelings. The attempt is made to see what kind of therapy is indicated and to formulate the focus of the collusion.

The second session begins with further clarification of the motivation for therapy and an account of the individual background of both partners' difficulties. Helga tells how she grew up amid the turmoil of war in Germany. When she was a child her father, a naval officer, was almost always away. She has an ideal image of him as a tall, strong, handsome man, and was very disappointed when he returned from captivity when she was eleven and attempted to lead a military regiment at home. He was not trained in a particular profession and felt inferior. Helga was furious that her mother allowed herself to be humiliated by him, and tried to stand up for her mother and resist her father. She saw Stani as the opposite of her father and believed that she chose to marry him, in part, to avenge herself on her father. She wanted to prove to her parents that she was capable of having a happy marriage. Since Helga left home her parents get along better, she thinks. Now she has the feeling that her father accepts her mother. Growing up alone with her mother as she did, Helga had little opportunity to have any realistic experiences with men, but lived in fantasies determined by her idealized father. So it hurt her very much when he called her a fresh little brat and rejected her.

In the session Stani expresses obvious skepticism about whether becoming more aware of things during therapy actually changes anything. He hints that he will be outmatched by his wife, who is more glib and better read in psychology. He also suspects that he may be manipulated by Helga or by me. So I devote more attention to the husband and have him tell me about his life. His was a difficult childhood, characterized in particular by the sickness and death of the people closest to him. He was born out of wedlock. When he was still very small his mother allegedly attempted suicide and tried to take him with her. She married when he was three. His younger brother died at the age of eight months, so that he was an only child. He spent a large part of his childhood in a day nursery. His mother was very sick for two years and died when he was ten. His father was half blind. Because of all this illness he had to be careful of everything he said and did in his home. He was not allowed to express ill-temper. He continually had to show consideration for his sick and handicapped parents. After his mother's death he was placed in a boarding school. His father married again two years later, but Stani continued to be skeptical and suspicious of his stepmother.

The atmosphere of this session is clearly different from that of the first session. Helga sits there like a big mother with a concerned look on her face, leaning forward and paying attention to Stani. She speaks in a warm voice. While we talk about his childhood Stani seems ambivalent: On the one hand, he shows a childlike need of protection and seems to enjoy the intensive attention devoted to him by his wife, and on the other, he is very defensive and tries to rationalize everything. He seems to experience Helga as the archaic mother: effusive in her emotions, but devouring and threatening in her aggressive love. He has the feeling of never having found security with a woman. He poses absolute demands on Helga and at the same time defends himself against forming any tie to her because of his fear that he will not be able to handle the pain if she abandons him. This episode continues as follows:

H: It's only natural that as time goes on one becomes less sensitive to certain experiences and disappointments.
W: I can't accept that, that's just something you've told yourself for one reason or another. With all the things you've told me—besides the fact that it makes me

Stani tries to play down his feelings about his difficult childhood, especially his lack of security with a mother whom he could not count on. At the same time he seems to enjoy the fact that Helga shows him such a strong emotional commitment and expresses the feelings he has delegated to her.

want to cry—I have always admired you no end and thought: "Yes, you can see that the environment isn't everything. How well Stani has turned out in spite of his childhood. I'd probably have gone to pieces with all that, I couldn't have stood it."

H: But it could also be the fact that I worked for a year—that was a deliberate choice. . . .

W: Yes, but you were already fourteen. But what Nelly [his stepmother] told us last year, that your mother had tried to commit suicide when you were three and tried to take you with her her. . . .

Th: Your natural mother?

H: Yes, that's what my stepmother said. I don't know how much of it is true.

W: Yes, all right, maybe. But you know how that is, she [your mother] may have felt bad about having an illegitimate child, and you know how good children are at picking up on tension. No doubt you felt some too, but didn't notice it.

Th: You said you cried when he told you the story? [The husband, who until now has sat there in an open, almost childlike way, now hides his face again behind his right hand]

W: I don't remember any more exactly how that was, but I could cry again now just thinking about it. It's simply awful. I really think it's so sad. I'd hate to do that to my children. Even if Stani doesn't feel it was so bad; for example in the afternoons when he was in the nursery, maybe he didn't miss it. I think it's very sad, I feel like crying every time I hear about it, especially of course because I'm close to him. (Her expression shows concern like that of a mother for her child)

Th: (To husband) Have you ever noticed how deeply affected your wife feels about your life?

H: (Defensive and clearly trying to play down his feelings) I've noticed it, yes; that time in the day nursery may be different, we always had the same teachers, and it was in the same rooms, and there were always the same children and toys.

W: Yes, dear Stani, but—

H: It was like a boarding school.

W: Yes, but we would fight tooth and nail to keep our children from being put into a nursery. (The husband tries to object). . . Please let me have my say; that is what you call a day nursery.

H: It wasn't only for little children, it was also for school-age children.

W: There are day schools for schoolchildren too!

H: But it isn't the same thing, in this case there's a difference between a school and a foundling home.

W: Yes, fine, but at some point we'd both fight tooth and nail and say, "No, our children mustn't get swallowed up in a crowd like that, we have to find a substitute parent so the child really has somebody." You always say, "It didn't matter to me at all." All the same we agree that we would never do anything like that to our children.

At the end the note of concern in Helga's voice mingles with a demanding tone. I have the impression that she is trying to make it up to Stani for all the mother-love he has never had. Stani's response is in part almost childlike, but at the same time he is growing increasingly defensive. Clearly a strong emotional bond exists between the partners on this mother-child level. Helga strikes Stani in a sensitive spot when she says that they would like to spare their own children the same fate he had. It is at once clear that she is referring to the danger that the two of them might be killed in an accident. But secretly she is also alluding to the effects of divorce on the children.

H: (With a warmer voice now that they are discussing the children) After all, I spent the whole day there, it's not as if I were continually being shunted from one place to the next.

W: All the same, Stani, I don't know why you're so defensive, I mean we've already talked about this kind of thing hundreds of times, that it's bad for a child if something like that happens. You always say, "Look, it didn't hurt me, I didn't get sick [from growing up the way I did]." That may be true. You aren't sick, but maybe during this difficult time you had to say to yourself: "In order to survive—I'll bury it all, start over." How can a person bear that? You always say: "No psychiatrist, I'm not sick."

H: (Laughs defensively) No, no, you said I was sick, a psychopath or schizophrenic.

W: No, no, I would never tell anyone he was schizophrenic, never . . .

H: You didn't say schizophrenic, but you said psychopath, I remember that clearly.

W: Yes, you also told me I wasn't normal, but of course we've both accused each other of that. But why are you always so terribly defensive, "Yes, but why do you say it bothered me? It doesn't matter to me in the least." It may have hurt you even so, and perhaps you would have turned out very different if you'd grown up in a proper home.

H: I don't doubt that.

W: But you mustn't be defensive about it.

H: I'm not defensive about it.

W: But you are.

H: I just feel that you want to use force to persuade me that [my childhood] was bad, and I really don't remember having had such a bad time.

As a woman Helga shows a greater ability to suffer and expresses more openness towards her feelings. She acts out Stani's feelings for him. On the one hand Stani is grateful for this because he would be afraid to have such strong feelings himself. On the other hand he is afraid of becoming dependent on Helga because she performs this service for him, and afraid of laying himself open to being manipulated by his feelings. Stani is delicate and very vulnerable and needs a certain amount of protection from the outside. His ambivalence is shown in the discrepancy between his defensive words and his facial expressions, which show a childlike pleasure in being coddled and mothered. Helga and I are now on the same footing and are showing Stani a therapeutic concern.

W: I'm not a psychiatrist, so I can't say; I'm not trying to talk you into accepting that it was bad, Stani, but would you want Klaus [their older child] to end up in a boarding school? Besides, there's the fact that your mother died when you were ten. I feel dreadful when I imagine that I'd die in three years and leave the children. And that's why we think so carefully about what would happen if something happened to both of us; after all we could have a car accident together. We've spent hours

talking about it. Why do you just say, "Oh, it wasn't that
bad." After all, you say too that it would be bad for our
children, so how could it not have been bad for you?

H: I didn't say that I want the same thing for the
children, and I didn't say that it was the best thing for me
either.

W: But you say it wasn't bad . . .

H: If I say I didn't feel it was bad, that doesn't mean
that I think it's the right thing in every case. I can
generalize, can't I . . .

W: (The couple seem at a loss for words. The wife
looks at the therapist, clearly expecting help. Softly,
almost inaudibly, apparently giving up her efforts) Yes,
I'm probably not so good at doing that.

Th: It just struck me, your wife says that even now
when she is hearing all this again, she has strong feelings
about it. It seemed to me as if your wife were having the
feelings for you.

H: You mean I don't have any?

Th: Of course you have feelings, but you don't dare to
let them show. Something in you resists it. (The husband
laughs) And that's completely understandable. The question is, To what extent can you yourself express the
things your wife is feeling? To what extent can you
yourself show them?

H: I don't know, I hear a lot of pity there. . . it is
pity she's feeling. (He looks expressively at the therapist)

*Helga tries
to help Stani
express his
feelings for
himself.*

   In response to my interventions Stani reveals some of his anxieties.
He is afraid of falling prey to self-pity, that is, of regressing and exposing
himself to feelings of grief, hurt and disappointment. But he is equally
afraid of being pitied by Helga and nothing more, and thus being devalued,
regarded as a poor, pitiable creature. This point is especially interesting in
relation to the collusion concept. To derive benefit from therapy it would
be important for Stani to be able to regress in order to experience his split-
off feelings and to work through childhood traumas. But this regression
would gravely threaten the balance of the couple's dyadic system because
Stani would feel inferior if he (instead of Helga) were in the regressive
position. As therapist I see myself caught in a dilemma, namely the
difficulty of encouraging the husband's therapeutic regression, on the one
hand, without at the same time placing a strain on his self-esteem and
causing his wife to ally herself with me in the progressive position of

therapist. Therapy can easily become a situation in which one patient remains a patient, while the other joins with the therapist in trying to help him. Helga's tendency to adopt a therapist's role with Stani becomes even more evident in the following interventions. I no longer feel very comfortable in this situation and hope for an opportunity to get things back in balance.

Th: Perhaps only to a degree.

W: Haven't you ever pitied yourself? I've often pitied myself no end, until I almost laughed. (All three laugh)

H: Maybe just for a moment, but then I thought, "This isn't going to help matters." I think very quickly, "What use is it if I'm sad, it doesn't change anything."

W: But it does.

H: (Annoyed, casting a meaningful glance at his wife) I'm trying to say how *I* feel about things.

Th: You wouldn't feel comfortable about pitying yourself?

H: I would think it was ridiculous and would say to myself: "What are you doing, what do you think you're up to?" That's more or less what I think, with other negative experiences too. What's past is past.

Th: Yes.

H: Maybe it's something one is taught, maybe it's—

W: Acquired.

H: I don't know. Certainly it's imprinted by one's life, but does that mean it's bad—she thinks it's bad. (Emphatically)

Th: You have the impression that she is almost trying to force you to feel that.

H: Let's say I don't understand how one can think it's bad.

Th: How one must think it's bad. You have the feeling that now she is almost imposing it on you?

H: Yes, so to speak. I'm supposed to think it's bad to be the way I am. (The wife's expression shows doubt) Yes, really she does almost impose that!

W: (Reflecting, after a pause) Yes—to the extent that you're saying, "I can't feel that happy and that sad, what's the point of all that?" I think it's really a shame when a person can't feel really happy. When I'm sad it usually passes quickly, but before that I'm completely

sad, from my toes to the top of my head. I also feel it
strongly on the physical level, it's a strange feeling.
Personally I find it much more beautiful when one can
feel so strongly. Stani, I think one is richer when one can
feel strongly, of course that's not always completely
comfortable, it works both ways, but I personally feel it's
an enrichment.

H: Yes.

W: Right away you switch on the defenses.

H: No.

W: Maybe I'm not speaking very carefully, I ought to
say that I *personally* feel . . .

H: Very often it's more categorical, you say: "It *is* an
enrichment. If one doesn't feel that way, one is poor."

W: No, that's just your defensive attitude.

Th: Yes, well, that's the way he feels about it and it's
his right to say so.

W: Yes, that's the difference, the way we think and
the way we say it.

(Several seconds pause)

Th: . . . To the degree that you really mean it
differently.

W: To the degree that we really do think differently.
(Reflects, then smiles) Yes, of course, if we really mean it
differently (Appears to catch herself), in that case I really
mean what I said . . .

H: I often find her intolerant. Often I make the
mistake of paying too little attention to the fact that
that's her way of expressing herself, that's her manner,
and then I make the mistake of not accepting that, and I
tell her, "You're being intolerant again." Naturally that's
a mistake, I know I shouldn't do that.

Th: (To husband) Apparently you feel she has a fixed
image of how you ought to be and imposes it on you?

H: I feel that she'd like to impose her notions on me,
that she'd like me to be something that fits her notions.

Th: (To wife) What do you think about that?

W: (Reflecting, inner-directed, no longer relating so
much to the husband) I'm just thinking about it. . . .

> Helga tends
> to pressure
> Stani to
> experience
> and to
> express
> feelings the
> way she
> does.

To restore the balance between husband and wife I encourage Stani
to express his sense that his feelings are being forced on him by Helga and

that she is dictating to him what he is supposed to feel. Helga tries to defend herself, and I challenge this attempt. Helga seems rather taken aback by this reversal in the mood of the session. Stani seems to feel guilty about this and tries to protect Helga against me.

Working out the nature of the interdependence of the two partners' behaviors is an important part of couples therapy. Helga feels, no doubt rightly, that Stani has not mastered his many childhood experiences of loss and frustration and he is splitting off all feelings that relate to them. She wanted to help him in overcoming these problems. On the other hand, the way in which she goes about helping him is shaped by her own problems in relating, especially by her tendency to force her partner to conform to a fixed image of what and how he is supposed to think and feel. The disadvantage of couples therapy, as compared to individual therapy, is that the therapist cannot give unilateral attention to the problems and inappropriate behavior of only one partner; but its advantage is that it enables the therapist to experience directly how the partners reinforce each other's inappropriate behavior. Stani's evasive behavior and his way of splitting off his feelings provoke Helga to dictate to him what he should feel, and Helga's overemphatic manner reinforces Stani's defensiveness towards his emotions.

Our time is almost over and we still have to decide how to proceed from here, so I ask the partners how they feel about it, at the same time making it clear that I am quite willing to treat them.

> Th: So, now the question is whether you would like therapy, and if so, in what form.
>
> W: I'm in favor of going ahead with it. After all, we're not the only couple who've had marital problems. A number of the couples we know are having problems, and the rest have a television.
>
> H: I've already said I wouldn't use a T.V. to solve anything.
>
> Th: (Laughing) Now you have a choice.
>
> W: Between a T.V. and therapy. (They all laugh)
>
> H: Rationally I think we ought to do it. For example, (Turns to his wife) you'd be glad if in time I were able to express more feelings, and I'd be glad if her lack of confidence—
>
> W: Self-confidence.
>
> H: Lack of self-confidence could be relieved, then probably she'd stop doing a lot of the things that bother me now: the boisterous way she makes herself the center

of attention. In this area therapy could really accomplish something.

W: Stani, it's not as bad as all that.

H: That's how I feel about it, you can't count the last few months.

W: But it's changed as a result of our talking about it.

H: You've also been making some effort. It's true, it hasn't been as bad as before.

W: I think you ought to take that as a positive sign.

H: I'm not thinking about the last few months.

W: But I think they're important, at least we've made a beginning.

H: Yes, that's true, yes. (To the therapist). If it's realistic for us to expect these things from therapy, if our expectations are not overblown, I'd be glad to go into therapy. What do you think?

Th: Hmm—yes—well, from what I've heard here today, it seems to me important for you (Turning to Helga) not to impose feelings on Stani, but that you (To Stani), on the other hand, accept it if Helga feels comfortable being the center of attention. It seems to me important that neither of you tries to impose on the other an image that doesn't suit him.

H: That's just the thing, that in this area she and I are different.

Th: I'm not so sure about that. I don't believe it's an accident that the two of you got together, I believe that you match each other, even if it seems that you're opposites.

H: I wouldn't call it opposites.

Th: The sessions are held once a week, a session lasts about ninety minutes, my fee would comply with your health-insurance rates.

H: What about breaks [in therapy]?

W: (To husband) Why?

H: Because now and then I have to go out of the country. Yes, but we could do it anyhow!

(We say goodbye)

Renewed discussion of the couple's motivation for therapy. Stani is able to take a more positive attitude but does not express a clear decision.

I am hoping that in this session my attitude has communicated to the couple two things regarding the motivation and goal of therapy. On the one hand, I have supported Helga in her efforts to help Stani to be aware of and express his split-off feelings about his childhood frustrations. But on the other hand, I also try to show that these efforts could be counterproductive if she presses Stani too hard. It seems to me important to show Stani that in therapy he will have a chance to work at being aware of feelings, but that he is not under any compulsion to do so. In this sense the therapy situation also acts as a model for the marital relationship, for both the therapy and the marriage necessitate that the partners show concern for each other while at the same time respecting each other's right to accept only such help as he chooses.

Evaluation of Indications for Therapy

At the end of the second session I thought about the indications for therapy.

1. Diagnostic Evaluation of the Marital Conflict

The Focus of the Collusion: The couple's conflict appears to be essentially a narcissistic collusion: Helga tends to *love Stani functionally,* as the image of the idealized father whose function it is to accept her and raise her self-esteem. But her internalized, negative father-figure leads her, unconsciously, to expect to be disappointed in this desire. Stani, with his weak sense of identity, has identified, on a primary level, with the idealized father image. But on a secondary plane he feels he has been forced to adopt a "false self" and evades the function conferred on him by Helga. The more he evades Helga's demands, the more pressure she puts on him, and the more pressure she puts on him, the more he evades her.

Stani's love for Helga, on the other hand, has substitutive traits: He wants Helga to supplement aspects lacking in his own personality—the capacity to experience and express strong emotions. Secondarily, however, he feels threatened by the very thing he feels he needs to make himself complete, for his emotional reserve is based not on lack of emotion but on emotional inhibition and fear of the destructive effects of emotion. So he devalues Helga's expression of emotion and by doing so hits her most sensitive spot. The more he rejects her emotionality, the more she feels her existence threatened, and is driven to emotional extremes.

Each partner's expectations place the other partner in a double bind. Each challenges the other to behave in just the opposite way from what is required. At bottom both are longing for an absolute, unconditional love, for fusion and oneness. The focus of the collusion for this couple can be formulated as follows:

"Disappointment at not being able to achieve a symbiotic fusion with my partner forces me to destroy him, for otherwise my very existence would be threatened."

Besides the narcissistic collusion there is a mother-child aspect to the relationship that greatly stabilizes it.

Systems or behavior-modification oriented therapists would try harder (than I do) to define one concrete problem that really could be changed. But couples like Helga and Stani do not show a distorted and lowered ability to solve problems; they show a deeper disturbance of their relationship. I think it is more appropriate to work on the disturbed relationship to clarify the feelings of both partners.

The Couple's Previous Attempts to Solve Their Problems, and the Motivation and Scope of Therapy: Both partners had attempted through extramarital relationships to validate themselves in their ability to form relationships and to define their separateness from their partner. Giving up these extramarital relationships would imperil their efforts to put some space between them. Given the husband's marked wariness about committing himself to anything, it is difficult to gauge his motivation for therapy. Where Helga is concerned, the question is whether she is prepared to change her model of marriage. External factors place almost no limits on the scope of therapy: Because of Helga's part-time work in a skilled profession, she is not to any great extent financially dependent on her husband. In external respects the couple are not yet so established as to make it impossible for them to separate. If they were to separate, the chief problem would be the fact that they have two children not yet of school age.

Conflict-Free Areas and Stabilizing Resources: The partners are well-matched in intelligence and education. Both are open to thinking on a psychological level. For the most part they have the same tastes in dress, behavior, interests and attitudes to life. Both show good survival skills, and in many areas of their relationship they get along well and work constructively together. They share the same circle of friends, with whom they keep in close touch. The raising of their children gives their relationship a firm foundation, relatively free of conflict. They do not appear to use their children against each other. The children are still small, and thus both parents are deeply concerned with building a positive family life.

2. Setting the Goal of Therapy

Ideally the goal is that both partners should free each other of their respective, contradictory expectations. The therapy should help Helga to develop a better father-image and to accept herself more—perhaps via a father-transference to the therapist. Stani should try to break down his emotional inhibitions in his dealings with Helga—if possible while under the protection of the therapy situation; and he should learn that the expression of aggressive impulses does not destroy the marital relationship (as his childhood experiences led him to expect) and that loving feelings do not obligate him to give up his own identity. Both partners should learn to separate themselves more clearly from each other. In real terms the goal of therapy would be for the partners to accept their own and each other's limitations, and learn to deal with the limitations of their relationship. If possible, they should give up playing destructive games involving the seesaw between intimacy and aloofness, and stop dragging third parties (extramarital partners) into their marriage as a provocative means of declaring their independence.

3. The Recommended Therapy Method

Couples therapy seems to me an appropriate method for treating the collusion and if possible for achieving the real goal. Couples therapy might also lay the groundwork for achieving a more intensive individual therapy aimed at self-improvement. The external prerequisites for couples therapy can be met. It is my impression that the couple can work constructively with the recommended therapy method.

4. The Therapist's Motivation

I have the impression that I have established a good relationship with both partners and am capable of emotional accord with them. The couple's problem is familiar to me through my own experience in marriage, but at the moment is not causing any conflict between my wife and me.

Third Session, September 26

Synopsis
Stani is afraid that therapy will obligate him to love Helga. Helga does not want to relax the absolute demands she makes on a relationship, preferring to break off the relationship rather than put up with lukewarm compromises. As the therapist I find Stani's tendency to evasiveness rather provocative. I try to nail him down to a firm decision for or against therapy,

and so involve myself with him in the same kind of collusion he has with Helga. The interpretation of this involvement as a therapeutic collusion *relieves the atmosphere considerably. Stani reveals conflicts very similar to Helga's: At bottom he too yearns for an exclusive love, for a wife who accepts him absolutely and unconditionally. Although he does not like Helga's violent emotional outbursts and demand for absolute loyalty, at the same time he is fascinated by them because he sees them as a proof of ardent love. His extramarital relationships primarily serve as something to fall back on if, as he fears, Helga runs out on him sooner or later. He has to keep several women—substitute mothers—in reserve. On the other hand, he feels deeply hurt that Helga has had extramarital relationships. He makes contradictory claims on Helga: On the one hand, she is supposed to be absolutely and unreservedly loyal and live only for him; on the other hand, she is not supposed to expect anything of him or make any claims on him. Helga hounds Stani, interrogating him until he hurtfully rejects her and confirms her distrust. During this phase I limit the couple's efforts to be absolutely frank with each other because they are threatening to use their frankness to hurt and reject each other.*

Continued Treatment:

Two months after the second interview I tell the couple that I would be prepared to begin a couples therapy. Then Stani telephones me and asks to speak with me alone, without Helga. Since we last met he has separated from his family. He must, he says, tell me that he is still continuing a long-term relationship with a second girlfriend, which he has kept secret from Helga and from the girlfriend he is living with now. Now he does not know whether he should confess this to Helga before he begins therapy. I make an appointment for him to come in for a private session, in violation of my basic rule that once I have begun a therapy I do not hold private sessions with one partner without the other's knowledge, and especially will not do so in order to be initiated into secrets that the other partner as yet knows nothing about. For in such a case it is all too easy to become one partner's secret confidant, and this reduces the therapist's freedom of movement. If, from the very beginning, I am informed only about things discussed in a couples setting, I am freer to get involved in the therapy process and express any ideas and interpretations the sessions suggest to me. In this case I do not feel that Stani wants to make me his secret confidant but that he has telephoned me in order to come to terms with therapy. We soon turn from the subject of the second girlfriend to the far more essential problem of setting a goal for the therapy. Again he expresses doubt about whether therapy is indicated for him and his wife. He believes he is a man who finds it difficult to tie himself to one partner.

He still finds other women sexually attractive. He really has no need for a close, exclusive relationship, he says. On the other hand, he does not want to dissolve his relationship with Helga, for the children's sake if nothing else. I have the feeling that Stani is very afraid of Helga's coercive and oppressive expectations, and thus is deeply concerned to preserve an external detachment from her and keep open sufficient avenues of escape. He is afraid of being forced to give up his identity if Helga once gets him under her thumb. But given Helga's clear all-or-nothing demands, it is questionable whether she can accept a marriage based on a compromise. I explain the goals of therapy to Stani. The most important thing seems to me to be open communication, combined with an effort on the couple's part to accept each other's capabilities and limitations, in the meantime leaving open the question of whether they both find this kind of relationship acceptable or would prefer to separate. It remains to be seen to what extent therapy could help them to feel closer and to intensify their relationship. Stani states his intention to end the external separation that has meanwhile taken place, to return to Helga, and to break off his extramarital relationship.

As a therapist I might have felt happy that after only two sessions the couple were giving up their extramarital relationships and that partners who had been living apart were now moving back together. Offers of this kind are often made at the beginning of a couples therapy. Frequently a couple may get along better after only a few sessions, and occasionally they even feel they are having a second honeymoon. But overnight successes like this rarely produce any lasting results, so that over the years I have found it is better if I urge couples not to make any external behavioral changes for the time being, and instead to concentrate on the underlying causes of their problems. For a premature change in behavior can enable one partner to evade the other's attacks and recriminations, and invalidate any intensive confrontation with the problem. In this respect I differ, to an extent, from many therapists who try to effect a rapid, concrete change in behavior. I advised Stani not to make any changes in his situation for the present. If he felt it was important to tell his wife about his extramarital relationship, he could bring it up during a therapy session. But I refused to do as he asked and tell Helga for him.

A few hours before the next therapy session he told Helga about his extramarital relationship. She arrived at our third session in tears.

What follows are excerpts from the third session.

Th: How are things going?

H: Good one day, not so good the next. Maybe we could talk about the fact that just this afternoon she said she couldn't go on this way. (Wife sits with tense, gloomy expression, the husband seems more active and involved) Maybe we could talk about what's bothering her.

W: Things vary a lot. (Shrugs her shoulders in a deprecatory way)

H: Maybe it would be better if first you describe the situation as it is.

W: Well, it varies. Sometimes it's good. Maybe I have a lot of mood swings, I'm always torn back and forth. It's simply that Stani is always around. Monday, Tuesday and Wednesday he puts the children to bed, and then he wants the car and brings it back next day . . . and it's the fact that he's always there, more or less. In part I feel that it's a good thing, and good for the children too, but I can't stand it any more. I feel attracted to him again, and then he doesn't feel anything for me, and then I see his slippers sitting around and they bother me, and then I tell myself, "Tomorrow it may all be different again." These constant ups and downs. A divorce would be the best thing for me. But then I say to myself, "He has a good relationship with the children; for them it's better if things stay as they are." But I can't stand it, I think it's awful, all this uncertainty. But then sometimes things are very different, we have a fine time. Sometimes I think, "Enough, that's the end of it." (She gestures as if she were trying to cut through something) Then at least I have something to go on. Then I know where I stand, and I can strike out in another direction, even if it's hard for the moment. I think I can deal much better with conclusive situations than with this uncertainty and hanging around. It would give me a clear guideline, even if things got worse for a while. Then too I could be a lot more active, otherwise I'll just hang around, be passive, wait and wait and wonder what's going to happen. When I have a clear guideline, I become much more active.

Helga thinks a divorce would clarify her continual uncertainty about Stani's love.

The atmosphere now differs considerably from that of the second session. In the second session Helga took the superior position of a therapist and Stani appeared childlike and regressive; this time he is sitting with a more composed air while Helga expresses her pain and despair in a tearful voice. Helga now appears more regressed, more insecure, less coherent and precise in her speech. I have the feeling that Stani is presenting me with his desperate wife and leaving it up to me to deal with her problems.

> Th: (To husband) Is this situation making you unhappy too?
>
> H: Much less so.
>
> Th: You're still more or less content with things as they are?
>
> H: Well, that would be exaggerating a bit, but I'm not really what you'd call unhappy. Mostly I tell myself, "Oh, that's all crap."
>
> W: (To husband) But last Thursday I really had the feeling you were suffering.
>
> H: Sure, sometimes I do.
>
> W: (To therapist) Yes, naturally things have their ups and downs, now they're one way, now they're another. I'm not always unhappy about things. And another problem is that I live in the same house with the kids, and Peter [her boyfriend] is always in and out. But so far the people who live in the building don't know that Stani's living somewhere else. I don't know what they think, and I'd rather go to the tenants and say, "I'm separated, my husband lives with his girlfriend and I'm living with my boyfriend." But the way things are now, I keep thinking maybe it wouldn't be good if they found out that all this is continually going on behind their backs, and so I'm always living under this strain, so that I think we shouldn't get into the car together. I'd rather tell them the truth straight out, and I've put up with all this long enough, the way you're so much cleverer at doing things on the sly and I always end up as the heavy. That's another thing that makes me suffer, I feel I'm at a disadvantage and think it's unfair.
>
> Th: Are you living with Peter?
>
> W: No, I'm not.
>
> Th: (To husband) Are you living alone or with your girlfriend?
>
> H: With my girlfriend.
>
> Th: (To wife) Why aren't you living with Peter?

W: Well, mostly because of the neighbors. The landla-
dy lives directly above us. She's an elderly spinster and I
don't know how she'd take it, she might even throw us
out of the apartment. I can't do anything about it, but it
makes me furious because it's just plain unfair. The strain
really gets to me. It gives me the feeling—maybe it's just
the way I was raised—that we're doing something wrong.

I don't feel very comfortable. Stani appears indifferent, and sometimes holds his hand protectively over the cheek he has turned to Helga, as
he has done in the past. Sometimes he stares into space and plays with his
fingers. There is genuine bitterness in Helga's complaints, but she too
appears uninvolved in the therapy. Feeling the need to "get back on the
track," to get the therapy going, I confront them with a challenging
question:

Th: But I'm really not clear on what it is that's still
holding you together?
W: What keeps the two of us together?
(Fairly long pause. At first both partners stare into space
without speaking, then turn to each other and look at
each other silently)
W: I'm still attached to Stani, I don't know exactly
why, I don't know exactly why I react the way I do. But
the last couple of days I've noticed I feel attracted to him,
even when I'm with Peter. Whenever Stani is there again,
I feel attracted to him, I don't know exactly why.
H: Isn't it just habit? You asked me too, and I said
that it's mostly habit.
W: This habit, this feeling of being used to something—I've really lost that. I don't know exactly.
Th: (To husband) Have you lost it too?
H: It's mostly the kids and the atmosphere; of course
that's true for her too. Family, home, everything we had,
I'd miss that and I'd like to hold onto it. Naturally I can
have that with someone else later on, but not right now.
Somehow I still have a sort of relationship with her. But
to a great extent it *is* just habit. I know what she's like. It
isn't that I have a need to be intimate with her, there's
nothing like that.
Th: Nothing at all?

In therapy,
too, Stani is
evasive and
impossible to
pin down,
which the
therapist
finds
increasingly
annoying.
The therapist
begins to
lose his
control, as is
shown by his
formulations.

H: No; that is, a couple of weeks ago I told myself I
could show her some affection again, but that's very rare.
Th: Is it really that you don't feel any need, or that
you think that if she would behave a little differently,
then you'd feel a need?
H: I think the attraction would get stronger again if
certain things were different, I do think so.
Th: What would have to be different?
H: Things would have to be really peaceful when we
were together. No matter what, there's always a tension
there, a lot of tension. Sometimes it's pretty nasty on the
surface, often it's only beneath the threshold. If it weren't
for that I might be much better able to feel close to her.
Probably that's true for her too. Then there wouldn't be
so much against us; but how much actual attraction I feel
I can't say, but I imagine (The therapist tries to intervene
but the husband raises his voice)—but I imagine things
could get better.
Th: I simply can't figure out to what extent you're
motivated to therapy. Essentially therapy would imply a
desire to be closer again, but there are certain obstacles to
this that, if possible, therapy is supposed to eliminate.
H: When you say "be closer again," of course you
mean emotionally?
Th: Yes, that the couple feel in some way that they are
a couple; that they matter to each other in a special way.

I feel frustrated by Stani's indolent air of resistance and wonder
whether we have enough ground for a therapy when he shows so little
commitment. I feel an annoyance that is revealed in my tense, more
expansive way of speaking. For the sake of my own commitment to the
therapy, it is important for me to find out: Is this couple staying together
out of habit and fear of the unknown, or do they have a positive
motivation to work on their relationship?

H: Of course it's very hard to say; if I were satisfied
with my wife, I wouldn't necessarily have any need to
seek satisfaction elsewhere.
Th: Uh-huh.
H: Naturally that's true for her too. Of course if we
were to go to New Zealand, we'd have to adjust to each
other and learn to cooperate. But the present situation

keeps us from doing that. On the other hand, I think both of us—or at least I—am afraid to throw all hesitation to the winds and start out fresh with her, which would mean putting up with this strained situation in the hope that some time it would get better.

W: (Shakes her head uncomprehendingly) Why did you—you said that not long ago, why are you afraid of losing everything now when you could have such a cozy, comfy set-up with someone else. Sure, you can't have any more children (Stani is vasectomized), but you told me you don't want any; but—

H: I wouldn't want to lose the ones I have if in fact I can't have any more.

W: But why are you afraid of losing everything?

H: It's not—

W: That's how you expressed it.

H: Well, sure, it's not a clearly definable fear, it's just the situation, it's uncertain. With this uncertainty, I sometimes feel that anything is possible.

W: What do you mean?

H: That I could come back to you, or stay in another relationship. Of course there's also the possibility of everything's being lost from your point of view. So I'm scared of losing it all too. Besides, maybe Renate [his girlfriend] could meet another guy, and of course you stir up this fear.

Now Stani seems more involved. He reveals something unexpected about himself. He not only attributes to his wife a feeling of continual uncertainty as to whether he will stay with her or leave her, but also voices his own fears of being abandoned by all women.

W: Yes, that's true, that's the way I'd look at it, because for one thing Stani wants a relationship with a woman who'll make him feel secure that she won't run out on him.

H: Won't run out on me, absolutely. I want to know I'm number one, let's put it that way.

Th: Yes—

W: (Interrupts the therapist) But you are number one to her; but you've said over and over that you don't feel you have trust and security with her. You said you'd like a relationship with a woman where you're secure, protected. Fine, if she runs out on you, you'd be able to take it, but then again there's the uncertainty about whom you can trust and whom you can feel sure of.

Th: (To husband) But you don't have that with Helga?

H: Not now.

Th: Does that in general seem to you something worth striving for?

H: As a general goal, yes.

Th: Would you like to be number one for your wife? Allowing for her running out on you now and then, but nevertheless that you'd clearly be number one? That you'd be a couple?

H: If I simply answer yes, it ties me down too much once we get into actual details. But I can't answer no either.

Th: It's simply always the same question, whether or not you're motivated for therapy.

H: (Tries to explain himself)

Th: (Not allowing him to talk and raising his voice) As a general rule, people who go into therapy ought to want it. It may be that you have certain fears, certain wishes about how Helga might be different, but basically it's a question of whether she's the woman you'd like to live with.

H: (Reflective) . . . If you put it that way, perhaps I'd have to say that isn't how I feel. The way our relationship is now, naturally she isn't the woman I'd like to live with. You understand, she's not my *ideal* woman.

W: (Sits with crossed arms, staring at the ceiling with a look of increasing strain)

Th: Well, of course, usually one doesn't find the ideal woman. (Speaks in a rather sharp and annoyed tone)

H: Exactly . . . well, I think we have a good chance of making things better, more secure and intimate, I do think that.

Th: So, would you feel you were concerned with working on your relationship in therapy to see whether you could get closer to each other again?

H: That was my reason for coming to see you again, the fact that I wanted to clear up this point. I would simply like to clarify our relationship. I think that once

Margin note (left): The therapist brings a great deal of pressure to bear on Stani to take a stand for or against working together in therapy.

we've clarified our relationship, found out why I'm still
scared the way I used to be and a lot of other things—
once such fears are out of the way—perhaps we could see
much more clearly whether we'd really like to start over
again.

My reactions as a therapist show increasing irritation, and I pressure
Stani to take some kind of stand as to what he'd really like. I am
increasingly annoyed at the way he evades questions over and over. I let
myself be provoked into saying things that do not really correspond to my
own theories. I stop portraying therapy as an attempt to clarify the
relationship and instead present it as the effort to restore the partners' love
for each other. Through my loss of control as therapist, I become
increasingly involved in a collusion with Stani. Stani structures his
relationship with me in such a way that the feelings I experience are very
much like those of his wife. Just like Helga I feel that Stani has betrayed
me; for in our first session he gave me the impression that he was
genuinely motivated to undertake therapy, and that although certain fears
were causing problems in their relationship, at bottom his desire to love
Helga was beyond question. I had believed that he was interested in
entering into a therapeutic relationship with me. My present reactions
show that I am expecting Stani to commit himself to therapy. The fact that
he continually evades this demand is a narcissistic insult to me as a
therapist, and I express my hurt feelings quite directly.

Th: Now you apparently feel some fear that if I ask
you this question, you'll be forced to commit yourself one
way or the other.
H: Yes, I was trying to explain that if now I simply
say yes, then later on you'd both tell me, "You said yes."
I think it's something that has to be clarified first.
Th: Yes, yes. (Pause)
H: I mean, the same is true with her.
Th: I think that that may be a problem for the two of
you, that you [the wife] perhaps have the tendency to try
to make him take a stand and he is particularly reluctant
to do that.
W: No, that's not really so. I mean—uhh—no, I
haven't tried to do that. I've really kept a tight reign on
myself.
H: But what I accused you of last night happens
fairly often, the way you always say, "You can't do

it . . . You don't really want to do it." But just tell me for once what *you* want, don't always expect things from me, talk about your own feelings for once. I have the impression that there's a lot there that could stand clearing up.

W: Yes—I've already said what I feel, I explained to you just a little while ago how I see it all—I don't know whether you keep on forgetting over and over.

H: You explain it in rather broad terms, in generalities. You evade the issue.

W: (In raised voice) You could always ask me what you didn't understand.

H: It's been the same way in other situations: You twist everything around so you can say to me, "You don't really want to anyway."

W: (Sits with her shoulders hunched up and casts a hostile sidewise glance at her husband)

The therapist sees that he has become embroiled in the same kind of conflict with Stani as Helga has, and works on it as a therapeutic collusion.

H: You've often twisted everything around.

W: Now I know as much as I did when we started.

H: You've gotten aggressive lots of times, and then we just stopped talking.

W: (To therapist) That often happens, he does that a lot, never remembering anything but the negative things.

H: Don't say "never."

W: Not remembering anything but the negative things. (Wife speaks in a shrill voice) He reacts only to the negative things and completely forgets the rest. He ought to think about the rest sometimes.

Th: Yes—I'm just now thinking how you [Helga] said you'd like to know where you stand, and that's just the problem one has with you [Stani], which I'm also feeling now—the fact that I too keep wanting you to tell me where we stand. I can see that probably it's hard for you to pin yourself down and place yourself under an obligation; but on the other hand, I can also understand why you [Helga] find that hard to put up with.

The partners' dialogue gave me some time to clarify my own emotional reactions. I was getting more and more tense with Stani and now have caught myself reacting to Stani exactly as Helga does. But thanks to a therapist's detachment I am in a better position than Helga to interpret the collusion developing between Stani and me. My demand that

Stani pin himself down, and his evasions of the need to take a definite stand, have led to an escalation of conflict. The interpretation I have just made is important to all three of us. First, I can relieve my own tension by understanding my emotional reactions. My interpretation is important to Stani, for one thing, because it enables him to understand better my increasingly strained reactions, but also because it shows him the extent to which he arouses in other people the same reactions he does in Helga. The interpretation is important for Helga because my behavior as a therapist can serve as a model of how to deal successfully with partner conflict. I show her that although I react to Stani much as she does and thus am able to identify with her, I also feel that persisting in this reaction leads nowhere and that I must accept Stani as he is without trying to make him live up to my ideal image. Clearly the interpretation I have offered within the framework of my collusion with Stani gives Stani the sense that he is understood, and subsequently he responds by showing an increased ability to explain his reservations about therapy.

H: Often I myself don't know where I stand. Perhaps that's why it's difficult to say it out loud. I have no relationship to her as a woman. To make up for that I have a sexual relationship with my girlfriend. Everything else is strongly in her [Helga's] favor.

Th: Are you afraid that it would be committing yourself to have sexual relations with her [Helga] again?

H: Less that it would be a commitment than a disappointment for both of us.

Th: What would be the disappointment?

H: That we didn't feel mutually satisfied.

Th: That sexually it wouldn't work?

Stani's fear of disappointing Helga is strongest in the sexual sphere.

H: Sure, in purely biological terms it works, but I'm afraid it won't work in terms of feelings. Maybe you can understand that.

W: (Appears self-absorbed)

H: After everything you've told me about Peter.

W: And you . . .

H: (Does not let her talk) And above all I'd like to learn to understand my attitude better, my desires . . . Uhh . . . Last autumn and also in the spring I thought that getting close sexually might do a lot—not everything but a lot—towards getting us close in general . . . For a little while we had this feeling that it might be right.

W: Not me.

H: Yes, in America.

W: Yes, back then.

H: Sure, sure, fine, but then other things were involved too.

W: No, that's not how it was at all. Before the sexual thing works you have to get rid of the other things that aren't working. I just can't go to bed with someone I hate. Maybe you can do that more easily; but I can't. And in America the conditions were right. The children weren't there. In time things got better between us, and then things went very well sexually too. After such a long time it can't go well again at the drop of a hat.

Th: When was all this?

W: In March . . . and then we came back home thinking, "Yes, it's really going to work okay again," and then Stani started up with another woman, and I had thought—because you had said so—

H: What did I say?

W: That it's so beautiful with me and that you were enjoying yourself and that you liked me, and naturally I thought, well . . . not that I went into raptures straight off, I just hoped to keep a spark alive between us, and then Stani started up again with another woman, and I shook my head and thought, "Well, nothing's changed at all." Before the summer holidays it was just the same, I was disappointed.

Th: Is part of it the fact that both of you are afraid it was better with each other's lovers, so that you [Stani] are afraid that Helga enjoys herself more with Peter, and you [Helga] are afraid that he enjoys himself more with his other women?

W: Yes, sure, that plays a big role.

H: Uh-huh.

Th: For you too?

H: Yes.

Th: Does that create a barrier between you?

W: Yes, very likely. (Helga now seems much more relaxed and cheerful, Stani rather reflective, keenly interested in the subject)

(Pause)

W: After such a long time with another partner, it's really hard I think.

Th: These other relationships that you both have, do you aim them at each other?

W: Naturally.

H: What do you mean?

Th: Well, that you each want to prove yourselves to the other.

H: We really don't talk much about it.

Th: Yes, and how do you feel about that?

W: Yes, absolutely.

H: Well, I don't really understand, to whom are you saying that?

Th: To both. If you have marital relations, are both of you inhibited because each one thinks that the other one enjoys himself more with the lover?

H: Yes, but also that one enjoyed *oneself* with one's lover. Not just that the other enjoyed himself more with his lover.

Th: Yes, and you're less inhibited with your other partners.

W: Freer, freer, that's only logical; and then there's the novelty too.

H: It's not only that I think you enjoy it more with Peter, but also that I think I enjoy it more with Renate. It's both.

W: Yes, it's only logical that that plays a role. (She seems disappointed, once again speaks in a shriller voice)

Th: And you use that against each other? There's a certain rivalry between you because of it?

W: And all that about Peter's potency, maybe that hurts you.

H: You do that [sort of thing], but I don't. I never make remarks like that.

W: Oh sure, but you did say too how beautiful it was with Susanne and with Hedwig.

H: That was last autumn, but now, during the last few months, I've stopped making cracks like that.

W: But you do make them, and then naturally I say something mean in return. I use the fact that I also have a partner who's better than you. (She has hurt him, for example with the remark that Peter is more potent than he is and has a bigger penis)

H: I haven't once—

Extramarital relationships serve both partners as a means of asserting themselves and confirming their value in each other's eyes.

W: Yes you have, about how sensual Renate is.

H: You asked me in very concrete terms, "What's she like?"

W: I'm simply interested in what kind of person she is.

Stani is now considerably more involved in the discussion. For the first time he shows Helga how much her extramarital relationship hurts him because he longs for a woman who will be absolutely loyal to him.

H: A case like that is different, but otherwise . . . You don't tell me any details and I don't want to know any, and you told me you didn't want to know any either. As far as that goes I'd like to talk to you about it. Yes, sure.

W: I told you, I don't want that at all. Naturally you don't express your feelings about that so openly and directly. Maybe you're not even conscious you're doing it, and you don't make me angry consciously, but you're simply very different from me.

Th: Is it also a sort of test when you have intercourse together?

W: It's been an eternity since we've slept together . . . but then it's not—

H: But yes, I often feel inhibited. I didn't realize that so clearly, now it's getting clearer. I feel inhibited with you because . . . I have the feeling that she'd rather not have anything to do with me, that she'd much rather stay with Peter, but she won't admit it to herself and is trying to live with me for God knows what reasons. This thought quite often inhibits my showing her affection, because I have the feeling that deep down she doesn't want to go on. Why does she always want to tie me down and demand that I change?

Th: (To husband) So you really don't feel sure whether you're loved by your spouse either?

H: Yes, maybe you could put it that way. It simply has to do with her attitude in the whole thing. I feel it isn't sincere. She ought to talk about herself, what *she'd* like, and not always just throw it in my face, "Well, you can't be faithful in any case." She ought to try to say how she feels about me, and not always, "You're this, and you're that. . . " that often inhibits me. I just realized it this very minute, and I think it's important.

Stani begins to defend himself against Helga's persistent accusation that he is incapable of being faithful. At bottom he measures love by even more absolute standards than Helga and thinks her incapable of fidelity. He suspects that her reasons for wanting to stay with him are superficial. His comments show how alike the partners are in their lack of self-esteem. Both suffer from the notion that they are not acceptable to their partner, not really loved for their own sake. Each partner has his own way of acting out his fear. The wife acts out her fear by directly and continually demanding declarations of love from her husband in order to allay her suspicions. The largely irrational fear that Helga is not absolutely committed to him and might leave him just as his mother did drives Stani to seek out a girlfriend; and because she too does not seem to him completely trustworthy, he needs to keep other girlfriends in reserve. The partners reinforce each other's need to play this game of persecution-and-retreat through a collusion based on the notion: "I would like to be loved unconditionally by my partner, but I cannot trust his devotion and so try to keep my distance from him by hurting him and driving him away."

W: And you always say, "Whatever you do, do it completely independently of my wishes"—but independently of my wishes you don't do anything either. Would you like me at all if I were absolutely free of Peter? (A trace of hope can be heard in the wife's voice)

H: (Immediately defensive again) I really wasn't thinking of Peter at all in this connection. I always talked about how I feel about you, about how little feeling there is in me. But when I think of you, Peter is always involved because he's a barrier where you're concerned.

W: Something about that isn't clear to me. You just finished saying that you feel inhibited because you think about what I have with Peter.

H: No, not that our relationship would be better without Peter, but that I feel inhibited about changing our relationship and making it better. (Again Stani is clearly being evasive)

Th: You asked him, "If I didn't have Peter, would you like me?" Is it a real advantage to you having Peter?

W: Yes, yes, of course.

Th: Is it that you feel that you have to use Peter to prove your value to him [Stani]?

W: More or less. Before I had someone else I wondered whether I was still a woman. I must say—no, I did not mean that now—now I know that I'm a woman. But if I didn't have Peter and if I were absolutely alone, would Stani be more likely to come home, and would he think things were better?

H: Then perhaps I wouldn't feel this barrier, that you're not being sincere.

W: I told you how I feel about that: One the one hand, I'd very much like to live with Peter, even though there are problems there too; but I don't want to try any experiments with Peter while I have two children. I've already broken it off with Peter twice, broken it off for good, really for good.

H: Yes, we've talked about that. (His tone shows that he is skeptical about this "for good")

W: Twice we separated, we were serious about it, but that didn't suit you at all, and then during our summer vacation I told you, "Regardless of whether or not I go on seeing Peter, I simply see that you don't want to do anything for our relationship," and then you said, "Fine, I'll do what I like." Then I thought, "No, I won't be that naïve, pulled first one way, then the other." I really broke it off [with Peter], seriously. But naturally if I give up Peter, then I make some demands of you. I mean, it's like this: Now I've separated from Peter, I've given up something for our relationship, and now we have to make an effort. Then I expect certain things that you're not prepared to do."

H: Peter as such doesn't bother me, he only bothers me indirectly. Because of Peter I always have the feeling that Helga isn't sincere in the things she says.

Th: What would she say if she were being sincere?

H: Just that she wouldn't all the time be thinking, at the back of her mind, "I still have Peter." She's not sincere because she'd rather live with Peter. When she says she'd rather live with me I don't believe her.

(The husband is now speaking with much more emotion, and his psychomotor gestures are less constrained; he emphasizes his words with a movement of his hands) I think she would rather live with him. In this sense it bothers me.

W: (Also appearing much more relaxed and open) Listen, Stani, I'm not denying at all that I'd really like to live with Peter. For the moment it's nice being with him, and we get along fine. But I've told you, Look, for such

But Stani could not stand it either if Helga gave up her boyfriend for his sake.

and such reasons I'm afraid to live with him, and if you come back again and I have a chance to live in a family with the children, that's what I'll do, regardless of Peter.

H: (Helga has the upper hand again) But it's because you'd like to be with him and the kids that you accuse me of things, saying that I don't want to do this and that and that I'm this way or that way; because deep down that's the way you want it.

W: No, Stani, look; it's true, I am exaggerating a bit now, but lately all you have to do is crook your little finger and I come running. You can talk me around to your side in a second. All you have to do is be a little nicer to me and I'm there like a flash. You just use Peter as an alibi. Either that or you are genuinely troubled by him.

H: Peter bothers me indirectly, through your behavior.

W: That's not true.

Th: Why isn't it true? I have the feeling you're both very ambivalent in your feelings towards Peter. Both of you get certain advantages and certain disadvantages from him.

On the surface the situation appears simple: Peter is an impediment to Helga and Stani's getting together. But at the same time Peter protects the two partners from each other, and that's why, in the final analysis, neither wants to get rid of Peter. Even if Stani is deeply hurt by Helga's relationship with Peter, he would find it even harder to deal with if Helga gave up Peter for his sake and thereby could place Stani under an obligation to live up to her claims. Helga cannot give up Peter because he's a trump card that she does not want to casually throw away. (I might be criticized for considering Peter, in the context of the therapy, only in his functional character, as a factor in the couple's relationship rather than as a human being who is himself affected by the relationships. My reasons for taking this attitude are traced in *Couples in Collusion*, pp. 171 and 178–182.)

W: That's true, yes, but I don't think that I'm being insincere. I really would very much like to be with Peter, if that was the only factor to be considered, but for various reasons I don't want to. I know about our problems [Stani's and hers], but I don't know yet what problems would arise with Peter, and that scares me a lot. No doubt there wouldn't be such a mess as there is with you, but Peter is—emotionally insecure. I tell myself that even if there aren't many problems with him right now, after a year of living together I'd see my problems are the same and one's partner doesn't make problems disappear but at most makes them a bit easier. Naturally that scares me. Better to have Stani in hand than Peter in the bush. I'm quite realistic about that. But in spite of it all, deep down I believe it would be possible for me to have a good relationship with Stani.

Helga suggests that both partners give up their extramarital relationships, a plan that the therapist finds questionable at this point.

H: For you, what would the preconditions for that be?

W: (Sighs) If only it were that simple. What I really think, even if it would be hard for the time being, is that we have to break it off with our lovers. Every time something goes wrong we can each scurry off to our lovers so that we don't have to put up with the tension in our relationship. I believe that if we wanted to work on our relationship, we'd have to separate from our lovers. Maybe it would be wrong to do that, and we'd both sit there all alone, feeling furious that we gave up our lovers for this. I don't know how it would all turn out.

H: I'm very much afraid that in no time we'd be blaming it all on each other.

Th: Yes, in particular I can picture each of you thinking, "Well, now I've made this sacrifice, now my spouse really has to show the sacrifice was worth it."

W: Yes, yes, that's true.

Th: I wonder whether it wouldn't be better just to keep your other relationships as they are and instead concentrate on trying to find out how you really feel about *each other*.

Depending on his values, a therapist may behave differently at this point. He might be glad that both partners are already seriously considering giving up their extramarital relationships and concentrating more on their marriage. A therapist might even take the attitude that as long as extramarital relationships enable the partners to continually avoid each other, there is no point to therapy. But the narcissistic structure of this couple's relationship, their high level of vulnerability to and fear of oppressive closeness, leads me to think that it would not be good for them to give up their extramarital relationships at this time, because I believe that for the time being they need these relationships as a barrier against the stress they feel as a result of the excessive intimacy of their marriage. Moreover, as I have already said, I am cautious about encouraging premature behavioral changes in couples therapy because it is futile to try to deal with the underlying factors in a marital problem if these factors have already been eliminated. Of course a therapist could also take the view that extramarital relationships are part and parcel of any modern marriage and that the desire to give them up is a symptom of regression. My professional experience up to now does not permit me to share this view.

Th: (To husband) An important thing to know would be whether you can really believe Helga when she says she'd like to live with you, or do you think, "At bottom the only reasons she'd like to stay with me is that it's convenient."

H: I'd like to get to the point that I could sincerely believe her.

W: Do you know, Stani, that you *can* sincerely believe me—no—no, that's wrong—

Th: (To wife) Why is it that you can't believe anything he says?

W: He's lied to me much too often.

H: It's fairly clear to me why she doesn't believe me. Because of the thing with Susanne she thinks, "That was a really dirty trick." That's understandable. As for why I don't believe *her*, that's less definable. I simply think that she tells me she wants to live with me because she isn't clear about her feelings.

Th: Do you believe in her feelings or don't you believe in them? When Helga tells you she would prefer to be with you, do you believe it?

H: It's easier for me to believe that, but when she starts to attack me, it's only because she wants to fight off her fear of being betrayed after she's gone and told me something like, "I want to be with you." That's why in the very next sentence she says, "But you don't want to, you're bad, you betrayed me and lied to me."

> Stani can understand that Helga feels betrayed by him. But he accuses her of using this against him to defend herself against her own fears.

Up to now I have felt that Stani's distrust of Helga is exaggerated when he says that she is insincere and does not say how she really feels about him. This suspicious attitude might derive from childhood experiences. Not until later sessions does it become clear to me that the husband's apparent exaggerations do have a basis in reality, namely in Helga's tendency to approach Stani seemingly without reservation, but then again and again to create a distance between them by discovering in him something that enables her to feel frustrated and rejected and that confirms her in her attitude of suspicion and accusation.

At this session, for the first time, Stani becomes aware of and expresses his distrust of Helga, for in the past her accusations always forced him to be on the defensive. Now Stani sees, quite correctly, that in her dealings with him Helga is acting out her own problems with feelings of distrust and insecurity. Instead of rejecting her partner directly, she makes him reject her, which in the end produces the same effect. Both partners long for fusion in a symbiotic relationship that nevertheless both are forced to reject because of the danger that they would be engulfed by it.

> Th: Perhaps it would be a good first step if each of you would say what he really feels, and try to assume that the other one is saying what he really feels.
>
> W: Each of us should accept that the other really means what he says. In some situations, I believe, we say just the opposite of what we said before, and still mean it. For example, if I say now, "I'd like to try it with you again," and then when something goes wrong again I say, "No, not for anything in the world," and then after a while I say again, "No, I'm wrong, it would work," I can still really mean it.
>
> Th: Perhaps an important thing to remember in that situation is that one ought not to force the other person to speak. Each person should say only as much as he wants to. This seems to me important where Stani is concerned because I imagine that you [Stani] don't like it when someone interrogates you and pressures you. Everyone should have the freedom to say, "I'd rather not comment on that."
>
> H: Actually that is a problem, that I've never been able to say, "I'd rather not say." But actually I *have* said that. I find it really annoying that you don't respect my wishes when I don't want to say something.
>
> W: That was because of [your lying to me about] Susanne.

H: Not just because of her, you used to be the same before her. You simply don't accept it when I say, "I don't want to say now."

Th: (To wife) It seems to me important to accept that, because otherwise he'll get into situations where he'll feel he has to lie again and again.

W: Yes, exactly, but sometimes he could volunteer some information.

Th: No, he has to be given the freedom to say what he wants to.

H: (In a concerned voice, to his wife) I really find it hard to tell you about my feelings because you smother them in sarcasm straightaway.

W: Yes, a couple of times that has happened.

H: But that annoys me, it inhibits me.

W: Last year we talked about a former girlfriend and he said, "Actually I still think she's nice," and then I said, "And you think this one's nice, and that one too."

H: Whenever I've tried to say something about my feelings . . . I'm far from indifferent to what you say about Hedwig. At the very least you could have listened without making any comment; but then there's the sarcasm again. So I really feel inhibited about saying anything about my feelings because it seems to me that you take advantage of it.

W: I don't believe that one little bit. If I'm sarcastic it's only out of self-defense, when I feel hurt. Of course I'm supposed to accept it that you're different and have to have three women at the same time. But then if I joke a little about the relationship between women in a harem, about Hedwig whom you claim you're so fond of, and about Susanne or some other woman, that's really wrong, oh yes.

Th: But you said you don't like hearing about all his women.

W: Yes, it hurts me.

Th: React directly then, show the hurt! Really, (To husband) I wonder if it makes sense for you to tell Helga all those things. One might say it's nice that you are so frank, but doesn't it also keep adding fuel to the fire, and isn't it much more important for the two of you to talk about *your* relationship rather than continually talk

The therapist expresses his doubts about the attempt to achieve unreserved candor.

about other partners? How do you feel about each other?
This is the area where you should try to be really frank.

My personal values and experience contradict the widespread view
that complete openness is desirable in a relationship. In therapy I often see
couples who have placed themselves under too much stress by trying to
live up to the ideal of total honesty about everything, even about what the
spouses feel for other partners. The above therapy excerpts show how
completely the therapeutic process is shaped by the therapist's personal
attitudes and values, even if the therapist makes an effort not to impose his
values on the patient. My intervention creates a safety zone for the
husband to protect him from the inquisitorial tendencies of the wife and
thus, even in the therapy context, imposes limits on the wife and compels
her to respect her husband's freedom to say what he chooses.

A short excerpt has been omitted in which Stani tells about Helga's
hypersensitive reaction to any criticism, and she confirms that she
immediately responds aggressively to any criticism and tries to pay Stani
back by running him down.

> W: I know that I run you down and that maybe it's
> wrong; and that drives me crazy every time, the way I
> know perfectly well that I really shouldn't say a certain
> thing and yet I say it anyhow.
> Th: Uh-huh.
> W: (Gazes intently at Stani for a short time without
> speaking) And it was the same way when you accused me
> of flirting at the chess club. Maybe it's a mean thing to do
> to men, but I've often flirted with them (Bursts into
> tears) to show you that I'm a woman too.
> H: Yes, but that was before.
> W: (Furiously beats her fists against her knee) No, no!
> H: But it was. That was at the very beginning when
> you flirted and stomped on my feet with your sharp-
> pointed shoes.
> W: (Her voice choked with tears) That's absolutely
> not true. For years I haven't flirted with anyone.
> H: I remember the Mardi Gras party at your place.
> (At that time they had only known each other for two
> weeks.)
> W: Yes, but that was at the very beginning, that was
> just insecurity. What did I do exactly?

H: Just a harmless bit of flirting, just when you were dancing you smiled a certain way at your partner. But I'd have preferred that you didn't.

W: Yes, I know it was wrong.

H: Wrong? But why did you do it then?

W: Of course it's wrong when someone doesn't allow his partner the same rights he accords himself; but you feel exactly the same way about it, and that's the way I felt about it too.

Th: Apparently things between you always build up and up.

Both: Yes, but it isn't like that any more.

Helga's comment on this excerpt from the manuscript of the book was: "Reading the 'scenes' between the couple I find I like the wife less than the husband, for example, in the way she tries to pressure him, or compulsively repeats things. I feel that the underlying factors, my fears, hurt feelings, despair, don't come out clearly enough."

Th: And yet you both hurt each other by having lovers.

W: Sure, he claims it doesn't matter to him at all. Either he isn't being honest and my relationship with Peter does matter to him, or it really doesn't matter to him, and I feel that would be a rejection of me.

Th: Yes, but apparently it does matter to him, he said that clearly today, but if he would tell you directly . . .

W: Then he'd be saddled with me again.

Th: Yes, or he'd be in a weakened position where you're concerned.

H: But of course my feelings vary. Sometimes I feel practically nothing when she goes away with Peter, and other times it bothers me. Most of all it bothers me indirectly, through the way she behaves. It's true that when I've told her it didn't matter to me, it did really matter.

Th: But is it hard to admit that because you're afraid that then she'll get the better of you?

H: No, it's completely unintentional when I don't tell her.

Th: Judging by what I've heard today, you've said very clearly that her relationship with Peter matters to

Helga had hoped that her extramarital relationship would provoke Stani so that she could reach his emotions; but he just withdrew more and intensified his own extramarital relationships.

you and that just like Helga, you place absolute demands on your partner, and any lukewarmness hurts you. But it isn't easy to let your partner see that you're vulnerable. (The husband raises the tips of his feet and crosses his arms. What I said is making him uncomfortable.)

H: No, I was trying to say that it bothers me only indirectly.

Th: But perhaps the fact that Peter's there does bother you, because you interpret it as meaning that Helga's feelings for you are not genuine.

H: Yes, all right, I'll accept that. It's not that I get depressed when she goes out with Peter. In fact she asks me fairly often whether it bothers me. I say no, and then she feels hurt.

W: (Gazing thoughtfully at the ceiling) Yes, that makes me feel, "Oh, what's the point, he doesn't give a damn what I do anyway."

Th: So it's like this: He doesn't show his feelings, so then you wonder, "Well, if it doesn't matter to him, what must I do now in order to get through to him?" You continually face the question, Can I touch him at all, or will nothing I do reach him?

W: Yes, he didn't react at all, and then I went too far. Then he withdrew more and more. In that sense it wasn't helpful when you took up with Susanne, because you could always withdraw and think about her and you didn't have to make any effort with me. You could withdraw into your own world and our problems never got solved. Then I was left high and dry. I know that I was wrong—I got aggressive because I was dissatisfied. Maybe we would have gotten through to each other sooner, you know, Stani, maybe things would have been different if you could have told me it hurt you, probably I wouldn't have done it then.

H: Back then I couldn't do that. We couldn't do that then. I can't say why exactly. We just couldn't. (Long pause. Both stare reflectively into space.)

H: Actually my relationship with Susanne meant a lot to me. But I think even so I could have been honest with you.

W: Last fall, Hedwig was sitting around in tears, I was sitting around in tears, and Stani was gaily riding off on holiday with his other girlfriend.

H: You can leave out the "gaily."

W: So, he was riding—no, I don't want to leave out the "gaily"–he was riding gaily off on holiday to Davos. I simply couldn't take it . . . (Pause)

Th: (After a long pause, it is time for the session to end) Well, we have to stop for today. I recommend that, if possible, you don't talk about this subject until our next session.

H: We've already tried that [not talking about things] on our own.

W: Sure, true, but never consciously like this. Of course we can do what you say.

Th: I think, for the time being, you shouldn't talk at all about the role your boyfriend and girlfriend play in your relationship, but keep that subject inside the protected zone of therapy. Also I think that you shouldn't try to continue talking at home about the things we talk about in therapy. If feel that in therapy it's easier for both of you to be more open, but the whole thing can easily get out of hand again if your conflict becomes too direct.

H: Yes, I think too that it's too difficult to discuss these things at home.

Th: I'd only like you not to talk about these particular topics, not stop talking in general.

H: Could you give up telling me your thoughts and making remarks?

W: Now listen, it's not as if I couldn't keep myself from talking to you for a week. After all, now there's a particular reason for it; it's not like before, when you simply didn't want to talk about it.

Th: Fine, we'll meet again in one week.

After the encouraging process made in this session, the therapist asks the couple not to discuss the subjects they have raised until the next session.

In view of the fact that one of the principal aims of therapy is to encourage couples to talk, it seems paradoxical that at the end of this session I recommended that Helga and Stani not talk about their problems. Substantial progress has been made in this session because both partners have revealed to each other sensitive areas that in the past they had closely guarded. Now there is a danger that they may nullify this progress and destroy something that is still very fragile if they use what they have heard in the therapy setting to hurt each other outside that setting.

Overall I feel that during this session we took a step forward in our work on the focus of the collusion: *"I'm disappointed that my partner does not get totally into me nor lets me get totally into him; so I try to hide my vulnerability by hurting him before he hurts me."* This formulation applies to both partners. Helga, deeply hurt, covers it up by trying to prove, by using Peter, that she is not dependent on Stani; whereas he tries to retreat from her provocations, which hurts Helga even more and makes her try even harder to challenge him.

One important goal of therapy is to enable the partners to reveal their sensitivity and vulnerability without them feeling compelled to stage a drama of defense and revenge.

Fourth Session, October 3

Synopsis
After the gratifying progress made in the previous session towards working out a therapeutic collusion between Stani and me, Helga now threatens to break off her relationship with Stani, and thus indirectly with me as therapist. In the therapy, the external divorce symbolizes the couple's inner divorce, the need of each to establish his separateness from the other and to accept the fact that in their love they must remain two separate people. I experience Helga's threats of divorce as intimidation and feel hurt after my efforts to help. I react with misplaced and hurtful interpretations of Helga's behavior. Because of my own problems I do not succeed in doing any therapeutic work on the collusion that forms between Helga and me. The more pressure is brought to bear on me by her threats, the more aloof and abusive I become, which in turn intensifies her attempts to force me to accept her and let her get close.

Th: So how's it going?

H: Well, some things have changed, and maybe we ought to talk about whether it still makes sense to go on with therapy. The last few days Helga has told me quite unequivocally that she doesn't want to live with me any more and doesn't want to have any contact with me even later on, and so there really isn't any reason for us to have therapy. But now maybe we ought to find out how genuinely she wants this, why this came so suddenly, out of the blue.

W: (She has just washed her hair, is wearing a brightly colored dress and looks radiant) Because of the therapy I've been thinking how I really feel about things, and I realized, no, in the first place I really have the feeling that Stani doesn't want to come back to me, that he'd like to have his children and his home but not to come back to me. After our last session I couldn't get away from it any more, then at night I couldn't sleep, that went on all night, and it's been up and down like that all year, and now I said to myself, "No more, I don't want to be dependent any more on Stani's moods, I'd like to take charge of my own life and not be dependent any more," and what Stani said to that was, "I don't want any damned liberated wife, I want a wife who'll spoil me." I'm simply fed up with that, then I look bad and people ask me, "Well, how are you, Mrs.——?" and I say, "I'm living it up and that's why I'm so tired." I'd just like a normal life again, I'd like to be in charge of my own life again, and not always pulled this way and that. It kills me, I said that the last time, it knocks me for a loop, I really want it to stop. And just during our last session I had the feeling, maybe it's asking too much of Stani, one can't expect him to give a clear yes or no; and maybe he can't say it, maybe that's how he is, and so on, but I can see that it's destroying me, I can't sleep, I feel attracted to him again and he pushes me away again; even if it is the worst choice and even if it scares me, I'd like us to simply split up. When Stani isn't there I feel much better, I feel relieved. I don't want to go on waiting and waiting; then I get passive, even in all the little everyday things, I just hang around. I'd like to get more involved in my work again, but I just don't have enough strength, I can't pull myself together; if I separate from Stani, I'll know that now I have to take charge of my own life, and then I know that I can get along a lot better.

Th: You feel dependent?

W: I've already said that, that I still feel very dependent on him, only a divorce will free me from that, maybe I'm impatient but the last time I saw that I'd like a divorce. Precisely because of what went on in our last

In the previous session Stani showed more genuine commitment to therapy, and now it is Helga who calls into question whether therapy should be continued.

Helga
believes that
she can
never become
independent
from Stani
without a
clear-cut,
external
divorce.

session, that Stani doesn't want to say either yes or no
and can't decide whether he wants to come back to me or
not, maybe one can't expect that from him, but it's
simply too hard for me. I'd really like a divorce, even if
things are rough for me afterwards. *I don't know how I
can become independent of Stani except by a divorce.*

Th: It strikes me that you see living with him exclusively in terms of possible dependency.

W: No doubt there are other ways, but I don't know
how to find them. For me I don't see any other way to
become independent than to separate from him.

Th: Mmm-hmm.

W: And my dependency makes me so furious again.
Then I say to myself, "I get nothing from him anyway,
and yet I'm dependent; but I don't know any other way."

Th: Mmm-hmm.

W: I don't know why I'm so dependent, I'm not
conscious of the reason. I want a divorce so I can be
independent.

Th: (To wife) Do you feel that he'd like to keep you
dependent? That he doesn't allow you any other kind of
relationship?

W: Probably—(Reflects)—probably he allows it to
me, but I don't know whether I can.

Th: (To husband) How do you see all this?

H: I think I could [allow her to be independent], I
think we could agree on many different kinds of relationship if . . . I see it pretty much the way she says, that
she can tolerate only the extremes. It's either all or
nothing, as far as I can tell about her reactions. It's too
bad that she's so geared to extremes and that for her
there's no middle ground.

W: Come on, don't talk to me about how there's no
middle ground. After all, the last time it was you who
said that you don't feel anything for me at all. When I try
to draw the logical conclusions from that, you start
talking just as sweet as pie about how we could do this or
that, and how nice that would be, and once upon a time it
was like that. Whenever—you may think I'm trying to
intimidate you, but I have to get a grip on myself—
whenever I see a clear-cut guideline to follow, then I can
accept it. Maybe I can't expect you to accept the idea of a

divorce, but after all, I have to look out for myself. I
don't know whether you [the therapist] understand what
I mean? I can understand that he can't say yes or no, but
then I have to figure how to get myself out of this.
Th: It's unbearable to be in such suspense.

After the previous good therapy session I was already looking
forward to going on with the therapy. When we exchanged greetings Helga
seemed more relaxed and lively than in our past sessions, so I was
expecting things to go well. So I felt all the more frustrated at the way
Helga's desire to separate was already jeopardizing the therapy again.
Once again I could not be certain whether or not the two partners really
wanted therapy. My last comment, about it being unbearable to be in such
suspense, was addressed not only to the wife's feelings, but was a discharge
of my own inner tension as well.

Looking at this sequence in terms of the dynamics of the therapeutic
triangle, the threat to break off the relationship, which Helga directs
against Stani, is also being transferred to me. Helga is not merely reacting
to Stani's comment that he cannot feel anything for her, but she probably
fears I may show a similar lack of feeling. During the last session the
balance of the therapeutic triangle shifted dramatically. Although at first
Stani created tension by his indecisive attitude towards therapy, on a
secondary level he received a lot of special attention from me and—as
Helga has sensed—my sympathy as well. She wants to redress the balance
by pressuring me into showing her the same sympathy.

W: Yes, and things have been like this for a year.
Basically I'm a happy person and like to have a good
time, but this just knocks me for a loop. Now I think it's
just got to end! And as soon as I saw my way clear to this
decision, I felt better right away. I have a good relationship with my parents and I could take the children and
move in with them. Naturally that's not what I had in
mind. They live in a small town. Sure, I'd be scared of
moving with the kids to a strange town, and perhaps it
wouldn't be the best thing from the financial point of
view either, but I can get along well there. And then I
told Stani I'm not separating from him *because* I have
Peter, but *while* I still have him. If we [Helga and Peter]
stay together, fine, and if not, that's okay too. That's how
I see it.

(Her husband sits with arms folded and a look of strain on his face).

In theory there's no reason why I have to be dependent, but I am. I mustn't be dependent, it's uncomfortable, the way, whenever he comes, I go through the whole gamut of feelings from joy to grief, from suspense to aggression, but I always react strongly to Stani and I don't know how to change that. I have the feeling that if I'm to find myself again, it would be better for me to separate from him.

Th: You have made him too much a part of you and now you're trying to separate him from yourself?

W: Yes, probably.

Essentially Helga's problem seems to be that she cannot separate herself from Stani, either emotionally or externally; she defines herself through him and so is handicapped in her own development and activity. Her desire for outward separation may imply, on a deeper level, a desire to separate herself more clearly on an emotional plane. In couples therapy expressions of the desire to get a divorce often have this implication. The therapist is then tempted to hold forth about the outward situation, counselling the couple for or against divorce and issuing directives. But as a therapist I see it as my duty to probe into the deeper experiential content of what goes on between the partners, and to help them to make their own decisions; perhaps eventually the decision to get a divorce.

Before her marriage Helga was self-confident and independent. But in her marriage she has become overdependent on Stani.

W: I don't know why I'm so dependent.

H: We'll have to have an exorcism.

W: I'm simply dependent and I don't see any other solution. (Pause)

Th: Do you think that you could get him out of your system if the two of you were outwardly separated?

W: I hope so, otherwise I wouldn't want it. I hope I'm really capable of doing that.

H: One thing that may be important to her is that she thinks that if we get a divorce we'll never meet again, and she wants to get free of me.

W: But Stani, when you tell me you're still around if I want you, then if things go badly with Peter, at that moment it would be a real temptation. But then by being around me you wouldn't appreciate me anymore, and it would just paralyze me again. It isn't a real solution, to think, "Sure, I'm getting a divorce, both of us can fool around a little, and then we'll get back together again."

Th: It's my impression that you feel you just can't be yourself as long as you have any relationship with him.

W: Yes, probably.

H: It's only with me that you can't be yourself, and otherwise you can.

W: I believe that in the past I was fairly self-confident. You said I was conceited. Maybe I was. Anyhow I was pretty uncomplicated and everything went fine. And over the years this self-confidence I used to have has broken down more and more. I didn't realize I had become so insecure. You've never given me the feeling that I was attractive. Maybe I'm not, objectively speaking, but one simply likes to hear that from someone one lives with.

Th: When you say, "Before I was so self-sufficient and now . . . ," do you have the feeling you've lost your identity?

W: It wasn't a deliberate losing of myself, it was passive, it just happened.

Th: You are defining yourself too much by him; you are completely dependent on his validation.

W: Yes, that's certainly true. I realized that when Peter told me I was pretty. Then he got very mad at Stani, and of course that made me feel good, but all in all I'd like to have heard that from you.

Th: It strikes me again that in many ways the two of you are very much alike, even though it seems as if you were opposites. I think both of you find it hard to be yourselves within the confines of such a close relationship. You [Stani] have the feeling that Helga gets too close to you and you have to struggle to keep hold of your own space, and you [Helga] are overabsorbed in him and so you can't find yourself either. Both of you find it hard to be yourselves in an intimate relationship.

> Both partners share the same problem: It is hard for them to be themselves in their marriage and to maintain separate identities.

Here I address directly the focus of the narcissistic collusion, namely the difficulty both partners have in resisting the tendency to lose oneself in one's partner in an intimate relationship; to be defined solely by one's partner. Helga gives up her sense of self for Stani, but in turn obligates him to behave in accordance with her ideals. For his part, Stani finds it hard to disappoint her expectations and yet feels that they alienate him from himself.

Stani is able to confess to Helga that with his girlfriends he has the same fear of being himself and disappointing their expectations.

W: Yes, I have that feeling too, and that's why I've decided I want to become completely myself. (Pause) And then so many things occur to me. He couldn't tell me the truth because he was scared, yes, I accept that. But you lied to Hedwig the same way you did to me. Does that mean you were scared of her reaction too? (Again the husband has placed his hand on his cheek in a protective gesture)

H: Yes, that's how it looked, maybe.

W: Then he went with Susanne for a year and didn't dare tell me that either; what are you scared of?

H: It wasn't fear, it was more the thought that I shouldn't tell you that, I don't know exactly why not. I didn't have the inner freedom and strength to tell you that. You wouldn't have had the strength either to say the things you're saying now.

W: Maybe not to you. True, a lot of things are clearer to me now, but I believe that even a year ago I did talk this way with a number of people.

H: I don't know, I wasn't capable of that, from the very first relationship on.

W: (Emphatically) You're a coward.

H: No, that's not a character trait. Today I can say that, I can tell my girlfriends too, but back then I couldn't; it's hard to say why.

W: Yes, right, it's true that you can admit it more readily now. But with the others [the girlfriends], you were scared of their reactions too, maybe more scared of mine. It always looks as if I was the only one who walked all over you and and beat you down; but you were afraid of their reactions too. Of course it may have been because of your experiences with me, but after all, they [the girlfriends] aren't gentle little doves either.

H: It's not so much that I'm scared of their getting mad. The situation can be more difficult when the other person is sad.

W: Yes, you're scared of all emotions.

H: (Softly) Maybe. (Prolonged silence)

Th: I'm still thinking about the question of separation. I think you two ought to separate . . . (Both partners stare at therapist in shock) The only question is, in what way. As I see it the crucial thing is that you have to separate yourselves more clearly from each other. I think that's more an internal process.

W: Mmm-hmm.

H: She sees physical separation as a necessary precondition for this process.

Th: I don't know, maybe it would be easier if you separated outwardly too, but the problem is that you can't separate inside, you can't define your boundaries. You [Helga] are too deeply absorbed in him, and he feels full of you. There's no clear boundary between you.

W: Mmm-hmm. (Looks at her husband)

Th: With no secure boundaries, a relationship is always threatening.

W: Mmm-hmm. (Pause) Yes, I've been really struck by that when Stani comes home; maybe you feel different, but for me it has to do with a physical separation. I think it could be easier if we don't see each other any more, or maybe only for therapy on Mondays. I think it's important that we make a definitive agreement to see each other or call each other up, and that's why I'd like a complete separation, because otherwise I couldn't do that!

Th: (To husband) How do you feel about that?

H: (Sighs) I can't say no; I think it's a good solution. For me personally there's the possibility of another solution, but maybe not for Helga. The fact is that I don't feel bad and I don't have such strong reactions; I can manage fine the way things are now, it's not the same for me as it is for her.

W: I'm amazed at that. The last time in therapy—when I said I was suffering over the way things are—you said, "No, I'm not really suffering." But then at home when I said, "Now I want a separation," you resisted the idea and encouraged me again. Actually we ought not to have talked about it between therapy sessions, but I just wanted to tell you so you could prepare yourself for the next session. At home you always talk about how bad you feel.

The therapist shocks the couple by approving their plan to separate. But he is referring to an inner rather than an outer separation.

H: You don't understand what I mean. The question is whether I have strong reactions when I see you the way you do when you see me. But even though I don't have strong reactions, I'm still depressed at the thought of having to give up everything, the children, the apartment, our home. There's no reason why that can't bother me, the two facts don't rule each other out.

W: (Increasingly angry) The Hungarian goulash and the warm sofa and the children, yes, all right.

(Long pause. The couple look angrily at each other.)

Th: The problem of defining your boundaries was relevant last time too, to some extent, when we were talking about extramarital relationships, and I saw that both of you had the same difficulty deciding "What's your problem, and what's my problem?"

W: Mmm-hmm, that's what I think too, as long as we're not together I believe that these relationships are his problem, but as soon as we're together I feel they're my problem too.

Th: Why is that?

H: It's always the same, as soon as I like someone else she feels it's a personal insult.

W: It could be that it is an insult. When we're not together I always think, "Go on, let him do whatever he wants"; but when we want to get together, it bothers me. And my feelings are variable. Sometimes I'm really mad at his girlfriends, and sometimes I think I don't hold anything against them at all.

My detachment enables me to see clearly that although to some extent I, as therapist, stick to the rules of the game, nevertheless I challenge the validity of the wife's behavior more than that of the husband's. In the following excerpt my own emotions clearly dominate my reactions to Helga's attempts to apply pressure, so that my attempt to sustain the role of therapist unconsciously becomes an abuse of this role. I take my personal feelings of grievance and of being threatened by an end to my work, and wrap them up inside therapeutic interventions, thus making my reactions more or less unassailable. At this point in our dialogue I was not aware of this, which shows once again how difficult it is in couples therapy for a therapist to come to terms with the bias induced by his own sex role and his own problems in relating.

Th: Sometimes I almost feel as if you need his girlfriends so you can differentiate yourself from him better.

W: In what sense?

Th: Because if it weren't for the girlfriends you and your husband would get too close.

W: Yes, that may well be.

Th: Because of his girlfriends you can push him away over and over and say, "Such an awful fellow, and there he's going with those women again, I'm so disappointed in him that I don't want to live with him any more."

W: That may well be, that's probably true. Clearly it's a lot easier for me to say, "You don't need me," so I can push him away. (She accompanies this statement with a powerful pushing gesture)

(Long pause, wife lowers her head, looks hurt)

W: Yes, probably the question is whether we ought to go on with therapy at all. (Tearful voice)

The therapist feels hurt by Helga's threat to separate from her husband and break off therapy, so he in turn hurts Helga with an "interpretation." Helga does not contradict him but questions the value of therapy.

My misguided interpretation is rewarded by Helga's threat to break off therapy. Helga is now in a difficult position in relation to me: Because of my comments she feels hurt and rejected, but she tries to accept them in order not to disrupt the harmony between us. Her difficulty with Stani is now transferred to her relationship with me, this difficulty being that she feels rejected if she can't maintain a harmonious bond with the people she is close to. I, in turn, under the pressure of her threat of divorce, feel she is forcing me to devote my full attention to her, and—like Stani—react by trying to pull away from her, which hurts her. At this point I am offered the chance to work on a therapeutic collusion between Helga and myself, but I do not take advantage of it because my personal involvement in my difficulties with Helga is too deep to allow me sufficient detachment.

H: Are you still sticking to your decision?

W: Yes, Stani! Things can't go on this way, and when I've distanced myself from it more we can meet on some other basis, not clinging to each other. For me it's simply unbearable having you always in the background and always there when I need you. With the little money that I have, I'm still proud of being able to make ends meet on my own, to show, "Look, I can do it." I want to show that I can do it alone and not always just think, "Now I'll see how much I can do on my own and if it doesn't

Here the therapist bypasses an opportunity to treat his strained relations with Helga as a therapeutic collusion.

work, there's Stani on the spot to help." The way things are now, I can use you any time I like.

Th: Do you feel handicapped by this so that it would prevent you from ever finding yourself?

W: I have that feeling now.

Th: That inside you still feel dependent?

W: Yes, that always makes me dependent, the fact that at bottom I never have to handle problems myself, that Stani's always there. That's part of the process of breaking free—not being able to rely on him. All right, I'll still need money from you, but then I can simply look on you as an employer.

Th: I think that finding oneself is more of an inner process, although perhaps the external situation makes it more difficult. But in this case the question is whether the actual physical contact between you could be structured in a way that would make it easier for you to become independent—for example, if you make a definite appointment whenever you're going to see each other and never telephone each other, so you know that now you really have to deal with problems yourself and can't wait until he drops by.

W: But often it's Stani who does the telephoning.

H: I said I'll accept your wishes; I just wouldn't like you to immediately break off all ties with me.

W: How do you picture things then? Are we supposed to separate and acquire our own identity with a view to having a future together later, or should we develop independently of any idea like that?

H: It's quite clear to me that if we have therapy, we have to do it with a view to the possibility that we may meet later and get back together again. I don't mean that that's necessarily what I want just now, so I don't want you saying later, "Back then you said such and such." All I want to say is that it might become possible [for us to be together], but now it isn't possible.

W: Yes, all right, but then you come back with the plan that we'd go abroad together. But that wouldn't change a thing. I'd get under your skin too much and I'd go on being dependent on you. Maybe the external threat could make it a bit better.

H: But now you know where we're making our mistakes, and so do I, and we could deliberately try something different from what we've done before. For me the only chance now is therapy. I don't see any possibility that I might come back to you and that we could try to get along. But if we have therapy now and you say, "In any case I don't ever want to be with you," then there's no need for us to get closer. And if you say I'm never to see the children again either . . .

W: Yes, as far as the children are concerned, that's another situation.

H: The thing is quite clear-cut if we look at the outward circumstances. Even though I'm not so close to my family that they're the only thing I want, still I think it's important for the children and our family to normalize our relationship so that we can really see a possibility of living together again, because outward circumstances dictate that we really ought to.

W: (Mockingly) Because I can cook the best goulash.

H: No, you understand, when you say that I can't give you a clear-cut yes-or-no answer when you ask me whether I want to live with you, what I say is—

W: "Maybe" (Sarcastic tone)

H: No, that's wrong, I do want to live with you, but not as we have in the past.

W: I wasn't happy either.

H: I can't just say a flat-out yes. It's a tricky question, and that's why I didn't answer the last time.

W: Yes, I know that, but when I ask whether you still care for me at all, you can't answer, you only mention the atmosphere, our home.

H: Of course.

W: It's quite clear we have problems, but there still ought to be something substantial there if people are even to try—

H: You mustn't forget that the physical attraction between people is very closely connected with their inner feelings; if I like you, I find you attractive, if I don't like you, I don't find you attractive.

Th: What do you think really, why does he come here [to therapy sessions]?

Stani urges that they continue therapy and rejects the idea of a definitive formal separation for the term of therapy.

Helga is
afraid that
she will stop
loving Stani
if she is
forced to
accept his
limited
capacity for
love.

W: (Staring into space, thinking, sighing; the husband holds his hand protectively in front of his face) Well, I have to think about that. Of course one can say his motivation is to normalize our relationship. (Pause) Yes, that's why. (Pause. Seems not very convinced.) But I have the feeling, maybe I'm wrong, maybe it'll turn out quite different, I have the feeling that once I've gotten away from Stani I won't want to go back with him, maybe I'm wrong, maybe it'll be better for me then, maybe I'll have a different attitude towards him.

H: Well fine, then at least it'll be a clear-cut solution, then you'll know that you don't want me back. We could have a good relationship all the same. I think it would simply be a pity if I didn't get to see the children again. At the moment they have three parent figures, and I don't see why we couldn't all remain on friendly terms.

Watching the video tapes again, I was struck by my tendency to expect the wife to adapt to the husband more than the other way around; an impression that Helga confirmed when we discussed the manuscript. In therapy I try to accept the husband as he is, and I expect the wife to adopt the same attitude towards her husband. This is asking too much of her, for after all she is not her husband's therapist. When Helga once again tries to pressure Stani into a declaration of his feelings, I try to mediate between them by asking her why she thinks he is coming to therapy. On a personal level it disturbs me that she shows so little willingness to admit that he is genuinely motivated to improve the relationship. Helga measures her own love, as well as his, by absolute standards: all or nothing.

The Twenty-Second Session, March 26

Synopsis
Six months have passed. The relationship between Stani and Helga has started to move. At times the partners are able to get closer; frequently each step forward is immediately followed by a step backward. It is difficult for Helga to acknowledge positive changes achieved during therapy because she doubts that they will last. She is much more inclined to believe the worst until Stani has proved to her that the change in his attitude and behavior is permanent. This demand hinders therapeutic change. Helga and Stani have had sporadic sexual contacts. Stani fears that these changes might lead Helga to expect too much and pushes her away, hurtfully accusing her of

being too fat for him. Helga takes an independent stand: She is not willing to lose weight on his account, but insists that either he must accept her as she is, or have nothing to do with her. In this way she makes it easier for Stani to define a position of his own and to confront her with it, which is difficult for him but less threatening than if she had not taken a stand.

During these six months, treatment continued to be focused on the narcissistic collusion. Again and again Stani places Helga in double-bind situations, rousing in her the need to fulfill contradictory expectations whose fulfillment, one way or the other, will lead to her being punished. He wants her to show him more tenderness, warmth and responsiveness, but cannot tolerate any expression of spontaneous emotion or any expectations that might make him feel he is under some obligation. But Stani has this same trouble with Renate too. Despite the fact that Renate is living with him, she is engaged to a student who is now abroad. Stani feels hurt that she has not broken off this relationship with her boyfriend on his account, despite the fact that under no circumstances does he want her to make any demands on him that might place him under some obligation. Behind this contradictory behavior lies his deep longing for an absolute, unconditional love that nothing can tarnish, the kind of love that he missed so desperately in his childhood. But the wish for this fantasized absolute love can never be realized, because in real life love will always be shaped by a full-grown woman who has her own dreams and expectations.

Certain contradictions have become more apparent in Helga too. At the beginning of their relationship she was fascinated by Stani because she hoped he would free her from her captivity in a respectable, bourgeois life-style. Stani seemed to her the opposite of her father. Her father's position was "This is where I stand, I won't budge an inch." But Stani was a man she could never completely understand. He was unpunctual, unreliable, a dreamer. Under pressure from her he had improved. But he had adapted to her only on the surface, and Helga was still uncertain who he was on the inside. His enigmatic and incomprehensible quality not only annoyed but also fascinated her.

Just before this session the partners' relationship seemed to be taking a marked turn for the better. Their resumption of sexual relations had brought with it some sexual dysfunction in Stani, apparently an exception. Helga was happy about their intimacy and during the last session reported that she felt absolutely secure with Stani and did not feel driven by their sexual encounter to form demands and expectations. Stani seemed unable to share her pleasure and appeared to be in an ambivalent mood. When asked about it he replied in a hurtful way, saying that it was hard for him to accept Helga because she was too fat for his taste. This remark instantaneously destroyed Helga's happy mood. To be sure, clarification revealed that Stani could not tolerate fervent intimacy with Helga and was afraid that she would once again become too open to him. The wounding remark he made was intended to push Helga away to a safe distance again and perhaps also to compensate him for the pain he had suffered over his sexual difficulties. The present hour begins with a dilemma: Should the wife lose weight in order to please her husband, or stay as she is and put up with the fact that he does not find her attractive?

Meanwhile Stani has grown a beard, which gives him the air of a revolutionary. Recently Helga has often worn a skirt instead of jeans, which makes her look younger and somewhat more girlish.

Helga and Stani resumed sexual relations. But then Stani immediately pushed her away again with hurtful remarks about her weight. Then Helga lost heart again.	**Th:** How's it going? **W:** It hasn't been going so well. Before the last therapy session—when we had slept together and our relationship was really good, or at least it looked that way, and we were happy—naturally I started building up false hopes again and thought, "Stani accepts me"—not that he thinks I'm ravishing, no man could feel that way about a woman after living with her for ten years, but all right, all the same I thought, "He does accept me, in any case more than before," and after we slept together we were still lying side by side, and we teased each other, "Yes, yes, the stardust is gone," and he said, "No, no, it really feels good." What else could he say? After the therapy session I started crying. What he said hurt me very much, especially because before then I thought I had really become emotionally free of what Stani thought. What he says or thinks about me doesn't matter to me now, I thought, or matters much less—and then I saw that what he said hurt me very much, and everything came up again—it's all the same as before—then I got upset, and the feeling came over me that nothing has changed in the least. The question is, How am I supposed to behave so Stani won't have this fear of me, whether that's even possible, whether it's possible in this set-up or whether it would only happen if I lost my identity entirely and turned gentle as a lamb. Is it even possible that Stani could someday lose his fear of me, and how should I behave without completely ceasing to be myself? I know that if I were soft and sweet and submitted to everything patiently, then he'd say I disgusted him by

acting that way. It's just the opposite of October, when Stani asked, "What should I do so that Helga will lose her fear, her suspicion?"

(Long silence)

H: Right, I don't think that being meek and saying yes to everything would be the right thing, I don't think so. I don't know exactly what one ought to do. What scares me again and again is that whenever I try to take stock and say what I'm feeling, that you immediately get upset instead of just saying, "All right, that's how it is, what can we do about it?" And you don't enter into my feelings at all. If you could just enter into my feelings, I think I'd be more willing to give in. I'm afraid to tell you because you just explode.

W: Well, if you'd tell me this way, tell me you have these fears, I think that then I'd be able to stand it. The sore point was the thing about losing weight.

H: All right, then let's ask Mr. Willi. What happened with the thing about losing weight?

W: You said there were a lot of things you couldn't tell me, and then Mr. Willi asked if there is something that you're afraid of.

H: Yes, and then I thought about it and thought that I couldn't tell you about the losing weight business because then you'd explode.

W: Yes, fine, so I just reacted to it and got mad about it again.

Th: (To wife) How should he have behaved in this situation?

W: There's nothing he could have done. If he thinks I'm too fat and can't say so, it's my problem because I can't take it and react so violently. He behaved properly, I should have taken it, but it was too hard a pill for me to swallow. It really hurt me a lot.

Th: How do you actually feel about your body?

W: (Reflects) Maybe I'd like to lose some weight, but not a lot, I'm really more or less satisfied, but I wasn't until Peter; because before, in America for example, I often stood in front of the mirror and thought I was so ugly that I thought, "Poor Stani, he really needs other women." I was genuinely sorry for Stani because I thought I was repulsive. But that subsided because Peter

Helga finds
it hard to
accept her
body and in
this area is
very
dependent on
her partner's
approval.

thinks I'm beautiful, and when a woman is accepted by her partner, she's more content about herself. When I'm with Peter, I feel completely free, he doesn't give a damn whether I lose ten pounds; on the contrary, he says, "I'd rather you gained weight because then you're in a good mood." (Helga smiles) Now of course I was dreadfully inhibited again about sleeping with Stani.

Th: It's not easy to be yourself where your body is concerned either, and not be too dependent on him.

W: I . . . felt so free before and thought, "Yes, now I'm myself," and now I'm so disappointed that things have turned out this way again.

The mood of this session is predominantly one of resignation, which affects all three of us. We had hoped that both partners had made some solid progress in defining their own limits. This self-definition proves particularly difficult for the partners in the sexual area. The problem in their relationship is most concretely expressed in physical terms. Helga finds it hard to accept herself and is very dependent on the unreserved acceptance of her partner.

Th: (To husband) How did you feel then?

H: (Sighs) At first I was disappointed, then later when she showed this strong reaction, I saw that I had hurt her, but I hadn't expected that afterwards she'd react so violently. What especially hurt me were the conclusions she drew, the way she said, "All right, now I'll get a divorce; I don't want anything more from you"—the way she immediately draws absolute conclusions and demands that I take a stand.

Th: (To husband) How would you have reacted if your wife had said something like that to you?

H: I think I wouldn't be so crushed. Probably I'd think, "Well, actually, I'd thought things were different." I'd be disappointed, but I couldn't react the way she did, so violently and negatively. My basic reaction would be, at most, to wonder what I could do so she'd find me attractive again.

Th: Would that mean, for example, that in a situation like this you'd set out to lose weight?

H: That's the way I do react in situations like that.

W: I don't.

H: Sure, I'm just saying how I'd react.

Th: Then you'd like to be what the other person expects?

H: Yes, if the other person's opinion matters to me. Then I'd think what can I do, and if I was fat I'd try to reduce.

W: That's something I simply won't do. Besides, you also said that you didn't know whether you could love me even after I lost the weight.

H: I believe the outward things don't play much of a role if people get along well in other ways.

Helga and Stani see that her weight is only a superficial problem concealing deeper problems of intimacy.

Stani's dissatisfaction with Helga's body is not really determined by her actual physique but rather is an expression of their disturbed relationship. Thus it would be useless to debate the question of whether or not Helga should go on a diet, because essentially the problem is not her weight but Stani's defensive reaction to having her close to him. Fortunately Helga is determined not to lose weight for her husband. For if she did this she would, to be sure, be complying with his wishes on the surface, but on the subconscious level she would just be intensifying his defensive reaction. Stani is bound to feel afraid if Helga is too compliant and thus later has a lever with which to pressure and intimidate him. Ultimately he is less afraid if she is faithful to her own feelings and is able to stick up for herself. Her being overweight is a concrete visualization of their problem in relating.

W: Then why did you say that about my losing weight?

H: Because we don't get along well in other respects, that may be why it plays some role.

W: Aha. (Pause)

H: But I also told you that for me it's not the essential thing; even if you lose weight, that won't change anything about my love for you. There's no cause-and-effect relationship.

W: So then, you love me first, and then I'll lose weight. (They both laugh)

H: If I loved you, then you wouldn't have to lose weight.

W: The simplest thing would be for you to love me, terrific! Then I'll be cheerful and happy and won't have to lose weight, that's terrific. (All three laugh)

Th: (To husband) How do you think Helga ought to behave?

H: In general terms, she should be less absolute.

Th: What do you mean by that?

H: In her reactions she's either up in the clouds or down in the dumps, there's nothing in between. (To Helga) Look, when all I say is that I find it hard to get close to you, you think I don't like you. (Helga shakes her head) But you do, that's the way you react, and then you up and say, "Now I want a divorce, tomorrow I'll start divorce proceedings."

W: No, Stani, that's not true.

Th: (To wife) You're saying he cuts himself off from you. I think that's your problem too, that is that you find it really hard to draw a clear dividing line between yourself and him. I believe there's no other way out for you but to learn to act on your own feelings. If you weren't determined so much by him, I think he might be less afraid of you.

W: Now and then, when we've hurt each other, we've been able to talk about it, but often I think we've made no progress at all from the way we were a year and a half ago. As for drawing a clear dividing line between myself and him, how am I to do that? All right, so I . . . (Long pause. Wife fights to hold back her tears, and sighs. The husband looks at her with deep concern, but at the same time holds his hand protectively before his face again.)

W: At bottom I don't really do so many things depending on Stani.

If Helga were a more clearly defined person, it would make it easier for Stani to define his own position.

Th: (To husband) I'd be interested to know how you feel about that? If Helga knew more clearly what she wants, would it be easier for you to get over your ambivalent feelings?

H: Maybe so.

Th: (To husband) I can really understand how Helga feels. She's repeatedly said that you have an ideal of a woman who is completely devoted to you and is very close to you, and at the same time you keep pushing Helga away the moment she tries to behave the way you want. That really confuses her.

H: You mean that I keep pushing away the ideal woman?

Th: Apparently that's a problem you have not only with Helga but also with your girlfriends. I have the impression that you find it difficult to take a clear position.

H: It's hard for me because generally I don't see things clearly myself.

(Long interlude in which the husband discusses this problem in detail)

As was discussed in detail in other sessions, Stani's loss of his mother in childhood, an experience that he has never come to terms with, continues to affect him even now in the form of his anxiety that if his behavior does not live up to his "mother's" expectations, she may die because she cannot be expected to endure any strain. This anxiety compels him, on the one hand, to seek total fusion with his "mother," and, on the other hand, to repulse her. Filled with hatred because her closeness threatens him, he can no longer be himself, and he is in danger of attaching himself to her too closely, so that he could hardly bear the pain if he were left alone.

Th: (To wife) Where your body's concerned, I don't see any alternative but to be loyal to it. "This is how I am! Either he can accept me or he can't."

W: That's just what I said the last time, and I won't lose an ounce.

H: (To wife) But you're not satisfied with yourself either.

W: But I am. Although naturally now and then one thinks— For example, I've thought it would be nice to have bigger eyes. Oh well, what does it matter? Actually I'm content with myself. (Her husband tries to signify disagreement) Yes, really.

H: That's not true. Quite apart from me you're not content, that's why you didn't want to go swimming with the kids, because people could see you.

W: Oh.

H: Yes, you said so.

W: Yes, but that's because you told me you think I'm so ugly.

H: It was the same way before.

W: Because you've been rejecting me for years. Can't
you get that into your head?
H: I find it really hard to accept that. If you were
satisfied with yourself—
W: I couldn't be satisfied because I was dependent on
you.

The problem of the wife's weight comes within the purview of the
focus of therapy. In this case there is no solution but that the wife stand on
her own two feet and try to accept herself as she is, without trying to see
herself through the husband's eyes. The tragic thing about every collusion
is that each partner exhibits those very behavior patterns that make it most
difficult for the other partner to make any progress towards improving the
situation and in fact is compelled by his own problem to prevent the other
partner from developing in a direction for which the latter may have a
desperate need; for to allow this would be to put himself at risk. Stani's
secret expectation that Helga will unite with him to form a single being
and his pain at her attempts to assert her independence make it doubly
difficult for her to overcome her personal limitations because these
attempts threaten the continuation of the relationship. Therefore I try to
show Stani that he would be less afraid of intimacy with Helga if he could
accept the fact that she is an independent person separate from himself.

Helga also faced the unavoidable necessity to assert her independence when Stani and his girlfriend Renate arranged a party and Stani did
not make it clear to Helga whether or not she was invited.

Th: I wonder whether you weren't asking too much of
yourself to have gone to this party.
(The wife shrugs her shoulders)
H: The party, you mean?
Th: Yes, a party you planned with your girlfriend.
W: Yes, when I found out you were throwing it with
Renate, right away I said, "No, I won't go," but you said
"No, it's completely casual."
H: Yes, but it's obvious if I'm living with Renate and
giving a party at her place, then I'll be with her, and you
wanted to come and expected me to pay attention to you.
W: No, no.
H: At least, that's how it seemed to me.
W: No, I neither thought that nor hoped for it. I
thought, "The whole thing is very casual"—that's the
way you described it to me.

H: It's not a question of whether we were the host and hostess; it's that if I'm there I'd like to dance with her without your making any claims on me and expecting things from me.

W: But I just don't get it. After all, Peter came too, and I said something like, "Mmm, there are some good-looking men, oh, I'm going to do such-and-such," and you took my arm and said to Peter, "Hey, Peter, I'll look after her."

H: Hold on, just hold on. Peter was sitting there looking depressed, and you said, "Oh, poor Peter" (Stani strokes Helga's shoulder comfortingly and sympathetically), and then I said, "All right, Peter, I'll look after her."

W: That's not what I care about. But you kept saying to Peter, "Come on now, come on now." I don't understand why you didn't say, "Hey, I think it's better if you don't come." Weren't you the least bit afraid there'd be some tension? And what about Renate, didn't it make any difference to her? Supposedly she feels threatened by me. But you told me she'd find it [the party] interesting. And I said I thought that was almost perverse. If I'm with another guy and feel threatened by his wife, I don't find it interesting.

H: She didn't feel at all threatened by you.

W: Fine, so I just imagined it.

Th: (To husband) I think you said here earlier that it would make Renate happy.

H: Not make her happy. She said, "Yes, it would be good if we felt free enough with each other to talk.

W: (Shakes her head) Free?

H: Yes, we don't have anything to do with each other, we can avoid each other if there's tension, but we can also talk together.

W: Nonsense! (Her expression shows that she considers this hogwash).

H: Fine, that was her notion, and you have a different one.

W: Yes, all right, it doesn't matter.

Th: I think it does matter. I have the impression that all of you, including Renate and whoever else is involved,

Stani organized a party with his girlfriend to which Helga was also invited. He hoped that the two women would talk. Helga is able to differentiate herself from him clearly.

are trying to be really tough. It's hard for me to believe that Renate could enjoy this.

H: She didn't say "enjoy."

Th: Yes, or that this was an opportunity to be together without any constraint.

H: She has already said several times that she'd like to talk to Helga some time.

W: But I don't want to talk to her.

Th: Isn't it more of a chance for them to look each other over so that then they can tear each other to pieces in a honey-sweet tone?

W: She's a social worker and completely altruistic; I'm saying that sarcastically. She's so altruistic that it really makes me sick. Naturally I feel threatened by her and am very subjective about her. But this whole way of doing things: "All four of us could get together, that would be so nice–" I say no! Stani says, "You really ought to talk to Renate some time, then she would tell you this and that." I say he ought to tell me himself. There's no need for Renate to do it.

H: I say that sometimes only when you say I have it so good, I don't have any children around, and so I wanted Renate to tell you how much that bothers me.

W: You can't tell me yourself that it bothers you a lot and that I'm wrong in what I think. All I'm saying is that he really has a good life, he can have his freedom whenever he wants it, and he can come back and have the children whenever he wants, he really has a beautiful life; so really why should he come back home? And then he always gets very mad. But he does have a beautiful life, at least more beautiful than I do.

The modern attitude that couples ought to tolerate extramarital relationships often leads them to arrange little "frank talks" or "friendly discussions" that place too much strain on them. Often they deny their real feelings, and each pretends to the other to be perfectly cool and under control. Helga sees this more clearly than Stani and again asserts her own opinion, contradicting her husband.

The following is an excerpt from a later phase of this session. Stani accuses Helga of behaving completely different in therapy sessions from the way she behaves at home, and thus of being insincere.

Th: That seems to me a very important point. Do you
have *the impression that the two of you behave differently
to each other during therapy than at other times?*
W: No, I don't think so.
Th: Do you have the feeling that you have to pull
yourself together more because of your fear that if you
don't, your partner will bring up the incident at the next
therapy session?
W: I don't fear that. At most I may think after I've
said something, "Wow, that really wasn't a very nice
thing to say."
Th: Why do you think that?
W: Because I'm embarrassed, because I've let myself
get carried away and done things that are very nasty.
Th: You're embarrassed in front of me?
W: Yes, I am. Maybe I've only done it to get in a
dirty blow at him, and I know that's wrong, and it isn't
very flattering if Stani brings up the matter here.
Th: Are you afraid that things you do will damage
your position with me?
W: No, that's not really so, but when I've had a
negative reaction that I actually ought not to have had,
and when he tells you about it, naturally it shows me in a
bad light.
Th: Mmm-hmm.
W: It's not that I'm afraid you'll punish me or prefer
him to me, it's simply that it's embarrassing for me.

In couples therapy one must always keep in mind how the couple's
life together is affected by their weekly meetings with the therapist.
Particularly there is the danger of "forced normalization," arising from the
fact that each partner is striving to behave laudably so that he or she will
be beyond criticism. The therapy sessions threaten to deteriorate into court
sessions in which each partner appears as both plaintiff and accused, and
where the advantage is felt to lie with the one who is innocent of any
provocation. In such a case an outward show of harmony in the
relationship can easily take on the appearance of a step forward in the
therapy. The therapist should remain on guard against the risk that
changes for the better may be only superficial, and continually discuss this
during therapy.

W: When one consciously does something that isn't nice, one feels embarrassed, or at least I do.

Th: Do you sometimes do certain things, as you say, deliberately, as a provocation?

W: Yes, I often do things quite deliberately.

Th: And what do you gain by them?

W: Probably it's purely and simply revenge; I don't gain a thing.

H: But you do.

W: Yes, I succeed in driving you away. I believe that *I hurt Stani out of revenge* because he hurts me. Above all I hurt him with ridicule because I have the edge on him there, because he can't make fun of things.

H: I don't like to do that.

W: You don't know how to.

H: Yes I do too, maybe you can do it better, but that doesn't mean I can't do it too.

W: All right, let's say you can do it as well as I can, but I feel I'm better at it than you are. And partly I just enjoy the play on words. I can also make fun of myself, I actually enjoy it.

H: But often it isn't just making fun, it's an insult.

W: Because I want to hurt you. That's exactly what embarrasses me about it; I know perfectly well that I don't achieve anything constructive by it.

As a male therapist I have to learn that a man and a woman have different ways of making people listen to them when they find themselves in an unsatisfactory situation. Men believe they can achieve most through logical, rational argument, whereas women react much more directly, emotionally and colorfully. In their fear that their complaints will not be heard and taken seriously, women tend to exaggerate their accusations and behave provocatively towards the people around them, in the process saying many things that do not stand up to objective evaluation. Psychiatrists designate this apparently ungenuine, theatrical and appellative behavior as hysterical. That is, they defend themselves against it by becoming aloof and detached and calling it by a deprecatory name. Women tend to react to this withdrawal by dishing out more of the same, i.e., their behavior becomes even more obtrusive and extreme so that they will be taken seriously. Helga is afraid that I might make the mistake of taking her emotional outburst at face value instead of asking her what she really means by it and what she wants.

Th: (To wife) In behaving this way you're trying to get close, but what you get is rejection and withdrawal. Perhaps one ought to ask whether you're really trying to produce this effect?

W: Probably. I hurt him much more deliberately than he does me; he hurts me more inadvertently.

Th: How would it be if Stani were really wild about you? Would that scare you?

W: (Thoughtful) Why should it scare me?

Th: The fact that you two were getting too close, that you were getting too involved again and would be disappointed again, so that often you'd rather smash everything at the start in order to keep it from going that far.

W: I don't know—I don't feel that way—maybe I'm not aware of it.

Th: (To husband) What do you think about that?

H: The idea that if she gets too involved she could be disappointed again, that's very likely true.

W: No, that's certain.

H: As for the fact that she keeps me at a distance with ridicule, no doubt that's true too. But to what extent it's really intentional . . .

Th: How much of a part is played by the idea: *I'll get involved with Stani again only if I'm quite sure he'll respond and will continue to respond.*

W: Probably, that's how it is.

Th: And as long as I'm not quite certain, I'd rather keep him at a distance.

W: Yes, that's it all right, we're on the right track. I haven't made any progress yet, I'm behaving the same way I did a year ago.

Th: What seems important to me is simply the question of *whether Stani isn't the only one who's afraid you may get too close, but whether you too are afraid when he gets close to you?*

W: You asked me before how I'd feel if he were wild about me and loved me, and I think I'd feel that was beautiful and I'd really like it.

Th: As long as you were absolutely positive that it would last your whole life long?

Helga does not achieve any intimacy by pressuring Stani but again merely causes him (and the therapist) to withdraw in self-defense, so that the therapist questions whether she herself finds it difficult to allow anyone to get close to her for very long.

W: And since I would know that things aren't like that in the real world . . .

Th: You ruin it over and over.

W: Yes, probably. (Silence)

W: Yes, but occasionally I get the feeling that now I can put up with things much better, that I'm much freer and more tolerant, and then suddenly it gets worse again, and now I never know exactly, when things get worse again, whether I've only imagined they were better, or whether it's just a relapse. I can't tell, I don't know.

Th: It seems that you have trouble trusting in any change, and that's why you always want a guarantee of your safety, and this very tendency to want a guarantee makes it difficult to achieve any positive change because Stani would feel obligated to live up to the guarantee and might feel, "I can't stick to it, and if I'm bound to disappoint her again in the end, I'd rather not make any changes to begin with."

W: Just last time I said I'd like to try changing, and if it goes wrong, then it just goes wrong; I sincerely wanted to try, and then after the last session everything was all in pieces again, and I was even disappointed in myself for having reacted that way. And now I'm very uncertain again.

Th: These ups and downs are a normal part of therapy.

W: It's normal for it to go on this way?

Th: Yes, it's normal to repeatedly arrive at the point of thinking that nothing whatever is changing.

W: Uh-huh. Now I actually feel better, now I have the feeling I might be able to do it after all, that I'm not expecting too much and that I wouldn't ruin things, or be compelled to ruin things, because my expectations aren't too high; now suddenly I have the feeling again that it would work. (Stani would like to raise an objection and looks at her. Helga looks back and says mockingly, screwing up her face in a venomous grimace:) What a sweet look you're giving me! (Stani smiles) Really aggressive and nasty.

H: No, no. I was just thinking, "What will I do if you can actually do it, how will I feel about that, and where do I go from there?"

The question is to what extent Helga's mockery and aggressivity represent reactions to the frustrations inflicted by Stani; and to what extent Helga is trying, by these means, to defend herself against her own exorbitant expectations and fears of disappointment.

When I replayed the tapes I was struck by the fact that I paid more attention to Helga's problems than to Stani's, which I clearly accepted almost as a given. In part this may have been due to my impression, during diagnosis, that because of her expansive personality Helga could profit more from an active therapeutic confrontation, whereas Stani, because of his hypersensitivity and tendency to withdraw, would make better progress if I avoided pressuring him and even protected him. But perhaps too, as a male therapist, I am more inclined to view the woman as a patient and to view her behavior as a problem. Stani's last comment, however, confirmed my impression that he was not simply holding himself aloof from therapy while I was occupied with Helga, but rather that he was better able to confront his problems in a protective setting.

Twenty-third Session, April 9

Synopsis
At the moment the problem in the therapy is that both partners now clearly perceive the collusion and also see how each of them has to change. But both find it difficult to give up their inappropriate behavior because each is afraid that any tangible change might cause his partner to develop exaggerated expectations about the extent and permanence of the change. Thus every step forward is followed by a step backward. Both are acting in accordance with the same fantasy: Because I cannot live up to my partner's image of me, I must nip his (her) hopes in the bud in order to forestall disappointment. This reaction is typical of this phase of therapy. When a person gives up a symptom of illness or an inappropriate behavior, other people raise their expectations, trusting that they will see an increased ability to endure stress and increased health and personal responsibility, all demands from which sick people are spared, and from which they derive the so-called profits of illness. It takes courage to get well. This is particularly clear in the sexual area. The man is afraid to resume sexual relations because he fears that his sexual addresses to the woman cannot continue, and so he would end by hurting her again. Helga perceives that she would have the tendency to hold Stani to his original behavior because of her fear that his change of attitude might not be genuine. Because of this fear she is inclined to admit that Stani has made progress only if she can be sure that she will not be disappointed in the end. A partner must also have courage to acknowledge his spouse's

progress, for if the spouse does change, he himself will have to change accordingly, i.e. he will have to give up his own inappropriate behavior that was a reaction to the inappropriate behavior of the other partner. Moreover, he must do so without any guarantee that the change made by the other partner is genuine and lasting. So each of them is afraid that he will be cheated in the end.

The couple have spent Easter with their children in a holiday cottage. Admittedly there were some violent quarrels, but, in general, they got along better than they had in the past. They also had marital relations. They turned up for the session looking quite relaxed. After Helga gave Stani an ultimatum, they agreed that in two months he would come back to her. An excerpt from this session will show how difficult it is for the partners to get together. Now, when supposedly Stani is ready to resume their life together by the date Helga stipulated, Helga sabotages his decision rather than being happy about it as one might first expect. The atmosphere of this session is clearly different from that of past sessions. The husband fights back, showing more emotion; the wife, who looks younger and rather pert, is more often in a defensive position. Despite the violent clash between them, the atmosphere is less hostile than in the past.

> H: Up until now Helga has always said, "Think about it until May 1." She's always said that she wanted to live with me, and I've expressed doubts about whether the only difficulty was whether I agreed or not, and she said, "Are you so dumb you can't see that?" So I really believed it was just a question of my making a decision, and that's the way I'd always formulated it. And now finally I say I'm ready to come back to her and she says she hasn't made up her mind yet. (Helga laughs as if she had just pulled off a successful prank) So, on the one hand, I was disappointed, yes. On the other hand, naturally I thought to myself, "Well, that proves that it's not up to me."
>
> W: Then naturally you added, "Of course there's also the possibility that you might stay with Peter and keep the children, and then if it ended with Peter in a year or two . . ." He always assumes that in a year or two—
>
> H: That's pretty clear.
>
> W: (Sharply) Why?
>
> H: Because he's a lot weaker than you.
>
> W: That's your opinion.

H: Yes, sure, that's my impression.

Th: (To wife) I'd be interested in knowing something. You said his tone is quite different when he's telling about all this here?

W: Yes, the tone in which he described me. That makes me laugh. It amuses me, maybe I said that, but I now know where you [Stani] stand, which I didn't really know before. He was even disappointed on the telephone, when I didn't react as if I was overjoyed.

H: Well no, not so much that.

W: And when I asked him, "Are you disappointed?" and he didn't say no . . .

H: Yes, I didn't realize straight off what I felt, people aren't always aware straight off how they are reacting.

Th: (To husband) I imagine that it was easier for you to have your wife behave with restraint than if she had immediately bubbled over with joy.

H: Restraint, sure, but she just backed away. Up until now it was clear that she wanted [to get back together]; what I was disappointed about was the way she said, "No, I didn't say I wanted us back together." Something like this happened once before, when I was really making an effort, and there was also a lot of strain over the whole relationship with Renate, and then I said yes, and she said (Making disparaging gestures), "I don't care, I haven't decided anything yet." Naturally I was disappointed; who wouldn't be? She really could have refrained from doing that, but that's really like her. Why has she been pretending to me for months that she really wants us to be together; what bothers me is simply that. I've already said a couple of times that I can't keep up with her, the contradiction between what she says and how she behaves.

Th: I can imagine that you [Helga] are very much afraid of being hurt, and you [Stani] are afraid of being pressured, and now you face the difficult question: When you're living together again, how will you manage to keep yourselves sufficiently separate and not too close? I think that's the problem on both sides now. I imagine that scares you both quite a bit.

(Pause. Both partners stare pensively into space.)

Helga has issued Stani an ultimatum demanding that they resume their life together. Now, when Stani is ready to do this, she turns him down.

Helga and
Stani are
both afraid
of being
frustrated if
they involve
themselves in
any
obligatory
intimacy.
Thus they
must destroy
every attempt
at intimacy
from the
outset.

H: Obviously that's frightening. I mean I know my relationship with her and my own situation. I know that I have too little feeling for her to begin with and that I'm not sure whether I can change that unless she helps somehow.

Th: And can you say how she could help you?

H: I've already said a couple of times that she'd have to try not to deliberately drive me away by her behavior. She knows what kinds of things drive me away, and she does them all the same.

Th: Mmm–hmm.

Th: (To wife) Are you aware of this?

W: Yes.

H: It's the same thing today. She realized she's mad and in a bad mood; fine, that's true. And she said, "I feel rotten," and I thought, "Okay." But then along come these continual gibes. I don't understand why you do that; you know what it gets you.

W: Yes, maybe that's what I want it to get me.

H: But then you can't at the same time expect my relationship with you to get better.

W: Yes, you know, that business of what you like, the behavior you expect, always seems to me like a child just before Christmas promising: "If you're nice and sweet and kind to me for a long, long time, maybe I can love you too." That behavior of yours always seems to me as if you were insisting on having everything just exactly the way you want it. But suppose something happens that *I* don't like? That's the way I see it.

(Again the husband is sitting half turned away from the wife, his hand protectively on his cheek)

W: Then I react defiantly, and say "No, I don't like that."

Th: I imagine that you reject him out of fear that he may reject you.

W: Yes, naturally, the fact that I quickly push him away like this (She makes a shoving gesture), that's the same old game, that I'm nasty as a preventive measure; sure it's true.

Th: Perhaps also in order to set limits to your own expectations?

W: Yes, yes, that's right.

The partners have made progress in that each of them is better able to describe how sensitive and vulnerable he is and what behavior on the part of the other partner provokes him to destructive reactions. On the surface it is easy to understand that if Helga does not feel a more decisive response from Stani, she would prefer to give him up entirely. But as therapy reveals at many points, Helga repeatedly sabotages any attempt by Stani to get closer to her because each such attempt makes her fear the overblown hopes it arouses, which sooner or later are frustrated in terms of her expectations. So she takes preventive measures, behaving in such a way that all Stani's overtures are nipped in the bud. Now when he makes advances, she no longer wants to commit herself. This seesaw phenomenon in which one partner suddenly adopts the same behavior he had fought in the other the moment the other partner gives it up is often observed during the therapeutic treatment of collusion. It is inappropriate for a therapist to feel satisfaction at the fact that Helga, who had hitherto continually persecuted Stani with her demands, reacts in the same defensive and anxious way as he when she is offered a chance of intimacy. It is easy to claim, in this case, that one partner is only acting as a representative of the other's resistance. For me, the most important thing is to show the couple that although they appear to be behaving in directly opposite ways, their behavior is linked by a basic problem common to them both. What the two partners have in common in this case is the fear of frustration they feel the moment the symbiosis they desire could conceivably come to pass.

H: (With strong emotion) I feel in any case that you don't understand me. I can't stand that now, it makes no sense any more for me to try to explain why I'm reacting this way. Then you'd just say, "Yes, I understand that, but . . ." Then let's just leave it as it is.

W: You feel I don't understand you. Why?

H: Because of your reactions. I can tell you exactly. You felt oppressed, you complained about my lack of tenderness, sexually there was a problem, and so you put on a big show, pure and simple.

W: Why do you feel you're not understood?

H: Because you keep attacking me.

W: That's a clear reaction, I don't . . . I can't understand why you feel you're not understood. Maybe *you* can understand that that hurts.

H: I can, but—

W: But why do you feel now that you're not understood?

H: Now you're saying that in such an objective tone, but when we talk about it alone, you say (He gesticulates and shouts with theatrical exaggeration), "And you've had other women, and now I want sex too," and I don't know—

(Wife tries to contradict him)

Here you react completely differently; you control yourself in front of Mr. Willi.

W: So do you.

H: No, I don't think I do.

W: Oh yes you do. First of all, here you have to listen to me sometimes; second, you don't yell at me, and—what was the other thing?—don't interrupt me—and, I've already said this in therapy, if Stani had a girlfriend now and then, I could easily understand it, but . . . That hurt me, and that's my problem, that when I was hurt I retaliated. In theory I can understand you very well, but I just got fed up. I understand your reaction all right, but it simply hurt me, and that's why I get mad. I don't know whether that behavior is so hard to understand.

H: But we don't get anywhere this way. Fine, you gave me a final date with time to think it over, and I've tried for a whole month to get close to you. Do you think anything's happened during this month? Absolutely nothing. It's exactly the same as it was three months ago, always throwing the past in my face, always destroying anything that might develop between us. Under these circumstances I'm simply scared of getting to June 1. That's why I asked you if we couldn't do the sensible thing and and talk about what we're feeling right now. I can't understand why you don't see that. And if I can't get closer to you again this way, then we'd better call it quits.

W: I haven't noticed that you wanted to get closer to me.

H: Yes—uh, then why are we talking? Why am I trying to get back together with you?

W: Yes, Stani, you wanted to get closer to me, that about getting closer, all right, *I'm trying to keep you at a distance because I'm afraid of your being close.*

H: Yes, exactly, that's just what I mean.

Th: It seems to me so important that both of you talk about the fears you have of getting closer, each of you from his point of view.

H: What each of us is experiencing right now.

W: You always accuse me of not talking about my fears. Now I'm going to take a tape and record what I say. It just isn't true. I do talk about my fears—after all they're obvious.

Th: I imagine that it would be easier for Stani if you talked about your fears rather than aggressively attacking him.

W: Yes, it's clear to me too that that isn't the best . . . that that's inappropriate behavior.

Th: But maybe it's not so easy after all to talk about your own fears instead of reacting to Stani.

W: (Raptly, to herself) I think I have one single great fear—my fear is simply that I won't be accepted. That's my really big fear. All right. Now I should tell myself that if I have such a big fear, I should try to be a bit nicer. I've already tried that, but I'm also afraid of being nice, because even when I want God-knows-what-all, Stani immediately gets the feeling: Oh God, oh God, now she's being nice, now she wants something again. Those are Stani's fears, which play a role in mine. Even back then when we slept together, I really didn't have grand expectations, I didn't think, "Now he thinks I'm terrific." I was really glad about it and joked about it and thought, "Things are all right, it's really just fine." I didn't have any grand expectations. I didn't think, "How lovely, now he loves me again." Nothing of that kind. It made me feel so free. And afterwards came this disappointment. I felt good after we slept together, I felt good because I was able to react with such moderation. That made me feel free. "Now you've moved a step forward," I thought to myself. And afterwards it was all gone again and everything was the way it had always been. Basically I'm really quite realistic and don't have any grand expectations. Of course I'm spontaneous with him. I may be cheerful, but there's nothing more behind it. And then right away he thinks, "Oh God, oh God"! (She imitates Stani's defensive gesture)

Both partners can now admit their fears of intimacy much more directly.

Th: You said, "It's so important to me whether or not I'm accepted." For you this is an either-or situation?

W: No, I don't think so, but—if at least he'd accept three-quarters of me or two-thirds.

Th: Or maybe one-tenth. Let's start with one-tenth.

W: Start with one-tenth and then wait to see whether some time it might get to be five-tenths?

Th: Without waiting for anything. Just accepting it's one-tenth.

W: One-tenth is simply not enough for me in a partnership. It doesn't work.

Th: He's talking in terms of small steps, and I have the impression that if you make it "either-or," he'll make it "neither-nor."

H: I've already said a couple of times that I find this extreme way of doing things very hard to put up with.

W: But if I have no hope of our being able to live on at least five-tenths, I say no. One-tenth isn't enough for me; that's not "either-or," but what I'm saying is that no, one-tenth is not enough for a relationship. And if I can't expect and hope for five-tenths, somehow that's—

H: And why don't you have this hope?

W: For five-tenths? Because I'm afraid that the thing has at most two-tenths to give. That has nothing to do with "either-or," but even the AHV [old age and survivors' insurance] gives you the minimum you need to survive, you know. (To the therapist) I wouldn't want to go on living with Stani any more, given what he feels for me now.

Th: What does he feel for you, actually?

W: (Musing to herself) Not much.

Th: How do you know that?

W: Because he's told me. "There's not enough there, there might be something more later on, but I don't feel anything for you at all as a woman." No, it's true, he did say once, "Yes, maybe it's not so bad"—of course we were in the dark when he said it. (She laughs, impishly) But (Now fighting back tears)—I have Peter, who thinks I'm pretty and attractive (Coquettish gestures), and then I say, "You can go to the devil!" That's my reaction, then I use Peter. It's a lot more pleasant too if you can be with a man who finds you attractive.

The two have come closer to meeting half-way. The wife, who at the beginning of therapy pursued the husband with her demands for absolute love, thus putting him on the defensive, now perceives her own fears of intimacy, whereas the husband is better able to express his own need for closeness to his wife and can show more emotion in his demand that she give him a loving response.

Twenty-Fifth Session, April 23

Synopsis
The collusion is gradually being disentwined. Both partners are less reactive to each other's behavior and, to an increasing degree, perceive the disorders in their relationship as manifestations of their personal problems. They both recognize their tendency, based on narcissism, to react to their partner's failure to live up to their expectations with feelings of deep hurt and a need, in turn, to hurt the other partner. Both are also suffering from their fear of the pointlessness of working to get closer and beginning to place their hopes in the relationship again. Both find it difficult to accept their partner's loving feelings. Each reacts defensively as soon as the other tries to get one step closer. Stani now perceives more clearly that the demand that he accept Helga one hundred percent stems not only from her but also from himself. His pain at being unable to live up to this ideal makes him react with feelings of guilt and hurtful behavior towards Helga. The partners have now found a strong bond in their common problems. Stani recognizes that he not only rejects but also envies and admires Helga for her spontaneity and emotional ebullience.

Stani tells about a new job prospect as a science teacher in a girls' boarding school. He feels uncertain whether he ought to take this post and move to the school with his family. He is, to be sure, aware of the danger that he might become involved in relationships with the young girls. Helga replies that she refuses to go along with the situation if it means having to compete with women who weigh less than a hundred pounds. She cannot live with him, she says, if she would have to live in continual uncertainty about whether he was deceiving her and lying to her.

W: Even if I don't keep an eye on him, just the feeling, the fear is still there, and if he comes home and I think, "Oh God, I'm losing him," then I just can't manage to be friendly to him. If there's an occasional fling, I don't want to know about it; that would still be okay.

Th: But there's simply no foundation for trust.

W: Yes.

Th: (To husband) And that's true on both sides. Basically you don't believe her either.

H: Yes, maybe less where fidelity's concerned.

Th: But where being loved is concerned?

H: Yes, I always see the same problem in me as in her: I don't want to tie myself down; I'm afraid of really tying myself down. I don't know why I have this fear. It's the same kind of tendency she has.

Th: Yes, but in part it's for the same reason as with her, namely the fear of being betrayed.

Now Stani can articulate better how he too is always afraid that his expectations may be disappointed by his partner.

H: With my other relationships too I've always taken a lot of care not to get hemmed in too much, not to get tied down; that might still be playing a big role in her mind.

Th: No doubt there are several reasons, but perhaps you see that it has to do with trust. There's a fear when one becomes too involved; one suddenly feels betrayed because the other person doesn't feel what one expected him to.

H: It's not so much that. It's more the thought that she doesn't give me what I want, what I expect. That I'll be disappointed in this sense and lose hope that we really suit each other. It's not so much that she'd cheat on me with other men. Of course, now and then that occurs to me too.

Th: It's more the feeling that you're not loved the way you expect to be loved?

H: Yes, more that.

The husband's share of the collusion can now be sifted out. He no longer experiences his problems in his relationship with Helga as a reaction to the way she badgers him, but rather as something grounded in his own nature. His problem is the same narcissism that Helga talked about during the first interview, namely the fact that his partner disappoints and hurts him by not thinking, feeling and being what he expects.

Th: Mmm-hmm—I think it's important for you to accept that that's a problem you both have in common. You're both hypersensitive, you're both troubled by the question: Does my partner really accept me or am I running the risk of getting overly involved and then being left alone, disappointed and betrayed? Maybe the thing is to accept that this is a problem you have in common. The question is, What's the most effective way for you to deal with this problem together? Now each of you is fighting it is on his own. But it's a problem you both share.

H: I was trying to say that that's something that doesn't just have to do with her, but that I have the same problems with other relationships.

Th: I think that both of you have the same problem in other relationships, whenever you get close to someone. (Silence)

(Wife looks questioningly at husband)

H: (To therapist) What do you think are the possibilities?

Th: I'm not thinking in terms of an external solution, but rather what we can agree on so that our mutual fear and suspicion will be reduced as much as possible. (Silence)

(Both are pensive)

W: (Sighs) I think the precondition would be that we accept each other as we are, as far as that's possible. I believe that would be an essential part of it.

Th: Yes, but for you that's just the problem: When one of you tries to accept the other, the other nevertheless feels that he isn't really being accepted.

(Both are silent. The wife looks inquiringly at the husband again. The husband holds his hand protectively in front of his face.)

H: (To therapist) Do you see any possibility that we could change that?

(The mood is one of reflection and, to some extent, perplexity.)

W: I believe we've already made considerable progress just to see that we share the same problem. It creates a common foundation when one can think, "Oh God, my partner has had just as rough a time over that as I have!" That's a very important basic thing we share.

The partners have in common the fear of not being really accepted by their partner and of being at a disadvantage if they commit themselves to a relationship.

222 Dynamics of Couples Therapy

Both partners see that the problem of being accepted is not so much caused by their partner as by their personal difficulties. The fact that they both share this problem creates a bond between them.

H: Yes, recently we've become pretty aware of the fact that basically we're very much alike in our fear of being disappointed.

W: But somehow I feel that all the same I'm a little more at a disadvantage. Maybe you feel that too. Because I still suffer over it. It's the same with the acceptance thing. If I tell myself, "Deep down he doesn't really accept me," still I also keep asking myself, "Why are you always worrying about being accepted?" I know now that Stani has fears, and I have fears too. Then I tell myself, "But you mustn't have any fears." *The fears are there. Even if you told me ten times over, "I think you're pretty and I like you," I still wouldn't believe it.* Even if you'd say, "Yes, I find you attractive" (She smiles in a somewhat embarrassed way, asking her husband and the therapist for confirmation), inside I'd think, "Sure, but— he finds others a hundred times more attractive."

H: *Everything you've said about yourself, I think the same thing applies to me.*

W: Yes, exactly, but then one feels it's completely unjustified when the other person feels that way. We weren't so aware of that before. Especially since we didn't try to do anything about it. Each of us thought, "He is much better off and I'm the one who's getting the raw deal."

We have arrived at a central point in collusion therapy when the two partners discover that their joint problem gives them a common foundation for their lives, namely the hope of being able to help each other overcome their problem. But Helga's hope of obtaining some kind of validation from Stani is already causing him to behave as he did in the past by backing away from her.

H: Now you're talking about your experience, not mine. I honestly have to say that I've never thought that, because I've always had the feeling you like me more than I like you, at least recently.

(Wife is clearly frustrated, hangs her head) (Pause)

W: (Subdued) All right, now I've explained how it is from my side.

Th: We've often talked about the fact that you share the same problems. But perhaps it would be something new if we were to ask, "What's the best way for us to work together to solve these problems?"

H: What's the best way for us to do that together? But part of that would be for us to draw up an inventory, so that neither of us thinks the other is, God knows, far removed from him in some respect. So that each of us is completely filled in on where the other stands.

Th: Yes.

H: That would be part of it.

W: I'd like to add the stipulation that each of us should tell the other where he stands on an issue only when he knows this himself and then says it.

H: But often one can't tell where one stands until somebody demands that he take a position.

The husband's remarks are unexpected and startling. He, who hitherto had always avoided taking any position and never wanted to commit himself to anything, is now pleading that both partners should be challenged to take a stand. The wife questions whether this requirement is realistic. In this area too the two partners have exchanged positions since the beginning of therapy.

H: Naturally it's hard, but the more one talks it over and the more one is required to take a stand, the more clearly one can unravel what one feels.

W: Yes, of course, it's true that one can formulate things more clearly when one is forced to, but naturally there's also the problem that he may—that to avoid a certain situation, he may decide not to be completely honest.

H: (Gravely and emphatically) But that's my main problem.

(Wife sighs)

The question is, To what extent is it a problem for *you*?

W: I'm afraid that then I wouldn't tell you everything, so I could avoid getting hurt. (Makes gestures indicating that she is putting distance between them) Can we really do that, get to the point of telling each other these things, and do we really want to know exactly where the other stands?

Th: (To wife) I just now had the feeling you were a bit hurt when he said that the love was mostly on your side.

Both freely and openly confess the defense mechanisms they use with their partner in order to avoid getting hurt.

W: (Moves her head as if she were pondering) Yes, that's true.

Th: Yes, I can easily understand that.

H: But that's something I've had happen to me over and over, that when you approach me I can't react the way I really ought to. But besides that I couldn't ever say, "I'm really fond of you," because you don't accept it when I show you signs of affection. You always pooh-pooh it as if what I feel for you were nothing at all.

It is becoming increasingly clear to both partners that they have the same problem accepting the other's feelings of love. The husband continually hurts the wife by rejecting her offers of love, but the wife also destroys any expression of affection from her husband by disparaging it and crushing it before it has a chance to develop. The husband now seems clearly determined to stop behaving purely defensively towards his wife and, instead, to learn to perceive and communicate his feelings for her more effectively.

W: But that came up in one of the last therapy sessions. You said you don't dare show your feelings for me because you're afraid they'd always hurt me. And then I said that naturally I didn't think it was exactly charming that your feelings for me always have to be the kind that would hurt me. And then you claimed you didn't say that.

(A violent quarrel develops over whether Stani did or did not say this, and I am called on to act as judge)

H: But look, everything hurts you unless I'm for you one hundred percent. This way, you can't help being always hurt. The only thing that doesn't hurt you is if every bit of me is there for you.

W: No, that's not true.

H: Fine, that's the way it seems to me.

W: It's really not so.

Th: (To wife) What was it that he said just now?

W: He said, "Everything hurts you, the only thing that doesn't hurt you is if I'm one hundred percent there for you."

Th: ". . . That's the way it seems to me."

W: Aha—

Each partner invariably reacts with hypersensitivity and defensiveness when the other tries to get close. Now, when the husband wants them to work at accepting each other more, the wife becomes afraid she may hear things that are only negative. This time the husband vehemently resists this imputation. To be sure, he does not say that he has positive feelings for his wife, but he unequivocally resists the notion that his feelings are purely negative.

Th: (To wife) It seems to me so important that you try to accept that this is simply the way he feels.

W: Fine, but once I've said, "Fine, I can accept that, that's the way he feels now," what am I supposed to do? I can't accept it one hundred percent—I have my limitations—I can accept it only seventy percent or fifty percent, and one feels it's all pointless.

H: I'm not saying that, I've never said it's pointless, not even back when I loved you zero percent.

Th: (To wife) My impression is that he senses your demand that he affirm you one hundred percent, and so he believes, "I can never fulfill her expectations, so it won't work anyway." And so it probably isn't any use for you to say, "That's not how I mean it." I believe that's simply the way he is, that's his problem, which causes him to react as he does, which may also cause him to hurt you because he has the feeling that he can never fulfill your demand [for one hundred percent acceptance].

W: Yes, I can try to accept that my expectations scare him, and I should try to lower my expectations.

Th: (To wife) Can you see that it may be these very expectations that drive him to hurt you so?

W: Yes, I understand that, absolutely. But it hurts me all the same. I can say to myself ten times over, "Stani reacts in such-and-such a way." But it hurts me all the same. That's the bad thing about it. Maybe the hurt is a bit less painful and doesn't last as long, but at that particular moment it hurts.

Th: I think that's already accomplishing a lot to be able to perceive the hurt so clearly and also to be able to express it.

Helga can understand Stani's limited ability to form relationships, but she cannot put up with it.

Step by step the collusion is unravelled. If Helga would stop demanding one hundred percent acceptance, Stani's defensiveness would cease to appear to be merely a reaction to her demands. Then it would become clearer to what extent his behavior is the result of his own problems, of the ideal that a man should be able to accept his wife without reservation; and to what extent he experiences guilt feelings as a result of his failure to live up to this self-imposed ideal and then is driven by these guilt feelings to hurt his wife. This question was treated in other sessions.

The course of therapy has resulted in the partners' improved ability to be aware of their feelings, needs and expectations and to communicate these to each other. Although the problems in their personal relationship have not been eliminated, much has been achieved towards enabling the couple to accept themselves and each other as people who have problems, so that they are less inclined to reinforce the problems by reacting to each other as they did before. The goal of this couples therapy is modest but concrete: The couple should come to understand each other's limitations and find in the awareness of their limitations a special kind of bond and love.

> W: I always have the feeling that I have to protect myself against you. I never have the feeling that you accept me as I am. I don't feel at all free in your presence.
> H: Yes, no doubt that's why you try to hurt me.
> Th: (To wife) In what sense do you feel unfree?
> W: In the sense that I'm continually thinking, "He doesn't like that." Of course I go ahead and do it anyway, but not spontaneously. I thought that just last weekend, "If Stani is there I can't show it if I'm feeling happy." Then I can't stop thinking, "That grates on his nerves. Calm down and don't shout so."
> (Helga then tells about the weekend she and Stani spent together in the mountains. There had been a deep snowfall. She was standing at the top of the hill with the skis. She let out a whoop of joy and plopped into the snow. He was standing down below. Perhaps she was a bit afraid too. She no longer knew exactly. Stani laughs, looking affectionately at Helga.)
> W: All the same I thought it was beautiful, and he said, "Come on down and don't shout so." It's just that I had fun plopping down into the snow. It's just that when I'm enjoying myself, I don't like to show it any more if Stani's there. I feel constrained. Often I do what I want

anyhow, but I don't have the same experience and feel the same pleasure. I'm much better at showing aggression.

H: That's true. Often I find it's just too much for me, and I think that I might be *jealous* that she's capable of that and I'm not.

W: (To husband) Strange, that's what I thought, "Maybe *Stani's envious because he can't feel this way too.*"

H: It's not that I can't feel it, I can too feel it, but *I can't express it that way. Possibly it is a kind of jealousy.*

Th: That seems to me an important discovery, because up to now you've always said that you just don't like her way of expressing things. But basically you wish you were that way yourself . . .

H: It just occurred to me that I may be jealous. In certain situations I can bubble with joy the way she does, and express it, but not in her presence, probably because I think, "She's thinking, 'That's a pretty sorry attempt he's making to show his feelings.' " It could be a kind of jealousy, my thinking that no matter what I do she's better at it than I am. Of course to some extent I really do dislike her ebullience; for example, when we're with other people and I think they may be thinking she's just being idiotic.

Th: You regret you can't show your feelings so freely?

H: Yes, and I'm scared that in her presence I can never learn how, and that then I'll show more [negative] reactions again because I feel stifled by her.

Th: You have the feeling you could never keep pace with her where showing feelings is concerned?

H: Yes, in that respect she's always way above me (Looks at the ceiling), and it bothers me that she's always so far above me.

Th: Perhaps it's important for Helga to see that her exuberance is something you don't merely reject, but also admire in her.

H: Yes, occasionally I've said that *I like and admire her spontaneity and I don't simply resent it. The rejection I do feel may stem from the fact that I'm not as good at that as she is.* If pleasure is spontaneous, I admire it. There are various reasons why it bothers me when she's so loud and

Helga feels that her spontaneity is inhibited by Stani's presence. Stani says that not only does he not reject Helga's exuberance, he actually admires and envies it. Stani thinks this could be related to the fact that he no longer needs her as a mother-substitute and she has trouble accepting this.

drowns out everything else—I don't know exactly. There
may be a bit of jealousy. She stifles me because then I
don't have any chance of getting a word in edgewise. But
her spontaneous behavior around the kids or her women
friends, or when she gets presents—that's more what I
admire in her.

Th: Yes, and maybe you'd even regret it if she didn't
have that quality any more.

H: *Yes, that's true, even now I miss that quality in
Renate, I regret that, roughly speaking, she's more like
me.* She feels things too, but she doesn't have a chance to
show it. I sometimes envy Helga that.

Stani's relationship with Renate is less stressful because she is more
like him than Helga is, but apparently it is also less fulfilling because she
seems not to complement him in those areas in which he views himself as
incomplete. The question arises, To what extent is his girlfriend's function
to provide a safety zone (now no longer necessary) whereby he can feel less
pressured by Helga?

Twenty-Seventh Session, May 15

Synopsis
*Helga has become increasingly desperate and depressed in therapy. She
finds it difficult to give up her absolute demands on a love relationship and
feels she cannot live up to the ideal of being more herself and of not allowing
all her feelings and aspirations to be governed by Stani. Stani feels
responsible for her survival, for her very existence, which causes him guilt
and fear. He demands that she be herself more and simply accept the fact
that if she is, many things about her will annoy him.*

Helga is   W: (Long sigh) I don't know whether I'll ever be able
depressed   to build a normal relationship with Stani. The way I
and out   behave— (Bursts into tears) I'm just having a stupid day
of it.   today—

               H: I think one factor involved is a mother-son
               relationship. At the beginning I was looking for a
               mother-substitute, and you accepted the role. It suited
               your expectations. I severed the mother-son relationship,
               and you're having trouble finding another role for

yourself. You think there's no other possible kind of relationship.

W: I didn't feel that way about it at all.

H: You treated me like a child, you determined my life; now I've separated from you exactly the way a son frees himself from his mother, and then the mother has lost the relationship and has problems.

W: You look for a mother in every woman.

H: That's part of every choice of a marriage partner. I never experienced our relationship as exclusively a mother-son relationship, but in any case it suited your nature.

Th: (To wife) In our second session, a year ago, you talked about the way he grew up.

W: . . . When I was reacting with pity and he said it hadn't been so bad.

Th: Yes. Back then I felt that there was a mother-son relationship on both sides. That is why you took his part like a good mother.

W: I know what you mean. Stani thought it wasn't so bad, and I started crying.

Th: (To husband) You were frustrated growing up and hoped to find a mother in Helga. You, Helga, accepted this role, and it's meant a lot to you too.

W: That's been over for two years.

H: That's also when our problems began.

W: This mother-son relationship stopped when I had my own children, for purely functional reasons.

Th: (To husband) How did you feel about having children of your own?

H: It made me very happy because it confirmed my feeling that I was grown up.

Th: Afterwards did you have to share Helga with the children?

H: No, I wasn't jealous of the children. After all, Helga didn't devote all her time to the children. When I lost her as a mother, I wasn't so crazy about the woman any more, and the problems began.

W: And you looked for a new mother in Susanne.

H: Quite possibly.

Th: Were you afraid that Helga, as a mother, might be taken away from you?

Stani's fear
of forming
ties is related
to the loss
of his
mother in
childhood, a
loss that he
transfers to
Helga and
his girlfriends
now that he
is an adult.

H:　　That could well be. I didn't see that so clearly before.

Th:　　Were you afraid of *losing your mother*—that she might die?

H:　　*Not die, but be lost.* My family and home might well be related to the mother role.

Th:　　Are you afraid of forming a close bond and then losing it again?

H:　　*I imagine it's fear of getting too used to something.* In the past I retreated from any close bond, and maybe that's also why I find it hard to break off relationships once they've formed.

W:　　You're not scared of losing me as Helga, but afraid of something ending?

H:　　It's burdensome for me that your decisions depend so much on me.

W:　　I've already told you I'd really like to be with you, but the problems are too big, so I don't want it any more. A definitive separation would be better. Then it would be easier for me to have some peace.

The striking thing is the change of atmosphere between this session and the second session, when the mother-son aspect of the relationship also came under discussion. In the second session Helga, as seen on the videotape, impressed one as the great bountiful mother, and Stani was the child she was tending; whereas now Helga is sitting there looking desperate and defiant like a lost child, but Stani speaks to her in a maternal voice full of fond concern. In losing her maternal function Helga lost a mainstay of her relationship with Stani. Without this function, which lent her stability and fortified her self-esteem, she fears that she may no longer be able to claim equality with Stani. She finds it hard to believe that she still means a lot to him even though she no longer completely fills his life and is no longer the foundation of his existence, and he is able to think, feel, and speak more independently.

Th:　　(To husband) I've repeatedly been struck by the fact that when Helga says she wants a divorce, you are much more affectionate to her.

H:　　When it gets final I'm afraid. Otherwise I don't have such a need to be with her.

Th:　　Helga gets the most affection when she doesn't want it any more.

W: We've played that game for years.

H: But now we're playing it without getting hurt.

W: In the past I often said I didn't want you, because then you wanted me. That bores me now.

Th: That shows how much you take your cues from each other. Probably it would be better if each of you could behave more as you really feel, and not simply react to your partner's behavior.

H: You always say, "When do you think it's time?" Why do you make it all depend on me? For once I'll ask, "When do *you* think it's time [to get back together]?"

W: I think I'd be better able to do that now.

Th: It might be easier for him if you also behaved in a more clear-cut way. When would be a good time for you?

W: I don't want to any more— (Bursts into tears). Of course I'm scared of a definite separation too. But I can't go on, I don't care whether or not I go on making the same mistakes in my relationships as I do with him. I'd just finally like to get some peace and settle down.

As soon as Helga tries to move away from Stani or leave him, he moves towards her again. He is afraid of ties and of a final separation.

Stani is not as alienated from Helga as he pretends. He becomes frightened whenever he sees that she is not in the background waiting for him. This behavior provokes Helga to play a game of intimacy-vs.-separation in which the more resolutely Helga threatens divorce, the more affection she gets. Helga is finding this situation increasingly unbearable. In the following sessions she asks Stani to move his things from their apartment. She wants to get him out of the apartment and thus out of herself. His belongings flaunt his presence and make it impossible for her to discover her independence and to give up taking her cues from him. Then Helga makes a rather forced effort to withdraw and stop exercising pressure on Stani. Stani disparages this effort, saying that her self-control is not sincere and that Helga ought to behave as she really is. Helga replies, "If I don't behave as I feel, I'm not myself; but if I feel aggressive and behave that way, then I'm not accepted." Stani replies, *"Be the way you are; then I can say what it is that bothers me. Allow me to be annoyed without always immediately reacting to me."* Helga says, *"All right, then I'll be 'me' without regard for the consequences."* Stani demands that she define herself and accept it when he does so and that they must live with the resultant friction as two separate but close individuals. But he also admits that it would be hard on him if Helga did not keep the relationship suspenseful, for he finds this stimulating and is afraid that a relationship might become pedestrian and boring and so fall apart. Thus when Helga behaves aggressively towards Stani, she is fulfilling his deeper expectations, although on the surface he is annoyed by her behavior.

Thirty-First Session, August 28

Synopsis
Today, after a two-month holiday break, Helga reveals her decision to finally go through with a divorce. She has, she says, given up hope that Stani will ever really be capable of a closer relationship. Granted, she can understand Stani better now, but she does not have any desire to perpetuate this unsatisfactory situation. I am disconcerted and disappointed by this decision. Stani regards Helga's decision as an overreactive act of will. Helga seems tense and desperate. Over the holidays she has made progress in standing on her own feet. She expresses the intention to separate from Peter too, because he is a good deal younger than she and still very childish and submissive, almost slavish. She has, she says, met with her former fiancé, who told her that in the old days he had felt oppressed by her strong personality. Helga recognizes one of her problems: When she cannot feel a man is weaker than she, she feels threatened and behaves aggressively in order to feel more secure. She would like to get into new relationships in order to find out which kinds of men suit her and what are the areas in which she can still make contact with other people. At least, in regard to other relationships, her demands are now very modest. A crisis has also arisen in Stani's relationship with Renate. We try to take stock of the therapy. Helga had expected that they would emerge from therapy a happy couple. I am not satisfied with the results either. To be sure, both partners have learned better how to recognize their deeper feelings and problems and to communicate them to each other. But I still regret very much that this couple, whom I like, are now going to go their separate ways. In the last few sessions Stani showed more clearly his deep attachment to Helga and how he wants to claim her undivided attention the way a child claims that of his mother. On the other hand, he fears that he may become too dependent on her and be unable to mature if he is with her.

This is the first, and also the last, session after a two-month summer break.

Helga wants a final separation.	Th: How did you feel coming here?
	W: I thought, "Oh dear, now we're starting all over again from the beginning." However, for now, I'm no longer afraid.

Th: But do you still have certain expectations?

W: No, I don't have any more expectations, I'm not motivated for therapy. *Now I've decided I'd like a divorce.* He says he doesn't know what he'll do professionally and personally. I don't know whether he'll go on being so ambivalent, but I know that I don't want to be part of it any more; I'm no longer willing to work at our relationship.

Th: Yes— (Turning to Stani) And you?

H: I'd like to try it; I still feel hopeful that we could have a better relationship and could get closer to each other. I have the feeling we understand each other better and that even if it doesn't last, sometimes we're closer. At least that's the direction things are heading, and I think that one day things could develop to the point that I'll want to live with her.

W: I believe things went well during the holidays because I no longer placed the slightest demand on Stani. I didn't ask him to say I was pretty or tell me he liked me and—in fact I didn't ask anything. But all in all I don't want a relationship in which I have to do without those things. If I have a relationship with a man, I want him to like me and accept me; I'm not willing to give that up. The only reason it went well is because I was able to tell myself, "Well, if he likes me that's fine, and if not, then he's simply not interested." But in the long run I can't do that. I ask myself, coldheartedly, "What will I get out of staying with Stani? Financial advantages?—social advantages?—because of the fact that I have a husband and the children will have a father who cares for them . . . But then he could do that anyhow. I don't want to spend any more time thinking, "Maybe someday it'll come." I know now that I can live alone, and I don't want to wait two more years to see whether maybe you can do it too.

Th: (To husband) (Disappointed, a bit annoyed, in a sharp voice) Can you understand that? (Passing the buck to Stani)

H: Yes, she's saying now that she's broken free, but to me it seems forced, and now she wants to destroy what we've built up. That's also why she doesn't want us to stay on friendly terms afterwards.

Helga does not want to settle for half-measures.

Th: (To wife) (Somewhat more composed) My impression is that you've thought a lot about this before making up your mind, but that it's still hurting you a lot.

W: (Sits with hunched-up shoulders, seems very tense) You [Stani] always gloat so and rub my nose in the fact that, on the one hand, I want a divorce and, on the other, I am still always at your beck and call. But this isn't an attempt to pressure you. It's not an act of coercion.

Th: More of a slow-developing, painful decision.

W: At first more a liberation, but now it's already beginning to hurt— (Fighting back tears) But— (Stani gives Helga a troubled look).

Th: In what way do you think it's forced?

H: Not forced, but that at bottom she doesn't really want it at all.

W: (Shakes her head thoughtfully)

Th: As far as I'm concerned, I feel her decision isn't at all an attempt to pressure anyone, but that she's serious about it.

Stani fears the finality of separation.

H: I feel too that it isn't an attempt to pressure me. But I can't understand why we can't go on being good friends.

W: But we can.

H: No, you've always said just the opposite, that you want to break off the relationship completely. That scares me, I'm afraid of finalities.

Th: For a long time in therapy it seemed that you had a hard time taking a clear-cut position because you felt pressured by Helga. Now, when you no longer feel pressured, you're still having a hard time taking a clear-cut position. No doubt that's putting a strain on Helga, and on you too, on both of you.

H: Yes, no doubt. It's just that I have a hard time making decisions and adjusting to anything conclusive.

Th: (To wife) How do you see that quality in him?

W: Often I think he could take a stand, but sometimes— On the whole that's his main problem, but at least he could make decisions on a small scale. (Cites an example of a weekend that they had planned to spend together, but Stani could not make up his mind to go

through with it until the last minute) At least in small
matters he ought to stick to his decisions.

The atmosphere is tense. The wife seems tense, as if she were finding
it hard to go through with her decision. The husband seems irresolute. He
is finding it hard to ask the wife to take back her decision. Although he
says nothing, it is clear how lost he would feel without the relationship
with his wife. I too feel hurt by the wife's declared intention to get a
divorce. I wonder whether Helga's decision is the result of my inability to
show more empathy with her despair. For this reason I ask her:

Th: (To wife) Do you feel that your decision is a
personal liberation, or do you have the feeling that in the
course of the therapy something in you was destroyed?
W: No, at this moment it's definitely a liberation. *Helga feels*
That became very clear to me during the holidays. The *that a*
important thing isn't the presence of one's partner, but *definitive*
whether or not one can be certain of his loyalty. It's also *separation*
become clear to me that I'll probably break off with Peter *brings a*
too. Now I can live alone very well. Over the holidays I *sense of*
met someone else and found I liked being able to form *liberation.*
other relationships and really find out the areas in which
I can click with someone else.
Th: Do you feel that you no longer place such absolute
demands on a relationship?
W: Yes.
H: You could only do that because you knew that
Peter was waiting for you at home.
W: No, this is something new for me. This is some-
thing I wasn't able to feel before.

Compared with past sessions, Helga now seems considerably more
controlled, resolute and clearly defined. Stani is obviously unprepared for
this change in Helga and tries in every way he can to disparage it. As the
session proceeds, Stani accuses Helga of provoking him with her plans for
divorce in such a way that he feels compelled to defend himself. In
response to a question from me, Stani states that he would accept the
divorce if he thought Helga was doing the right thing from her point of
view. But from his vantage point, he says, things between them might get
better. We talk about whether Stani might get more help for his personal
problems from individual therapy, particularly from psychoanalysis.
Although he basically agrees that this is necessary, he is afraid that

analysis might upset him to such a degree that he would not be able to concentrate or continue work. First he must get a solid foothold in his profession. At the moment, however, he wonders if he ought to look for a job abroad. Helga mockingly expresses her regret, and *the two of them start squabbling again. Basically the mood is not hostile.* In general, the couple, especially Helga, are trying to draw up a balance-sheet.

Despite their plans for divorce, Helga and Stani have positive feelings about therapy.

Th: (To wife) If your therapy were to end in divorce now, what would you think about the therapy as a whole?

W: Actually I have very positive feelings about it. I believe I've been able, to a large extent, to get rid of my aggressive feelings towards Stani, which I couldn't do anything about in the past. I've been able to see that this is really the way Stani is, and I don't expect anything more; I feel this is a big gain. Without therapy I'd probably still be just where I was before; maybe it would even have become worse. I'd probably be much more disappointed than I was a year ago.

Th: (To husband) And you?

H: Actually I feel the same, mainly because I have the feeling that we have a new understanding of each other. We see better why it all happened and why we react the way we do. Now I really know what it's like for the two of us to feel sympathy and understanding for each other; in the past that wouldn't have been possible and it wouldn't have become possible without outside help.

W: I honestly have to confess that I expected something different when we entered therapy. I thought that the purpose of it was for us to come out a happy couple, even though we were told that its purpose was to clarify our relationship; but for long stretches I still went on hoping. In the end I'm not disappointed that things turned out this way, but for quite a long time that's what I expected of therapy; though in the end I didn't so much any more.

Nevertheless, Helga's voice holds a pronounced note of disappointment. Helga's comment when we discussed the manuscript was, "It was hard for me to say that without getting very emotional, because at that time it still hurt me a lot."

Although I did not express this directly, I too was disappointed by the outcome of the therapy. In theory I may not hold this view, but emotionally I generally feel dissatisfied when a therapy ends in divorce. I wonder to what extent I failed as a therapist. In this case I felt particularly strongly that—despite the fact that the couple's relationship was handicapped by deeply-rooted personality problems—it was a rich and valuable one. Although I found it hard to accept that divorce was the outcome of the therapy, I did not try to persuade the couple to stay together. I felt that I had failed rather than they. I wondered whether I had been unable to show the wife enough sympathy and understanding; whether her obtrusive manner had pressured me into adopting the same attitude as Stani; and whether her decision to get a divorce stemmed from disappointment, or even a desire to take vengeance for my destruction of her high standards for marriage. Several times I tried to talk with her about this. She said that my fears were groundless. Taking into account her efforts to maintain an idealized, conflict-free relationship with me, I wondered whether she did not feel compelled to deny that any conflict existed between us. Before this session I had asked our female psychologist, Therese Kohler, to re-test the couple with the Joint Rorschach Test because I was finding it difficult to determine my orientation towards the therapy as a whole. At the moment I was giving my full attention to the wife's intention to divorce, so that I was not in a position to see to what extent therapy might have achieved positive results in terms of the personality development of the two partners.

W: What were the results of the Joint Rorschach Test?

Th: Well, I was particularly concerned in your case. The test showed that communication between the two of you is substantially better and clearer than at the beginning of therapy, that you can work together better; but on the level of experience, you [Helga] show signs of resignation, apathy and anxiety. I'd be interested to know how you were feeling then [during the test].

W: I know I was feeling really bad when I started the test. It was shortly before the holidays. I was feeling pretty aggressive and had had a drink too, and thought that instead of identifying [a certain inkblot] as "butterfly," for once I'd say "evil vulture"; I was really mad. But I have the feeling that during the test that subsided; it may be that I felt resignation. Maybe in part that's still true.

The re-test of the Joint Rorschach Test shows a distinctly different diagnostic picture than at the beginning of therapy.

Th: But was that more in relation to Stani, or do you just in general have a feeling of resignation, apathy, forlornness?

The therapist tries to address his concern about Helga's emotional development in terms of a therapeutic collusion. Helga does not accept this.

W: (Pause) (She gazes reflectively into space) I don't know, I can't tell. (Pause) Maybe it's because of a certain apathy I felt that things went well between Stani and me, I don't know.

Th: I've been wondering, concerning the last few sessions, whether you had the impression that Stani and I had formed a kind of alliance.

W: Not really. I guess that from time to time there were always situations in which I had the feeling, "Now he's siding with Stani," but there were others when I felt, "Aha, now he's backing me up," but on the whole I didn't have that feeling.

Th: Mmm-hmm.

Th: (To husband) With you it's turned out—and of course this is a positive thing—that at the beginning of therapy there was an extreme polarization: Helga was all feeling and you [Stani] were the one who defended himself against feelings. When you [Helga] showed strong emotion, you [Stani] closed down, and even in the [first] test you didn't show you were relating to your feelings. And then you got much closer together, both approaching a middle ground, and you [Stani] were able to respond with considerably more emotion in the test. That would really seem to be a good sign. But in fact that may mean too that you don't need each other so much any more. Before, Helga acted out your feelings for you, the emotional part of you, so that you've made progress there, and now you aren't simply compelled to ward off your feelings, but also to experience them.

H: Yes, I think so too, and also that in many ways—in the personal area—I can make many decisions more easily. I think that's so too. (Pause)

For some time we go on talking about what will happen next. At the moment Helga does not feel motivated to undertake further therapy, but she cannot decide to terminate therapy either. Stani too anticipates nothing new to be gained from our weekly sessions. For this reason I suggest that we meet at longer intervals for some follow-up talks with the aim of carrying through the divorce in a constructive way that will not be damaging to the children, and will make it possible for both partners to grow from the crisis. We agree to have a follow-up talk in two months.

The Therapy Results as Reflected in the Joint Rorschach Test

For me as therapist it became increasingly difficult to keep my perspective about the course of the therapy. A therapist is in much the same boat as a parent who finds it more difficult to perceive changes in his growing children than an outsider who sees them less often and who is less personally involved with them. Moreover, therapy is a discontinuous process in which advances, again and again, are succeeded by setbacks, so that the therapist, as well as the patient, may easily be overcome by a feeling of disorientation and resignation. In this situation a test like the Joint Rorschach Test (*Willi*, 1973) can be of great assistance in providing supplementary information.

In the Joint Rorschach Test both partners perform the Rorschach Test, with the additional feature that they must agree on one interpretation of each of the ten inkblots. The formal elements of the couple's performance reveals the structure of their communication and their capacity for cooperation. But the peculiarity of the test is that interpretation of the couple's interpretations of the inkblots simultaneously reveals the character of their deeper emotional experience, their needs and fears and the individual and joint defense mechanisms they use to overcome them. As a rule we conduct the Joint Rorschach Test at the beginning of a therapy and towards the end. The results of a couples therapy can be judged by the following five criteria:

1. The structure of the partnership (the distribution of function according to economic or neurotic factors, anxiety-ridden role fixations, double-bind role expectations), the definition and openness of the system towards the outside world

2. Communication, processes of exchange

3. Cooperation (ability to function as a couple or family, problem-solving behavior)

4. Personality-development in the partnership, interdependent interactional personalities

5. Subjective satisfaction in the partnership

Criteria 1–4 can be determined and interpreted in an objectifiable and quantifiable form. The test and re-test of this couple has already been described in detail (*Willi*, 1976), so that here I would like to discuss only those findings that are important in the present therapy situation.

At the beginning of therapy the test reveals good cooperation between the couple in externals, which however was greatly disrupted in emotional situations. Often joint solutions could be arrived at only by the curtailment of individual differentiation. The partners showed little ability to enter into each other's feelings but attempted to hold on rigidly to their own fantasies vis-à-vis their partner. There was an extreme polarization in role behavior. The husband appeared emotionally constrained and formalistic, whereas the wife was expansive and had few personal resources for control and guidance. They had divided their functions so that the wife expressed the feelings and the husband brought her feelings under control. The wife attempted to assert her feelings vis-à-vis the husband by acting-out and manipulation, on the one hand idealizing and stylizing his masculinity, on the other, disparaging and tearing it down. The husband defended himself by disparaging her feelings. Nevertheless the husband, in his emotional experience, was stimulated and fascinated by the wife's uncontrolled behavior.

The test results show much more pronounced and positive changes than the therapist expected on the grounds of the present therapy situation.

At the end of therapy the quality of cooperation was much better, mainly because of the increased flexibility of the partners and their improved communication: Each is able to draw a clearer distinction between his own and the other's interpretations. To what extent can I adapt to you without losing myself? Which of your interpretations, although I may not find them ideal, are still acceptable to me? The husband is less rejecting in his judgments of the wife, and she no longer manipulates him or exerts pressure to the extent she did before. The partners have a clearer perception of each other as separate, autonomous individuals and have a better understanding of each other's deeper feelings. Both are better able to formulate their own feelings and views, to comprehend those of their partner, and to search objectively for constructive solutions. A particularly important finding is that the partners, who formerly were extremely polarized in their emotional processing of experience and in their emotional behavior, have drawn closer together. The husband can now perceive and express his feelings better. He seems more impulsive and more capable of relating. He exposes himself more readily to his fears. The wife, on the other hand, is less expansive and has lowered her demanding standards. She controls her feelings and her behavior better, without shocking and provoking her husband by theatrical acting-out. The husband feels less pressured by her and can restrain his defensive attitude and the rationalization and critical tendencies that go with it. However, the impression, derived from therapy, that the wife may have paid a high price for her renunciation of manipulation and expansive acting-out is confirmed by the re-test. The content of her interpretations is no longer characterized by "phallic and castrating" rivalry, but is more depressive and anxiety-ridden. To be sure, *this emotional upset is revealed only in the content of her interpretations, whereas the formal manifestations of her experience suggest a more stable personality.*

There is hardly any indication of the partners' male-female rivalry and of the game, which they formerly played, of emotional ebullience versus emotional control. On the other hand, problems involving their mothers and feelings of insecurity, which neither partner has solved, have now become prominent in both. (Possible connection between these problems and the planned divorce as a prelude to life alone?)

Contrary to my rather pessimistic evaluation of the therapy at this point, the Joint Rorschach Test shows highly positive results: In the re-test the partners demonstrate improved cooperation and communication, the wife improved emotional control and the husband an improved ability to experience emotion openly.

Follow-up Talk, October 23

Synopsis
Contrary to my expectations, during the two-month interval since our last meeting Helga has taken no concrete steps to obtain a divorce. The atmosphere in this session is clearly different. The partners have established a subtle balance by which, while preserving their outer and inner separation, they are able to display and to accept delicate signs of love without immediately trying to pressure each other or engage in hurtful defensive reactions. In particular Helga's wounds, i.e. her disappointment over the fact that therapy did not validate her ideal of marriage, seem to be healing. The withdrawal of her demands on Stani is not leading to a decrease of affection

on his part but instead is affording him space to show her affection for the first time. Considerable unspoken tenderness is visible, mainly in the way the couple turn towards each other and smile. It is as if they can allow none of this to be directly verbalized because then it could all fall apart again. There is tacit agreement that the partners like each other. On the outside the image of the couple has greatly altered, almost reversed, since the beginning of therapy. In the beginning Helga accompanied her words with sweeping, almost theatrical gestures that contrasted strongly with Stani's inhibited, paralyzed attitude. Now he speaks with strong emotion that is expressed in energetic body language, whereas Helga seems to be more contained and reflective. Helga sees that she needed to make the decision to get a divorce in order to achieve emotional detachment from Stani, but that at the moment this decision is no longer important. She appears to be more emotionally detached from Stani, but at the same time still seems depressed. She appears to be still working through her period of mourning for her lost ideal of marriage, and probably needs time to deal with this loss.

The relationship now seems much more relaxed and loving.

Th: We haven't seen each other for a long time. When was the last time?

H: Oh, I forgot, I've misplaced your bill somewhere.

W: Did you look in the chess newspaper? You might have put it in there.

H: Yes, I'll have to take another look.

W: (Archly) Obviously you don't have a woman around the house to tidy up. (All three laugh)

Th: Well, how are things?

W: At the moment it's still fine, but I don't know what kind of state I'm going to be in when I leave here. (Both laugh) I've often found that when I arrive for a therapy session I'm really feeling quite well compared to how I feel when I leave.

Th: Yes.

H: Well, it's been quiet since I saw you last. For me, of course, it's important to have things quiet (Smiles ironically at himself), but it wasn't just quiet. Now and then there were also moments when I had the feeling—not only about myself, but also about her—that, yes, now there could be something there, not something oppressive and frightening, but positive.

Th: You mean you felt this in Helga too?

H: Yes, in fact particularly in her.

Th: (To wife) Is that true?

W: Well, yes—I just don't have any more aggressive feelings towards Stani and we haven't been together any less or more often than before. Our points of contact are the same and—this is a big relief to me—I no longer have the same feelings for him. I noticed that on Sunday—last Sunday when he telephoned saying he'd like to drop by, I immediately thought, "That's not such a good idea [because Peter was there]," but he came anyhow, and we had supper together, and in the past I always felt so sorry for him and I always kept thinking, "Oh, here I am, sitting with the children and Peter, and now poor Stani has to leave us again." I didn't feel that way this time. I always used to be so sorry for him, and I also felt guilty. Now somehow that's gone, and it feels really good. Or, for example, his job took him abroad for a few weeks, and he wrote to me; I thought that was nice, but I didn't think any more about it than that. He wrote that he realized he didn't like living alone and kept thinking about us. I didn't react to that nearly as much as I would have before. I don't know exactly whether I did it quite consciously and closed off my feelings in order not to be disappointed again, but it felt good to have no hopes and expectations; I was simply happy about it, nothing more. I don't know whether I've lost all feeling now, or whether I've genuinely detached myself from him; I'm saying that cautiously because I've often thought I'd detached myself from him and then I've seen that it's not true. I really feel very good about that.

Helga has not taken any concrete steps towards divorce, but emotionally she has separated more from Stani.

Th: Now you don't feel so bitter about the situation?

W: Yes. It wasn't just bitterness, more the fact that I no longer react so strongly to everything he does, I used to react so to the positive things too, and now there's less of that. (Pause) It's not really bitterness, but sometimes I'm—sometimes I feel the children are hemming me in. Sure I'm fond of them and, no matter what, I'd like to keep them with me, but the idea that I'll have them with me constantly for the next fifteen years scares me sometimes, because I have to bear all the responsibility alone, and then sometimes I get mad and think, "Stani has it good, he can be free," but at the same time that's all he's got, obviously. But sometimes, all the same, I think, "He has it good." And the last time in therapy you

Helga would feel divorce is a loss all the same.

asked me whether *I feel that divorce is a relief or a loss. I said, "Sure, it's a relief," but afterwards I realized that I would feel very strongly it was a loss.* Now I really don't know any more, (Sighs) I just don't know. I haven't come to terms with it in the meantime, I've just let it go. We saw each other briefly, and it was very nice. But we haven't reached the point of being able to talk together about the positive aspects of divorce; I think it would take me quite a long time before I could feel divorce was an enrichment (Smiles) and probably Stani will go to Munich to work in the spring, and I'd be really glad to have some physical space between us too.

Th: Would you be glad?

W: Physical separation is really important to me too because unless we're a long distance apart we still see each other very often and that always hurts, which wouldn't happen any more if there's lots of space between us.

Th: (To husband) How do you feel about that?

H: (Sighs) I can't say exactly. When she says something like that, then naturally I think she's already decided in Peter's favor. (The atmosphere grows warmer and more relaxed) (Long pause)

Stani's new job takes him to another city.

W: (Pensively) My big problem—the thing that preoccupies me the most—is the children. I'm terribly afraid too. The children see our separation as a temporary thing, and they see that we fight less now, and I've told them that Stani may go to Munich to work and then we'll go to visit him during the holidays, and Christoph [the younger son] said, "No, Stani shouldn't go away, he should stay here," and so on . . . And I keep thinking, "How am I going to tell them?"

H: Well, we mustn't tell them, "Now I'm going to Munich for five years," but we should simply say, "Now I've gone to Munich."

W: I don't know whether one day the moment will come when that won't work any more. They may think, "Well, I don't know if he's ever coming back." Someday they really ought to be told that it's a clean break. "Stani is our father, he loves us, we'll see each other during the holidays, but he won't live here any more." I don't know which way is better. I just think that when people get a divorce the children should be told.

H: Yes, of course, if things have really gotten to that point.

W: And that's something I'm pretty scared about, how they're going to react.

Th: (To wife) In the past you always said that the suspense was unbearable for you, and a decision had to be made in a hurry.

W: Yes, but now, at this moment, I don't care about that again. Things can go on the way they are for a while yet. (Husband laughs bitterly)

Th: I wonder whether the two of you have adjusted to a situation in which you accept the loosening of the ties between you, and don't feel it's so painful any more.

H: Yes, probably because she knows it's only going to last a certain length of time.

W: No, that's not why; it's that I no longer react so strongly in my relationship with you. That has nothing to do with time, and at the moment I tell myself, "The question of whether or not I should get a divorce really isn't relevant any more." Yes, that's true. I don't know whether it's out of a kind of resignation that I've given up placing such demands on Stani. But I don't have any wish to commit myself or try anything new with him either, absolutely not.

Th: But to me it no longer sounds as if you're saying, "I find this situation completely intolerable."

W: No, no, definitely not.

Th: Perhaps there's a lot that still binds you together after all. (Pause) (Stani looks at Helga questioningly, with an almost entreating gaze)

W: Maybe there's something to it, but I wouldn't know how to formulate it. I don't know exactly what it is. (They look at each other)

H: A couple of times before the holidays there was a certain—I don't know how to express it—it was as if we were flirting, that kind of atmosphere.

W: A certain tension.

H: Yes, crackling tension, but not in a bad sense, and I interpreted that to mean that you too have at least some

Stani is suffering because Helga has detached herself from him and wants to be sure of her love.

positive feelings—that you're interested in what's going on inside me—that you're interested.

W: Sure, I mean naturally I'm interested in what's happening to you, obviously.

H: But it isn't so obvious any more.

W: You're right, no.

H: Sometimes you say you don't give a damn now.

W: Yes, but after all, we were together for ten years; I'm interested even in boyfriends I was with for two years.

H: It isn't that; this tension shows that there's something more there than nothing.

W: (Reflects. Pause. Very softly) Yes.

H: I can admit that now without being afraid that you'll jump on it straightaway. I think perhaps you could admit the same thing.

W: Yes, I've told you that when we're right in the middle of the thing too, when we were having coffee, for example, and also recently in the post office when I told you, when you looked at me that way, "Oh, you're making my heart pound."

H: Yes, but then why do you always retreat a couple of steps?

W: Just for the fun of it. (Helga's comment during our discussion of the manuscript was, "It was really out of fear.") Well, I've admitted that I said . . .

H: When I see that you still have some feeling for me, I don't feel any more that it makes me anxious or that you're being possessive.

W: Probably because I said I've made the decision to get a divorce.

H: No, recently we haven't talked about that at all.

W: Well, I left our last therapy session convinced that divorce was really the only thing to do. You said then, "She still feels something for me, she doesn't really want a divorce." But even if it hurt me ten times as much, it's still the only possible solution. Quite reasonably, I strongly resist the idea of trying to work on any relationship with you. It was, I don't know . . .

Th: I feel that the two of you have reached an understanding that's still very fragile, that I hardly dare address.

The partners can hint to each other about their feelings of love.

H: Maybe.

W: At the moment I feel capable of putting up with considerable stress.

Th: *The new thing for me is that both of you are able, in the same session, to hint and to accept without resistance that you are very fond of each other and really don't want to go your separate ways, but that you can't get too close either.* I have the impression that now you can accept that without bitterness.

W: Yes, essentially we're getting along just fine like this.

H: I think the advantage of this situation is that we don't react aggressively to each other, that it gives us a better chance of understanding each other. If we can go on talking together like this, it's better and more comfortable.

W: Yes, that's true Stani, but in the past I've always found that when I said clearly and unequivocally that I'd like us [to talk openly], you felt boxed in. Yes, at the moment things are really going very well for me, some time or other I'd still like to get divorced, that is I wouldn't like to let things go on as they are for another ten years. The situation now has the advantage that we can understand each other without getting into fights, but I think that all the same we'll grow farther and farther apart.

Th: I feel that you're much closer now than you used to be.

H: I feel that too.

Th: You're much less constrained with each other and much more relaxed . . .

W: Mmm-hmm.

Th: . . . than in any of our earlier sessions. I wonder whether you can get closer if the external separation between you is more pronounced, by using a lot of delicacy and skill, but having a less intense relationship.

W: Mmm-hmm.

H: I also find that I feel more secure with her and that I'm not afraid now; it's easier for me to do or say what I'd like to. This makes it easier than it used to be for me to get close to her.

Helga and Stani have found a new kind of limited closeness, a way of remaining separate within the union of love.

Th: (To husband) I can understand that you find the situation easier to tolerate when you have this clear-cut separation between you. On the other hand, I always had the feeling that you [Helga] don't like it much, and no doubt even now it's hard on you, but perhaps now you don't feel as bitter as you did in the last few months.

W: (Drops her eyes, fights back tears, saying nothing) Yes, actually that's true—if we tried to get closer—now I'm very far apart from Stani, so I can put up with anything, but if we tried to get closer, I'd start making demands again.

Th: Perhaps you can get closer only within certain limits.

W: Yes, I know. We could have a friendly relationship even if we're divorced.

H: But not long ago you said you didn't want to have any relationship with me at all any more.

W: Yes, now I see that somewhat differently. In the past I thought I couldn't ever do it, I'd always be aggressive towards Stani, but now . . . (Lowers her eyes and is clearly trying to hold back the tears. Long pause. The husband looks involved and concerned about his wife.)

Th: What are you feeling now?

W: I was just thinking what will happen later. Because if we can't get closer anyhow because we can't stand that, what kind of relationship can I have with Stani?

(Long pause)

My impression is that the partners are beginning to achieve a delicate balance. Their external separation and their basic decision to get a definitive divorce are helping the couple to consolidate an inner separation that is not yet firmly established. Thanks to this physical and, to some extent, emotional separation, they now find it easier to approach each other, to show each other understanding, and to communicate hints of their affinity and loving feelings. But this state is still precarious. Clearly Helga is suffering more than she can express. As Helga struggles with her tears, I try to fortify her control over her feelings because I am afraid that an uncontrolled eruption of emotion could upset the balance they have laboriously achieved.

W: (To husband) What do you think about it?

H: I still feel that you're suppressing something. Your decision to get a divorce is allowing you to suppress something you don't want to see. Maybe some feeling for me. It really comes through very strongly.

W: And what if that were true? What use is it to me if I love you? The way you are and the way I am, there'd be tension every time we got close.

H: Yes, probably.

W: And that's why I say that if we can't be close, it's better for us to get a divorce. If you were my boyfriend, we could have a relationship without ties. After all, we can still be friends if we're divorced.

The decision of whether or not to get a divorce is qualified and loses its meaning.

H: I don't think divorce would necessarily be all that final. It wouldn't be the first time that people got together again after a divorce. It's not really so much a question of divorce.

W: But it is for me, in the sense that then I'd have a better chance to look for a new partner. The bloom is off the rose; now it's time for me to open my eyes and look for another partner. If I were still twenty-five I'd still have time to mess things up.

H: (Smiling) True.

W: But now, at thirty-five, the firelight's burning low. I'm being quite realistic about it. I can't afford to be choosy. Thank God, nowadays there are lots of divorces; but the poor husbands are mostly fed up from their first marriage. (She laughs) Naturally I could tell myself, Stani isn't preventing me from looking for a new partner . . . (Pause. She reflects.) Yes, right, actually that's true.

Both partners see more and more clearly that the divorce is an external event that will not definitively end their relationship. On the one hand, they see that divorce could make the relationship freer, a thought that appeals to them. Moreover, even after divorce they could continue seeing each other, so essentially the divorce need not change much about their present relationship. I feel that we might all do well to ponder on this fact, as too many people—including couples therapists—tend to regard divorce as something final. In reality the years a couple have spent together can never be wiped out—especially if they also have children. These years are now an inalienable part of both their lives. Besides, their later lives will be built on a foundation that includes their past marriage. People can try to forget an earlier relationship in a second or third marriage, but it will always live on, in one form or another, in the later relationship. Often this fact is repressed and denied.

Th: (To wife) I'm not really clear about this: Are things going better for you, or do you perhaps have a tendency to cover up your feelings in order not to give in to them too much? Things haven't really been going well for you the past few months.

W: I asked myself the same question, whether I really feel good or have built up a defensive wall. Before the holidays I really didn't feel at all good. (Looks at her husband) We both said we were feeling rotten. I was very discontented and irritable then.

H: It all has to do with biorhythms.

(They both laugh)

Helga's newfound stability is still precarious.

W: I don't believe there is such a thing. But, for example, during the summer I felt fine. I have the impression that now I even recover much better from the bad spells and that the spells aren't so violent any more. At the start of the vacation I had the feeling that I couldn't feel so intensely any more, and I was even disappointed because I no longer had such strong emotions. Even before I didn't like that so much; I prefer to have intense feelings, both positive and negative, and now I don't quite know if I've covered myself with a protective shell or if I'm really feeling well, and I thought, "Today when I leave therapy I'll know if I'm really feeling well or if it's only covering up. (She smiles and wags her index finger admonishingly)

Th: I have a strange feeling about that too. In spring and summer I felt you were really deeply hurt by what had resulted from therapy, and now it seems to me as if the wounds are healing, and I almost hesitate to go into it much because I'm afraid of opening them up again. My feeling is that we should just let it rest a bit until everything has stabilized. But I'm not quite sure: Is that the right thing to do, or is it just an evasion of problems we still ought to talk about?

(Helga's comment during discussion of the manuscript: "I was very grateful to you for saying this.")

Helga has highly ambivalent feelings about the change therapy has produced in her. One important reason for not wanting to give up her absolute demands on Stani was her fear that doing so would result in a reduction of her capacity to feel. As a rule therapy leads to a better adjustment to reality, to more insightful behavior. As this example shows, clinging to absolute demands in a love relationship does not bring about more intense intimacy, but actually prevents intimacy. An increase in demands leads to a decrease in what can actually be attained, and vice versa. In this sense a more "rational" and "realistic" attitude does not lead to a loss in the ability to love, but is the only factor that makes it possible for people to get close. This truth may deprive love of some of its mystique, its fantastical and dreamlike character. This loss can be experienced as painful and hard to accept.

W: I can't really judge that myself. But sometimes I really have the feeling that I'm getting along fine. And if I were just covering up, I think I wouldn't feel as well as I do. I think I may cover up a bit in my relationship with Stani simply so that I can make my protective shell a bit thicker. That may be.

Th: Maybe you actually need a protective shell, and that's why at the moment I feel reluctant about challenging it and probing into it. Perhaps you need it, at least for a time.

W: But as for getting hurt, I've noticed that I get through the bad patches much faster now.

(The husband is sitting at an angle in the chair, one arm supported on the armrest, bending towards his wife, and deeply attentive. This shows a degree of involvement that he has never displayed in this way in any of the earlier therapy sessions.)

H: And maybe we haven't hurt each other as deeply as we used to do.

W: For example, after therapy the last time I felt really awful. After the session you said I had such a haughty look that you felt like slapping my face. (Wife bows her head, fighting tears. The husband looks deeply touched.)

Th: I see you're in pain and that a lot of wounds haven't healed yet.

W: Yes, we'll have to wait until some grass grows over them. (Long pause)

The couple
have
achieved a
delicate
stability.

Th: I think it might be a good idea after all for us to meet after fairly long intervals; then we'll see to what extent you're just trying to protect yourself, repressing things in a way that won't last in the long run.

W: Mmm-hmm.

Th: It's my impression that you've distanced yourselves from each other more and that you need this distance. Naturally the question is whether you can tolerate it; I think that you [Stani] tolerate it a good deal better.

H: Yes, when I was out of the country she telephoned me once. In the past I would have been alarmed or angry: "Oh, what does she want *now?*" But this time I was glad, I noticed that I felt glad about it and didn't feel anything unpleasant like, "*Why* is she calling?" Anyhow, before I found out what she wanted I was simply glad she called.

Stani is now turned towards me and is making vigorous gestures with his hands. Each partner now displays just the opposite posture and gestures from those of the first therapy session. At that first session Helga accompanied her words with animated body language, whereas Stani was restrained and made very few expressive movements; now Stani's words are accompanied by many gestures and he speaks in a strongly modulated, spirited voice, while Helga looks introspective and self-reflective.

H: And I think that's good; after all, for a long time things weren't like that. [If she had telephoned me] I would have felt she was keeping track of me. And because I felt glad [she had called], it was easier for me to call her later and chat with her a bit; it was really easy for me and I enjoyed it. It's because of the distance that I felt glad and didn't immediately think, "Now she's jumping on me again." At the moment I simply felt glad, without thinking for a long time about what she had in mind. And it would be good if things could go on that way. Then we'd see what's possible for us.
(Pause)

H: (Turning towards his wife) How did you feel about that?

W: (Defensive) To me it seemed completely ordinary. For a long time now I haven't thought about the fact that when I telephone you, you might think I was checking up on you.

H: Not checking up, I simply saw that in the past I'd reacted negatively when you called.

W: I think it has to do with the fact that now there's so much distance between us. Now you tend to think, "That's really a shame, now she doesn't have any more claims on me." So it's easier for me to approach you. And another thing that may be playing a role is that apparently things aren't going too well any more between you and Renate and now you're more inclined to pull away from her (Makes gestures indicating a drawing apart) because her demands are getting to be too much for you.

H: Yes, it's true about Renate, but now just in general I'm better at expressing what I want, and I can really make things better, not only with you but in general. And that's why I'm getting along better.

W: But it's also because I'm not making any demands on you any more.

H: Yes, of course, one also needs the outward framework.

W: Even if I had seen that earlier, I simply couldn't do anything but get furious and say all sorts of dreadful things to you and feel really awful, but I couldn't have done anything else. I simply had to get rid of my fears and hurt feelings, smash! (Beats her fists through the air) But despite my aggressive behavior I really still expected you to love me. That may have been asking too much because I really wasn't pleasant.

(Pause)

Th: (To wife) What's new is that you no longer feel that this situation is completely intolerable. In the past you always said, "I can't stand it any more, it's better to destroy everything than go on in this suspense . . ."

W: Yes, but then I was really still hoping that we'd get back together completely. *Maybe I needed to tell myself, "Now it's over for good, it's a thing of the past."* And maybe I still need that in order to be able to behave

Helga needed to decide in favor of an external divorce in order to achieve an inner divorce.	this way. Perhaps I'd have trouble with that again if we got closer in external terms. Th: I think we have to wait and see how things develop from now on. W: (To husband) In any case I won't get a divorce before May 20 [six months from now]; that would be our anniversary. When I've been married for ten years I'll be entitled to a pension, and of course I'm not going to let that slip past me! (All three laugh)

Even after this follow-up talk it is still not clear how the couple's outward situation will develop. What is certain is that the partners feel more satisfied, even-tempered and happy with each other and have a considerably more constructive, differentiated and open relationship. As Helga emphasizes in the last excerpt, she still needs the idea of divorce in order to relate differently to Stani. I believe that it is not so much the idea of outward divorce that has changed her attitude, as her acceptance of inner divorce, the recognition that she must accept the frustration of remaining separate in the experience of love, and that she has to take into account her partner's limited abilities to relate to her. In this last session Helga still seems somewhat depressed and pent-up. She still has to mourn a bit more for the loss of her ideal of marriage. She seems softer and more vulnerable than at the beginning of therapy. Her voice is warmer and more subdued. She appears more open and willing to change.

I saw the couple again three months and then six months later. Both partners described their relationship as a good deal more positive and happy. To be sure, they had not yet moved back together. A new external problem had arisen. Because of the recession Stani had not been able to find work in Switzerland, so he had had to go to Munich. Professionally it was more satisfying for him there, but it was hard for him to make the move because Helga could not and would not move too. Renate would have been willing to go with him, but he did not want this, because he had grown away from her since his relationship with Helga started to improve. Helga and Stani have also resumed sexual relations, which both of them regard as satisfying. Stani is no longer disturbed by Helga's weight. Helga no longer seems depressed but is much more self-confident, calm and decisive. Towards Stani she exhibits a critical understanding and a benevolent detachment.

At the time of our last talk Stani had come from Munich, as he often did, to visit Helga and the children. He was still looking for a job in Switzerland and was determined to get back together with his family as soon as circumstances permitted.

Reflections on the Results of Therapy

It is a complex and delicate task to evaluate the results of this therapy. Therapists who work purely on a systemic or behavioral basis and insist on clear-cut problem-definitions, and on clear arrangements and decisions, would not be satisfied with the results of this couples therapy. They probably would not have taken this couple into therapy. But I think there are many couples whose problems are the same as or very similar to those of Helga and Stani, and they, too, could benefit from couples therapy. Those who believe that therapy should at least clear up the question of whether a couple want to continue their marriage will not be satisfied either. But those who are willing to draw subtle distinctions will perceive that both the partners and their relationship have changed in the course of these thirty-one sessions. To be sure, the couple have not arrived at a relationship that corresponds to the traditional model of marriage, but I believe that they have found the particular form of relationship that is possible for them given their present stage of personal development.

Many people are offended by the suggestion that a close marital relationship may not be conducive to their health. They feel that they are not fully worthwhile human beings if they do not prove capable of living in a traditional marriage, and indeed tend to further exaggerate their idealized notions about marriage by demanding the maximum openness, intimacy and intensity in their relationship. But the facts show that an intimate form of marriage is unsuitable for many people and that both they and those close to them are unhappy in this kind of relationship. However, they are capable of meaningful and fulfilling relationships if they are not compelled to fit into such a narrow and expectation-ridden framework. An intimate and exclusive marital partnership is, culturally, a new development, a product of Western industrialized society, and it has by no means been adopted by all the world's peoples. I believe that the acceptance of one's own limitations and the desire to find a form of relationship that suits each individual are not symptoms of a circumscribed, neurotic personality, but rather a sign of maturity. I believe that in this sense Helga and Stani made progress in therapy. The greater congruency between ideal and reality achieved by both partners affords them increased satisfaction, and keeps them from continuing with destructive games in which they are compelled to hurt and punish each other and make each other's lives miserable. They no longer use extramarital relationships to create space between them and to hurt each other or find compensation. The breakdown of their neurotic interaction has also been accompanied by personality changes. The two partners, formerly so polarized, have each made a move in the other's direction. Helga has become more independent. She can deal better with her overblown emotions. She no longer needs to express them in an exaggerated form, and is better able to accept Stani's limitations without continually reproaching him. Stani is better at experiencing and expressing feelings. He is less timid about sticking up for what he feels, and can define his position more clearly in relation to Helga's expectations, without being forced to hurt her and drive her away.

Today the partners do not need each other as before in order to compensate for their own deficiencies. They are freer and more independent in their behavior.

Even if they should eventually get a divorce—which at the moment is still an open question—I believe it will be a freely made decision and not a provocative attempt to put pressure on each other or take revenge.

What are we to make of the fact that at the end of therapy Helga seems more depressed? Is it a typically male response to feel that a therapy has been successful if female patients end up more subdued and less aggressive than they were before? Does a male therapist feel, "I love you more when you're depressed? Did I, as a male therapist, not have a tendency to diagnose as "sick" that aggressive and expansive behavior Helga showed before therapy, that is, to view her as needing treatment in order to better defend myself from her? In the long run Helga's depression showed all the marks of being a transitional phase representing a period of mourning, and it gradually lifted a few months after the termination of therapy. In the follow-up talks she reported that she was more even-tempered and happier than before therapy, and generally lived a more active and independent life. During our later talks, which took place when Stani came back from Germany to visit, he, not Helga, was the one who seemed somewhat lost and lonely. He complained that he lacked drive and a sense of purpose when he was working in Germany. Without the structure imposed on him by Helga he seemed to have increased difficulties finding a direction for his life and developing initiative.

During our discussion of the manuscript Helga reported that during the course of therapy she had been amazed at how she had repeatedly fallen into her old patterns of communication and reaction, long after she thought she was completely over them.

She says, concerning the divorce, "The wish for divorce was the wish for independence. Today I have accepted—I don't know whether because of the therapy or through the passage of time—the fact that I can never break entirely free from Stani and so I no longer feel that divorce is so necessary. As long as he lives, a person can never completely free himself from his parents, and in the same way I cannot turn a ten-year marriage into something that never happened. I think it would be beautiful to grow old together the way I can see my parents doing now. Strangely enough I did not succeed in becoming freer of Stani until he was able to accept me. Before that it was as if I were under a spell. My self-confidence, damaged as it was, depended on Stani. Before I married, I was more self-confident. Then something inside me said, "You robbed me of my self-confidence, and you have to make amends for it." It was important to me to have the approval of the person who hurt me. Perhaps that has to do with my father. In the time when I was constantly fighting with him all he used to say was, "I won't talk to a brat like you."

The feeling that she had not been accepted by her father continued to affect Helga. Stani had his work cut out for him to make up for what she felt her father still owed her. *Norman and Betti Paul* have pointed out that unachieved mourning and unsettled conflicts with parents can play a central role in the development of marital disorders.

During the follow-up sessions I tried to learn from Helga why she had not entered into my repeated attempts to clarify the problems in my relationship with her. She said that she had not wanted to (call into) question the unbiased role of the therapist. "For me it was important that my relationship with you remain inviolable and that I keep you as an ideal on a pedestal. It would have been too much for me to have had to challenge and work through my relationship with my therapist [on top of all the rest]. It would also scare me to feel he was not completely above the whole situation. This would destroy the basis of my trust. If the therapist is viewed as an authority, then he must not have any problems and must be able to keep things under complete control. I thought to myself, You mustn't have problems with him too, because if you did it would mean, 'Now here's another man who finds you a pain.' I had the feeling that I had to defend myself against you or, 'He too will like you only if you change.' " These comments seem to me important in relation to the therapist's handling of therapeutic collusion; they show that under no circumstances ought he to force the patient to deal with the collusion, but should merely reveal his willingness to work on the therapeutic relationship if the patient wants to. It is also clear that patients often impose on the therapist role behavior that may make him feel constrained. I would have liked to have clarified my problems with Helga during the therapy, not only for her sake but for mine; but she wanted to keep me in the position of the superior therapist. I had to accept that. Many patients need to feel that a therapist or doctor is superior and infallible because it is only under the sway of this image that they can allow themselves to become involved in therapy. This often sets limits on the therapist's efforts to refrain from pretending to be more than he is. If I had to undergo an operation, I myself would not want to hear that the surgeon does not feel completely equal to the task.

13

WHAT THIS BOOK CAN TEACH

This book is intended as a practical supplement to *Couples in Collusion,* in which I described the deep yearnings that can involve a couple in a lasting relationship and can later entangle them in seemingly insoluble conflicts. As a learning tool, it was the purpose of *Couples in Collusion* to help people understand the unconscious interaction of two partners, and to convey "knowledge and information" about the concept of collusion. The present book is concerned with skills (What should I know how to do?) and the therapeutic attitude (How should I behave?). Can this knowledge be acquired by reading? No doubt only to a limited extent. I wanted to give the reader a concrete insight into the process of couples therapy, in the hope that he will learn to empathize with the complex relationships involved in the wife-husband-therapist triangle, and that he will see more clearly what couples therapy is like. The records of a therapy, complete with commentary, take up a substantial portion of this book and demand that a reader be willing to tune into the therapy described.

Any description of psychotherapy always strongly reflects personal attitudes. For me the important results of this study are those which show that the differences between different schools of therapy have less bearing on the results of therapy than their passionate struggles and claims to the truth would lead one to believe. A more important factor in the results is the personality of the therapist. Patients, too, ascribe more importance to their relationship with the therapist than to his theoretical orientation and specific methodology. Thus I have attempted to describe not so much a particular technique of couples therapy as the practical configuration of the complex triangular relationship of wife-husband-therapist, which is central to any form of couples therapy.

This is not to suggest that it is superfluous for a therapist to undergo training in a particular method of therapy, provided that he is a strong, mature and committed individual. But my experience has been that couples therapy reveals his limitations to the therapist more clearly than anything else, so that for me training in couples therapy to a large extent represents training in the purposeful application of one's limited powers so as to make them as productive as possible. The purpose of the collusion concept, as outlined in *Couples in Collusion*, was to aid the therapist in viewing every phenomenon as not merely the concern of one or the other partner, but as a statement made by the two of them together; whereas the present book shows every phenomenon in therapy as a matter concerning the therapeutic triad, which also includes the therapist.

The psychodynamics of the therapeutic triangle is a problem in any therapeutic approach to the problems of couples, either directly, when the therapist confronts both partners at once, or indirectly, if he is treating only one partner. In couples therapy the therapist can, according to his methods, try to minimize his personal involvement by structuring the therapy process through a series of exercises, or, as shown here, he can bring into the therapy his personal involvement in the therapeutic triangle.

Meeting

is the beginning of parting

— Japanese proverb

BIBLIOGRAPHY

Balint, Michael *Der Arzt, sein Patient und die Krankheit*, Stuttgart: Klett, 1957.

Therapeutische Aspekte der Regression, Stuttgart: Klett, 1970.

——, Ornstein, Paul H. and Emil Balint, *Focal Psychotherapy*, London: Tavistock Publications, 1972.

Bateson, Gregory *Naven*, Palo Alto, California: Stanford University Press, 1958.

Beck, D. *Die Kurzpsychotherapie*, Bern: Huber, 1974.

"Das 'Koryphaen-Killer-Syndrom,'" *Dtsch. Med. Zschr.* 102, 303–307 (1977).

Beckmann, D. *Der Analytiker und sein Patient*, Bern: Huber, 1974.

"Paardynamik und Gesundheitsverhalten" in *Familie und seelische Krankheit*, ed. by H. E. Richter, H. Strotzka, J. Willi, Reinbek bei Hamburg: Rowohlt, 1976, pp. 123–130.

"Selbst- und Fremdbild der Frau," *Familiendynamik* 2, 35–49 (1977).

——, Braehler, E. and Richter, H.E. *Neustandardisierung des Giessen-Tests (GT)*, unpublished manuscript (1977).

Bellak, Leopold and Leonard Small *Emergency Psychotherapy and Brief Psychotherapy*, New York: Grune & Stratton, 1964.

Bellville, T.P., Raths, O.N. and Bellville, C.J. "Conjoint Marriage Therapy with a Husband-and-Wife Team," *Amer. J. Orthopsychiat.* 39 (3), 473–483 (1969).

Berman, E.M. and Lief, H. "Ehetherapie in der amerikanischen Psychiatrie: ein Überblick," *Familiendynamik* 1, 238–266 (1976).

Boszormenyi-Nagy, Ivan, "Mann und Frau, Verdienstkonten in den Geschlechtsrollen," *Familiendynamik* 2, 1–10 (1977).

—— and Geraldine Spark, *Invisible Loyalties*, Hagerstown, Maryland: Harper & Row, 1973.

Bowen, M. "Die Anwendung von Familientheorien in der klinischen Praxis," *Ehe* 12, 1–33 (1975).

Buehler, Charlotte *Die Rolle der Werte in der Entwicklung der Persönlichkeit und in der Psychotherapie*, Stuttgart: Klett, 1975.

Burgard, R. *Wie Frauen "verrückt" gemacht werden*, Berlin: Frauenselbstverlag, 1977.

Cartwright, R.D. and Lerner, B. "Empathy, Need to Change, and Improvement with Psychotherapy," *J. Consult. Psychol.* 27, 138–144 (1963).

Christ, J. "Treatment of Marriage Disorders," in Grunebaum, H. and Christ, J. (ed.), *Contemporary Marriage: Structure, Dynamics and Therapy*, Boston: Little, Brown & Co., 1976, pp. 371–399.

D'Eaubonne, F. *Feminismus oder Tod*, Munich: Frauenoffensive, 1975.

Deutsche Hauptstelle Gegen Die Suchtgefahren, Bulletin of July 22, 1977.

Dicks, Henry Victor *Marital Tensions*, New York: Basic Books, 1967.

Duss, J., Stierlin, H. and Welter, R. "Lernen und Lehren von Familientherapie," *Familiendynamik* 1, 186–208 (1976).

Duss-von Werdt, J. *Die junge Kleinfamilie* (in preparation).

Emma: Zeitschrift für Frauen von Frauen, Heft 2, Cologne: 1977.

Erikson, Erik Homburger "Das Problem der Identität," *Psyche* 10, 114–176 (1956/57).

Freud, Sigmund "The Future Prospects of Psycho-Analytic Therapy," Vol. XI (1910) of the Standard Edition of the Complete Psychological Works of Sigmund Freud, ed. by J. Strachey et al., London: Hogarth, 1957.

"The Dynamics of Transference," Vol. XII (1912), Standard Edition.

"Observations on Transference Love" (1915a), Standard Edition.

Fuller, F.F. "Influence of Sex of Counselor and of Client on Client Expressions of Feeling," *J. Counsel. Psychol.* 10, 34–40 (1963).

Giovacchini, P.L. "Treatment of Marital Disharmonies: The Classical Approach" in Greene, B. (ed.), *The Psychotherapy of Marital Disharmony*, New York: Free Press, 1965.

Goldberg, Herb *The Hazards of Being Male: Surviving the Myth of Masculine Privilege*, New York: Nash Pub., 1976.

Greene, B.L. *A Clinical Approach to Marital Problems*, Chicago: Thomas, 1970.

Grunebaum, H., Christ, J. and Neiberg, N. "Diagnosis and Treatment Planning for Couples," *Int. J. Group Psychoth.* 19, 185–202 (1969).

—— and Christ, J. (ed.), *Contemporary Marriage: Structure, Dynamics and Therapy*, Boston: Little, Brown & Co., 1976.

Haffner, S. (ed.) *Gewalt in der Ehe*, Berlin: Wagenbach, 1976.

Haffter, C. *Kinder aus geschiedenen Ehen*, Bern: Huber, 1948.

Haley, J. "Familientherapie mit gestörten Jugendlichen," *Ehe* 12, 148–161 (1975).

Problem-Solving Therapy: New Strategies for Effective Family Therapy, San Francisco: Jossey-Bass, 1976.

Heigl, F. "Indikation zur Psychotherapie," *Nervenarzt* 47, 217–224 (1976).

Heigl-Evers, A. "Zum Konzept des implizierten Ehevertrags," *Gruppen-psychoth. u. Gruppendyn.* 6, 134–146 (1972).

Heimann, P. "On Counter-transference," *Int. J. Psa.* 31, 81–84 (1950).

Hoeh, R. and Kulms, A. *Scheidung—Befreiung oder Katastrophe?,* unpublished manuscript, Hamburg: 1977.

Hollender, M.H. "Selection of Therapy for Marital Problems" in Masserman, J.H. (ed.), *Current Psychiatric Therapies,* Vol. 11, New York: Grune and Stratton, 1971, pp. 119–128.

Jung, C.G. *Psychological Types,* Vol. 6 in The Collected Works of C.G. Jung, ed. by Sir Herbert Read et al., London: Routledge and Kegan Paul, 1971.

Kaplan, H. *The New Sex Therapy,* New York: Brunner/Mazel, 1974.

Kaufmann, L. *Familie, Kommunikation, Psychose,* Bern: Huber, 1972.

Kraus, A. and Lilienfeld, A. "Some Epidemiological Aspects of the High Mortality Rate in the Young Widowed Group," *J. Chron. Dis.* 10, 207 (1959).

Laing, R.D. *The Divided Self,* London: Tavistock Publications, 1960.

—— *The Self and Others,* London: Tavistock Publications, 1961.

Leslie, G.R. "Conjoint Therapy in Marriage Counselling," *J. Marriage and the Family* 26, 65–71 (1964).

Liberman, R.P. "Behavioristische Ansätze für die Familien- und Ehetherapie" in Sager, C.J. and Singer Kaplan, H.S. (ed.), *Handbuch der Ehe-, Familien- and Gruppen-Therapie,* Vol. II, Munich: Kindler, 1973, pp. 398–417.

Macoby, E.E. and Jacklin, C.N. *The Psychology of Sex Differences,* Stanford University Press, 1974.

Malan, David H. *A Study of Brief Psychotherapy,* London: Tavistock Publications, 1963.

Mandel, A., Mandel, K.H., Stadter, E., and Zimmer, D. *Einübung in Partnerschaft durch Kommunikationstherapie and Verhaltenstherapie,* Munich: Pfeiffer, 1971.

Mandel, K.H., Mandel, A., and Rosenthal, H. *Einübung der Liebesfähigkeit: Praxis der Kommunikationstherapie für Paare,* Munich: Pfeiffer, 1975.

Manika, C. "Sind Frauen 'fraulicher' und Männer 'männlicher,' wenn sie in der Paarsituation aufeinander bezogen sind? Untersuching mit dem Individuellen and Gemeinsamen Rorschach-Versuch," *Familiendynamik* 3 (1978), now being printed.

Masters, William H. and Johnson, Virginia E. *Human Sexual Inadequacy*, Boston: Little Brown & Co., 1970.

Meerwein, F. *Die Grundlagen des ärztlichen Gesprächs*, Bern: Huber, 1969.

Miller, Jean Baker *Psychoanalysis and Women*, New York: Penguin Books, 1973.

Minsel, W.R. *Praxis der Gesprächspsychotherapie*, Vienna: Böhlaus, 1974.

Moeller, M.L. "Zur Theorie der Gegenübertragung," *Psyche* 31, 142–166 (1977).

Nichols, J. *Men's Liberation: A New Definition of Masculinity*, New York: Penguin Books, 1975.

Parin, P., "Das Ich und die Anpassungs-Mechanismen," *Psyche* 31, 481–515 (1977).

Parkes, C.M., Benjamin, B., and Fitzgerald, R.G. "Broken Heart: A Statistical Study of Increased Mortality among Widowers," *Brit. Med. J.* 1, 740–743 (1969).

Patterson, C.H. *Counseling and Psychotherapy: Theory and Practice*, New York: Harper, 1959.

Paul, N.L. *The Divorce Process*, unpublished manuscript, 1977.

—— and B.B. Paul, *A Marital Puzzle: Transgenerational Analysis in Marriage Counseling*, New York: Norton, 1975.

Pizzey, E. *Scream Quietly or the Neighbors Will Hear*, Short Hills, New Jersey: R. Enslow Publishers, 1977.

Rapaport, David *Die Struktur der psychoanalytischen Theorie*, Stuttgart: Klett, 1959.

Redlich, F.C. "Die Psychoanalyse und das Wertsystem," *Psyche* 13, 481 (1959).

Richter, Horst-Eberhard *Eltern, Kind und Neurose*, Reinbek bei Hamburg: Rowohlt, 1967.

The Family as Patient, New York: Farrar, Straus & Giroux, 1974.

"Zwei-Wochen-Paartherapie," *Psyche* 10, 889 (1973).

Lernziel Solidarität, Reinbek bei Hamburg: Rowohlt, 1974.

Flüchten oder Standhalten, Reinbek bei Hamburg: Rowohlt 1976.

Rogers, Carl Ransom *On Becoming a Person*, New York: Houghton Mifflin, 1961.

Becoming Partners: Marriage and Its Alternatives, New York: Delacorte, 1972.

Rosenthal, D. "Changes in Some Moral Values Following Psychotherapy," *J. Consult. Psych.* 19, 431–436 (1955).

Sager, C. "The Treatment of Married Couples" in Arieti, S. (ed.), *Amer. Handbook of Psychiatry*, Vol. 3, New York: Basic Books, 1966, pp. 213–225.

"Transference in the Conjoint Therapy of Married Couples," *Arch. Gen. Psychiat.* 16, 185 (1967).

Sandler, Joseph "Gegenübertragung und Bereitschaft zur Rollenübernahme," *Psyche* 30, pp. 297–305 (1976).

——, Dare, Christopher and Holder, Alex *The Patient and the Analyst: The Basis of the Psychoanalytic Process*, London: Allen and Unwin, 1973.

Scheu, U. *Wir werden nicht als Mädchen geboren—wir werden dazu gemacht*, Frankfurt am Main: Fischer, 1977.

Skynner, A.C.R. *Systems of Family and Marital Psychotherapy*, New York: Brunner/Mazel, 1976.

Smith, J.W. and Grunebaum, H. "The Therapeutic Alliance in Marital Therapy" in Grunebaum, H. and Christ, J. (ed.), *Contemporary Marriage: Structure, Dynamics and Therapy*, Boston: Little, Brown & Co., 1976.

Spark, Geraldine M. "Grandparents and Intergenerational Family Therapy," *Family Process* 13, 225–237 (1974).

Sperling, E. and U. "Die Einbeziehung der Grosseltern in die Familientherapie," in Richter, H.-E., Strotzka, H. and Willi, J. (ed.), *Familie und seelische Krankheit*, Reinbek bei Hamburg: Rowohlt, 1976, pp. 196–215.

Spiegel, J.P. "Some Cultural Aspects of Transference and Countertransference," in Masserman, J.H. (ed.), *Individual and Familial Dynamics*, New York: Grune & Stratton, 1959.

Stierlin, H. *Eltern und Kinder im Prozess der Ablösung*, Frankfurt am Main: Suhrkamp, 1975.

Von der Psychoanalyse zur Familientherapie, Stuttgart: Klett, 1975.

"Familiendynamische Aspekte der Übertragung und Gegenübertragung," *Familiendynamik* 2, 182–197 (1977).

Straus, M.A. "Cultural and Social Organizational Influences on Violence between Family Members," in Price, R. and Barrier, D. (ed.), *Configurations: Biological and Social Factors in Sexual and Family Life*, Lexington (Mass.): Lexington Books, 1974.

Stuart, R.B. "Die operante-interpersonale Behandlung von Eheproblemen," in Sager, C.J. and Singer Kaplan, H.S. (ed.), *Handbuch der Ehe-, Familien- und Gruppen-Therapie*, Vol. III, Munich: Kindler, 1973, pp. 626–642.

Toomin, M.K. "Structured Separation with Counseling: A Therapeutic Approach for Couples in Conflict," *Family Process* 11, 299 (1972).

Uchtenhagen, A. "Psychische Störungen bei Frauen," *Schweiz. Arch. Neurol. Neurochir. Psychiat.* 117, 55–64 (1975).

Watzlawick, Paul "Diskussion zum Vortrag auf den Lindauer Psycho-
therapiewochen," quoted in E. Enke-Ferchland, "Die psychothera-
peutische Zweier-Beziehung aus der Perspektive der sozialpsycholog-
ischen Forschung und der psychoanalytisch-psychotherapeutischen
Praxis," *Praxis Psychoth.* 22, 63–73 (1977).

―――,Beavin, J.H., and Jackson, D. *Pragmatics of Human Communication,* New York: Norton, 1967.

―――,Weakland, John H., and Fisch, R. *Change: Principles of Problem
Formation and Problem Resolution,* New York: Norton, 1974.

Weis, K. and Borges, S.S. "Victimology and Rape: The Case of the
Legitimate Victim," *Iss. Crim.* 8, 71–115 (1973).

Wickler, W. *Sind wir Sünder?: Naturgesetze der Ehe,* Munich: Knaur,
1969.

Willi, J. "Die hysterische Ehe," *Psyche* 24, 326–356 (1972a).

"Die angstneurotische Ehe," *Nervenarzt* 43, 399–408 (1972b).

Couples in Collusion, Pomona, California: Hunter House Publishers, 1982.

Der Gemeinsame Rorschach-Versuch, Bern: Huber, 1973.

"Die Beurteilung des Behandlungsergebnisses einer Paartherapie," in
Richter, H.-E., Strotzka, H., and Willi, J. (ed.) *Familie and seelische
Krankheit,* Reinbek bei Hamburg: Rowohlt, 1976, pp. 278–300.
"Die psychosomatische Kollusion am Beispiel einer herzneurotischen
Ehe," *Familiendynamik* 1, 319–333 (1976).

―――― and Rotach-Fuchs, M. "Über die spezifische Struktur und
Dynamik der Ehepaar-Therapiegruppe," *Ehe* 4, 165–168 (1970).

Zuk, G.H. *Family Therapy,* New York: Behavioral Publ., 1971.

Zweiter Familienbericht, Bundesminister für Jugend, Familie and Gesund-
heit, Bonn-Bad Godesberg, 1975.

INDEX